The Anointed One

The Anointed One

The Complete Life Story of Jesus Christ

Rodney S. Laughlin
Susan Tough

FIDELIS
PUBLISHING

FIDELIS PUBLISHING®

ISBN: 9781956454345
ISBN (eBook): 9781956454352

The Anointed One: The Complete Life Story of Jesus Christ
© 2023 Rodney S. Laughlin

Cover Design by Diana Lawrence
Interior Layout by LParnell Book Services
Edited by Lisa Parnell
Maps and tables by Clyde Adams

Order at www.faithfultext.com for a significant discount. Email info@fidelispublishing.com to inquire about bulk purchase discounts.

Fidelis Publishing, LLC Sterling, VA • Nashville, TN
www.fidelispublishing.com

Scripture quotations are taken from The Readable Bible®. Copyright 2022 by Rodney S. Laughlin, Leawood, Kansas. Used by permission of Iron Stream Media.

Manufactured in the United States of America

10 9 8 7 6 5 4 3 2

Contents

Appendix

Maps and Tables

To the Reader

This is the complete biography of the person who has influenced more people than anyone in the history of the world. More than two billion people claim to follow him today, just over 30 percent of the world's population. And many irreligious people hold to his values of love, justice, and mercy.

The name *Jesus* may mean something to you, or it may not. Almost everyone has a positive, negative, or neutral view toward him. But most people have not read a full account of his life. We suggest that you put your view on hold and consider this account of what he did and said. Let the book, based on the records written by eyewitnesses to his life, enlighten you with the truth about him. This is your opportunity to do that and to make a fully informed decision about what you believe.

This book is primarily a compilation of what was written about Jesus by four people:

- Matthew and John, men who walked with Jesus thoughout his ministry;
- Mark, a young man who observed Jesus and his work, and who accompanied the apostles Peter and Paul on their missionary journeys; and
- Luke, a doctor who "carefully investigated everything from the beginning to write an orderly account."

Here those writings are supplemented with other biblical writings about Jesus as well as fictional elements to help you understand the context, see the people mentioned as thinking, feeling human beings and to make the ancient writings read as smoothly as a modern biography.

Much of what you are about to read may seem ordinary, and much of it will seem extraordinary. How should you understand it? Read it normally, just like any other book. Jesus spoke as speakers do today, with emotion, using exaggeration, raising and lowering his voice, pausing and gesturing. So when you come across a passage where he is speaking, consider reading it out loud. Put yourself in the situation, picture the moment and the people involved in the dialogue, and find their emotions. Then imagine the words as they were originally spoken.

You may want to read this book as you would any other biography, just for the enjoyment of understanding more about the life of someone of great accomplishment. Or you may read it with an eye open to Jesus' claim that he is God. He was the long-awaited Messiah,* the Anointed One. In that case, you may want to highlight as you read. At the end of each sitting, review what you've highlighted and think about it.

Many who have read Jesus' story have concluded he is the Son of God, that he died for their sins and offers salvation as a gift through faith in him. You may conclude that, or you may not believe. If not, at least you'll be able to truthfully say, "I've read all about Jesus." If you reject him, let your rejection be fully informed.

When you finish reading, if you find yourself believing Jesus is who he claims to be and want to know more or have a relationship with him, find a Bible. You will be amazed at the revelations you encounter as you read the world's most-read book. We believe those who read it can find the life that can't be found anywhere else: eternal life.

Rodney A. Laughlin

Susan Tough

---

* "Messiah": the English transliteration for the Hebrew word *mashiach*, which means "Anointed One." He would come and save the Jews (i.e., lead Israel into a time of victory and/or peace). He was expected to do this under the direction of God in the power of God.

Prologue

The apostle John, writing some sixty years after the death of Jesus, made this amazing statement about him:

> He was with God in the beginning. All things came into existence through him. Apart from him nothing came into existence that has existed. In him was life, and that life was the light of all humanity. The light shines in the darkness, and the darkness has not overcome it. . . .
>
> The true light (who gives light to everyone) was coming into the world. He was in the world, and the world was made through him, yet the world didn't know him. He came to his own people, but his own people didn't receive him. Yet to all who did receive him, to those who believed in his name, he gave the right to become children of God, born not of human descent, nor of sexual desire, nor of a human's decision, but born of God. . . .
>
> For the Law was given through Moses; grace and truth came through Jesus Christ. No one has ever seen all of God. The one and only God (*i.e., Jesus*), who is in the closest possible relationship with the Father, has made him fully known.

Surely it benefits all of us to consider the record and come to our own conclusion.

Part 1

Family, Birth, and Childhood

Chapter 1

Beginnings

As Zechariah neared the temple, he felt a sense of anticipation he hadn't experienced in years. Even the atmosphere seemed charged with expectation, or could he even say hope? Yet at his age, what was there left to hope for? The brutal King Herod was ruling Judea. And Zechariah and his wife, Elizabeth, never had the pleasure of being parents. Though they'd prayed for years, Elizabeth had never conceived. Now because of their advanced age, she never would. Yet he never gave up on his faith in God. He continued to serve as a Levite priest and did his best to obey God's commands. He always looked forward to coming to Jerusalem when it was his turn to serve for a week at the temple, and it was his turn again.

He greeted the Levites from his division then washed and prepared himself, like he had every other time. But this was not like every other time. They informed him he'd been chosen by lot to burn incense in the Holy Place in the temple. Elated to be this close to God's presence and knowing the people were praying outside, he stepped toward the incense altar. Suddenly, the area around him lit up like a thousand suns. Blinded by the light, he froze, petrified with fear. Shading his eyes, he peeked out and saw an angel of the Lord standing right next to the altar.

The angel said, "Don't be afraid, Zechariah. Your prayer has been heard. Your wife, Elizabeth, will have a son, whom you are to name John. He will be a source of great happiness for you, and many will be pleased when he's born because he will be great in the Lord's sight. He will be filled with the Holy Spirit even before he's born, so he must never drink wine or alcoholic drinks. He will minister in the spirit and power of the great prophet Elijah, preparing people for the coming of the Lord. He'll turn many in Israel back to God, and he'll turn the hearts of parents back to their children. Those who disobey God will come to understand their need to get into a right relationship with the Lord."

Zechariah asked the angel, "How can this be true? I'm an old man, and my wife is an old woman."

The angel answered, "I am Gabriel, the one who stands in the presence of the Lord, and I've been sent to tell you this good news. Now listen—what I said is really going to happen. But because you didn't believe me, you won't be able to speak until John is born."

Zechariah was both awestruck and heartbroken—awestruck to have seen this heavenly vision and hear this wonderful news but heartbroken to have failed God with his unbelief. Meanwhile, people were waiting outside the temple, wondering where he was. Still shaking from the miraculous encounter, he walked out, anxious to tell everyone what happened. But when he opened his mouth to speak, words wouldn't come out. He was completely mute! They realized he'd seen a vision because he kept making signs to them but was speechless.

It was all Zechariah could do to complete his week of service at the temple before he could return home to share the news with Elizabeth. And just as the angel had promised, Elizabeth became pregnant in her old age. She isolated herself for five months, but she let it be known, "The Lord has done this for me. He's blessed me and allowed me to have a child!"

❧

About the same time, Elizabeth's young cousin Mary became betrothed to Joseph the carpenter, and betrothal was a pledge that could only be broken by divorce or death. Betrothed couples, though they did not live together, were considered husband and wife.

Six months into Elizabeth's pregnancy, Mary was busy preparing for her wedding in the town of Nazareth. Lost in thought about her upcoming marriage to Joseph, she was startled when a blinding light suddenly filled the room as if lightning had struck. She shielded her eyes and was almost too afraid to look, but curiosity got the better of her. There in the middle of the room stood an imposing man in shining robes.

His voice boomed when he spoke. "Hello, favored one! The Lord is with you."

Mary felt the energy drain from her body, and she could hardly stand. She grabbed hold of a chair to stop her hand from shaking so much. She was barely able to comprehend this vision let alone understand what his words meant.

The man continued, "I am the angel Gabriel sent to you from God. Don't be afraid. You have found favor with him. I've come to tell you that you're going to become pregnant and have a son. You will name him Jesus. He will be great and called the Son of the Most High."

Mary was speechless. First of all, how could she have a child when she'd never been with a man? Second, what did he mean by "Son of the Most High"? Was the angel saying he would be God's Son? This news was too wonderful to take in. She remembered how God had promised to bring a Messiah through a descendant of King David:

> "I will make him my firstborn, highest of the kings of the
>   earth.
> I will maintain my lovingkindness for him forever;
>   My covenant with him will stand firm;
>   I will establish his family line forever,
>   And his throne as endless as the days of heaven. . . .
>   Once for all time I swore an oath by my holiness—and I
>   will not lie to David—that
>   His descendants will continue forever, and
>   His throne will be as the sun before me—estab-
>   lished forever like the moon is established as a
>   faithful witness to the sun's presence in the sky."[1]

Then Gabriel said, "The Lord God will give him the throne of his ancestor King David, and he will reign over the house of Israel forever. His kingdom will never come to an end."

Now Mary knew both she and Joseph were descendants of King David, but it had been more than five hundred years since any Jewish king had reigned in Israel. But she also knew God had promised through the prophet Jeremiah to raise up the Messiah from the line of David. Could her child be him? She finally found the courage to ask the angel, "How is this going to happen since I'm a virgin?"

Gabriel answered, "The Holy Spirit will come upon you, and the power of the Most High will overshadow you. So the child will be holy and called the Son of God. And listen to this—your cousin Elizabeth has become pregnant in her old age. Though she was never able to conceive, she's now in her sixth month. You see, nothing is impossible with God!"

Mary believed all he said and answered, "I am the Lord's servant. Let it be done to me as you have said." Then the angel left her as swiftly as he'd come. And just as Gabriel had promised, she became pregnant by the Holy Spirit while she was betrothed to Joseph, but before they had come together.

ॐ

After Mary heard about her cousin Elizabeth's miraculous pregnancy, she immediately made the three-day trip to Zechariah's home in the hill country of Judea. She couldn't wait to tell Elizabeth the incredible news she herself had received from the angel. When she reached the house, she knocked and called out to Elizabeth.

When Elizabeth heard Mary's voice, her baby leaped inside of her. Elizabeth was filled with the Holy Spirit and cried out, "Blessed are you among women, and blessed is the fruit of your womb!" Then she asked Mary, "Why has the mother of my Lord come to me? My baby leaped for joy when I heard your voice. You're truly blessed for believing what the Lord told you would happen."

Mary was astounded. How could Elizabeth possibly know all that happened to her when she hadn't yet told her? She thought,

"God himself must have revealed it." Filled with happiness, these words poured out of her:

"My soul glorifies the Lord, and
my spirit rejoices in God my Savior!
  He looked at the humble condition of his servant.
    From now on, all generations will call me blessed,
      for the Mighty One has done great things for me.
  His name is holy.
  From generation to generation, he shows mercy to those
    who fear him.
  He has done mighty things:
    scattering the proud,
    bringing rulers down from their thrones,
    lifting up the humble,
    filling the hungry with good things, and
    sending the rich away empty.
  He has helped Israel and remembered (as he promised to
  our ancestors) to be merciful to Abraham and his descen-
  dants forever."

Mary stayed with Elizabeth for three months before returning home.

When Elizabeth's pregnancy reached full term, she gave birth to a son. Her neighbors and relatives heard about how the Lord had blessed her, and they celebrated with her. On the eighth day, friends and family came to the circumcision ceremony required by Jewish law. They planned to follow the Jewish tradition and name the boy after his father, Zechariah. But his mother Elizabeth intervened, "No! He is to be named John."

Everyone objected, "But none of your relatives are named John," and they made signs to his father to find out what he wanted him named.

He asked for a wax writing tablet and, to everyone's astonishment, wrote, "His name is John." Immediately Zechariah regained his speech and was filled with the Holy Spirit. He began blessing God, and speaking under the influence of the Holy Spirit, he said:

"Praise be to the Lord, the God of Israel, for just as he promised through his holy prophets long ago,
He has visited and redeemed his people.
He has raised up a powerful Savior for us from the family
of his servant King David,
to save us from our enemies and all who hate us;
to show mercy to our ancestors; and
to remember the holy covenant he swore to our ancestor Abraham, promising
to rescue us from our enemies so we can serve him
without fear in holy righteousness all our days.
And you, my child, will be called the prophet of the Most
High. You will go ahead of the Lord
to prepare the way for him,
to show his people how to be saved through the forgiveness of their sins
that comes because of God's tender mercy,
by which the sunrise will come to us from heaven
to shine on those who live in darkness and in the
shadow of death, and
to guide our feet into the way of peace."

The people listened in awe, and throughout the Judean hill country, they spread the news about all that had happened. Everyone who
heard about these things kept them in mind, wondering, "What will
this child be?" They knew the Lord was with him.

As John grew up, he became strong with the Holy Spirit's power.
And he went to live in the wilderness.

Chapter 2

Birth

Joseph was building some furniture when he got the news. Just as the angel Gabriel had promised, Mary became pregnant by the Holy Spirit while they were engaged to be married but before they'd been together as a couple. He could hardly focus on his work. What would people in the village think when they found out Mary was pregnant? Would they assume he was to blame? Or that she'd slept with someone else? When Mary told him she'd seen an angel and what he said to her, it was beyond belief.

Joseph paced back and forth, hammer in hand, trying to figure out his options. What could he do and remain faithful to God's law as he always had? Finally, he laid down his tool and sat down on a log to think. The heat of the day was getting to him—or was it the pressure of his dilemma—and he mopped his forehead with a cloth. He truly loved Mary and didn't want to disgrace her within their community. Though they hadn't been married yet, a pledge to marry was as binding as marriage itself. He decided the best thing to do was to quietly divorce her.

One night when Joseph was in a deep sleep, an angel of the Lord appeared to him in a dream and said, "Joseph, don't be afraid to take Mary as your wife, for her baby is from the Holy Spirit. She will have a son, and you are to name him Jesus because he will save his people from their sins.* This will fulfill the prophecy the Lord spoke through Isaiah: 'A virgin will conceive and give birth to a son, and they will call him Immanuel'"² (Hebrew meaning "God with us").

---

* "Jesus" means "God saves/rescues/delivers." This is summed up in the term "Savior."

Joseph jolted awake. Mary really had seen an angel, and now he had too! And the angel even said Isaiah's prophecy from more than six hundred years ago was about to be fulfilled through him and Mary! He knew what he had to do. So he followed through with his marriage to Mary and pledged to keep her a virgin until after the baby was born.

❧

Several months passed until it was almost time for Mary to give birth. The situation the couple faced was challenging enough but became even more so when Joseph received word that Caesar Augustus had ordered a census be taken of all the Roman Empire. This was not good news because everyone had to return to their ancestral hometown to register. Joseph was a descendent of King David, so he and Mary were expected to make the long trip from Nazareth to David's birthplace, Bethlehem! How could she make this difficult eighty-mile journey over mountainous terrain in her condition? Though the timing couldn't be worse, they had no choice, as Governor Quirinius expected everyone to comply by the deadline. They both prayed for God's help in making the arduous trek. They encouraged themselves by remembering what the prophet Micah said more than seven hundred years ago—a ruler of Israel whose origins were eternal would come out of Bethlehem.[3]

When they arrived, they searched for a place to stay, but with all the people in town for the census, they couldn't find a room. Joseph was frantic with worry, knocking on door after door, pleading, in hope that someone would take them in.* But Mary appeared calm and peaceful even when her labor pains began. At that point, Joseph knew her time had run out. He saw a stable where livestock were being kept and led Mary there. He put their blankets on the ground and helped her lie down. There Mary gave birth to her firstborn son.

---

* The traditional idea of Mary and Joseph asking an innkeeper for a room is not in any historical record. It is unlikely that a small community like Bethlehem had any inn, but it may have had a brush arbor shelter for travelers. Perhaps it was filled with others returning for the census. There is no record of anyone helping them.

She wrapped him in cloths and placed him in a manger (an animal feed trough).

Genealogy of Jesus*

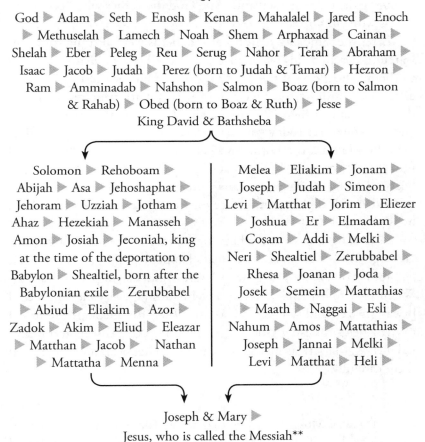

God ▶ Adam ▶ Seth ▶ Enosh ▶ Kenan ▶ Mahalalel ▶ Jared ▶ Enoch ▶ Methuselah ▶ Lamech ▶ Noah ▶ Shem ▶ Arphaxad ▶ Cainan ▶ Shelah ▶ Eber ▶ Peleg ▶ Reu ▶ Serug ▶ Nahor ▶ Terah ▶ Abraham ▶ Isaac ▶ Jacob ▶ Judah ▶ Perez (born to Judah & Tamar) ▶ Hezron ▶ Ram ▶ Amminadab ▶ Nahshon ▶ Salmon ▶ Boaz (born to Salmon & Rahab) ▶ Obed (born to Boaz & Ruth) ▶ Jesse ▶ King David & Bathsheba ▶

Solomon ▶ Rehoboam ▶ Abijah ▶ Asa ▶ Jehoshaphat ▶ Jehoram ▶ Uzziah ▶ Jotham ▶ Ahaz ▶ Hezekiah ▶ Manasseh ▶ Amon ▶ Josiah ▶ Jeconiah, king at the time of the deportation to Babylon ▶ Shealtiel, born after the Babylonian exile ▶ Zerubbabel ▶ Abiud ▶ Eliakim ▶ Azor ▶ Zadok ▶ Akim ▶ Eliud ▶ Eleazar ▶ Matthan ▶ Jacob ▶ Nathan ▶ Mattatha ▶ Menna ▶

Melea ▶ Eliakim ▶ Jonam ▶ Joseph ▶ Judah ▶ Simeon ▶ Levi ▶ Matthat ▶ Jorim ▶ Eliezer ▶ Joshua ▶ Er ▶ Elmadam ▶ Cosam ▶ Addi ▶ Melki ▶ Neri ▶ Shealtiel ▶ Zerubbabel ▶ Rhesa ▶ Joanan ▶ Joda ▶ Josek ▶ Semein ▶ Mattathias ▶ Maath ▶ Naggai ▶ Esli ▶ Nahum ▶ Amos ▶ Mattathias ▶ Joseph ▶ Jannai ▶ Melki ▶ Levi ▶ Matthat ▶ Heli ▶

Joseph & Mary ▶
Jesus, who is called the Messiah**

---

* Ancient genealogies such as this are incomplete; skipping lesser-known persons was common.

** Matthew's Gospel finishes this genealogy with the statement, "There are fourteen generations from Abraham to David, fourteen generations from David to the deportation to Babylon, and fourteen generations from the exile to Christ." Ancient genealogies commonly mentioned numbers of generations that do not tally with the number of names in the tables. While theories have been proposed to explain this anomaly, there is little agreement.

Here was the baby Jesus, about whom later the apostle Paul wrote, "Being in very nature God himself, he did not consider equality with God something to be held on to. Rather, he emptied himself by being made in human likeness and appearing as a man. He humbled himself by taking the form of a servant." And God the Father said, "Let all my angels worship him."[4]

Later the same day, a group of shepherds were keeping the night watch in nearby fields when an angel of the Lord suddenly appeared to them. The glory of the Lord, a visible manifestation of his presence, shone around the angel, and the shepherds were terrified. But the angel said to them, "Don't be afraid. I have great news for you and everyone else! Today your Savior was born in the town of David! He's the Messiah, the Lord. And here's how you'll know him: you'll find a baby wrapped in cloths and lying in a manger." Then a huge heavenly army of angels appeared, praising God and saying, "Glory to God in the highest, and peace on earth to everyone with whom he is pleased."

As the angels returned to heaven, the shepherds said to each other, "Let's go to Bethlehem and see what's happened." So they quickly left and found Mary and Joseph with Jesus, who was lying in the manger. When they told them what the angel had said, everyone who heard it was amazed and wondered about it. Then the shepherds returned to their fields, praising God for all the things they'd seen and heard. Exhausted, Mary treasured all these things in her heart and considered them carefully.

❧

Now the law of Moses stipulated that every male child must be circumcised eight days after he is born, and tradition is that a child should be named on his circumcision day. So Jesus was circumcised on his eighth day, and Joseph named him Jesus, the name the angel had given him before he'd been conceived.

The law also said all firstborn sons were the property of the Lord and had to be redeemed by paying a price of five shekels (two ounces of silver, about five days' wages) to the temple treasury. So about six weeks later, Joseph and Mary took Jesus to Jerusalem to offer a sacrifice to complete Mary's purification* and to present Jesus to the Lord and pay the price to redeem him. Since they were too poor to offer a lamb, they offered a pair of doves, and they paid the priests five shekels to redeem Jesus.

Now there was a godly man in Jerusalem named Simeon. He had been waiting for God to rescue Israel by restoring the people's loyalty to God and their power as a nation. The Holy Spirit was on him and had revealed he would not die before he'd seen the Lord's Messiah.

Led by the Holy Spirit, Simeon went into the temple courts at the same time Joseph and Mary brought in the baby Jesus to redeem him. And the Lord revealed to Simeon that Jesus was the Messiah! So Simeon took him in his arms, blessed God, and said, "Lord, now I can die in peace just as you promised me, for I've seen the Savior. He's the light that will make you known to the Gentiles and reveal your glory to your people, Israel."

Mary and Joseph were amazed at what he'd said about Jesus. Then Simeon blessed them and told Mary, "Listen, this child is destined to cause the rise and fall of many people in Israel and to be a sign that will be rejected. He'll be a sword that pierces even your own soul. And the thoughts of many hearts will be revealed through him."

At that very moment, the prophetess Anna came up to them. She was eighty-four years old, a widow for most of her life. Sadly, her husband had died when they'd been married only eight years. Yet she remained faithful to the Lord. She never left the temple but worshiped there night and day, fasting and praying. She spoke just as Simeon had, praising God and speaking about Jesus to everyone who was waiting for the redemption of Jerusalem.

After Joseph and Mary redeemed Jesus and completed Mary's purification ritual, they returned to Nazareth, filled with anticipation about what Jesus' future held.

---

* According to the Jewish law, a woman was ceremonially unclean after giving birth and had to make a sacrifice at the temple to be purified.

Chapter 3

Childhood

About two years after Jesus was born, magi from the east came to Jerusalem.* They asked, "Where's the one who's been born king of the Jews? We've seen his star in the east and have come to worship him."

When King Herod heard this, he was troubled (and when Herod was upset, all Jerusalem was on edge, for he was a cruel person given to excess). Herod wondered, who was this so-called "king" who might threaten his throne. Such a threat needed to be nipped in the bud. So he met with all the chief priests and scribes and asked them, "Where will the Messiah be born?"

They replied, "In Bethlehem in Judea. The prophet Micah wrote seven hundred years ago, 'But you, Bethlehem in Judah, are in no way least among the towns that provide Judah with rulers, for out of you will come a ruler who will shepherd my people, Israel.'"[5]

Then Herod met with the magi secretly and discovered the exact time the star had appeared. He sent them to Bethlehem and said, "Search carefully for the child. When you find him, report it to me so that I can go and worship him too." He was lying of course. He had no intention of worshiping anyone but himself. He was just trying to gain their trust, so they'd reveal the child's location.

When the magi left, the star led them until it stood over the place where the child was. Elated to have finally found who they were

---

* "Magi,": a transliteration of a Persian word traditionally translated "wise men." They were astrologers, priests, dream interpreters, and practitioners of other secret/mysterious arts. In Scripture there is no mention of how many came or their place in society, but the value of the gifts indicates they were wealthy, perhaps even kings.

searching for, they hurried to enter the house where Mary was with her child. When they saw the baby, they were overjoyed and fell to the ground in worship. Their long, tiring journey had paid off. They gave Jesus gifts of gold, frankincense (a plant resin—dried sap—used in anointing oil, perfumes, and incense), and myrrh (a plant resin that was as valuable as gold). When it was time to go back to their own country, they went home by a different route because God had warned them in a dream not to return to Herod.

After the magi had left, Joseph reflected on their visit, marveling that these wise men from the east had traveled so far—more than a thousand miles to honor Jesus! That night, after he'd finally drifted off to sleep, an angel of the Lord appeared to him in a dream and said, "Get up! Take the child and his mother and flee to Egypt. Stay there until I tell you to leave because Herod is about to search for the child to kill him!"

Joseph jumped up out of bed, waking Mary. "Joseph, what's come over you?" she said. "Why are you so agitated? You'll wake Jesus."

"Mary, there's no time to waste—Jesus is in danger!" Joseph started gathering up the bedclothes. "We have to leave—now!"

After he told Mary what the angel had said, they both began packing all they could carry into their sacks. They wrapped Jesus in warm clothes and headed out the door to start the 250-mile journey to Egypt. This led to the fulfillment of what the Lord had said through the prophet Hosea more than 750 years earlier: "I called my son out of Egypt."

When Herod saw that he'd been tricked by the magi, he shook with anger and went on the warpath. Based on the dates he'd learned from them, he sent soldiers to kill every boy two years old and under in and around Bethlehem.

❧

After living in Egypt until Herod's death, Joseph was once again visited by an angel in a dream. The angel said, "Take the child and his mother back to Israel. Those who sought the child's life are dead." But when Joseph heard that Archelaus, Herod the Great's son, was ruling in Judea, he was afraid to live there. (Archelaus was known for his cruelty and had murdered many Jews.) So the family passed through Judea to Galilee and settled in Nazareth. This fulfilled what the Lord had said through the prophets: he would be called a Nazarene. He became strong and wise, and God's favor was on him.

℁

Every spring Joseph and Mary went to Jerusalem for the Passover Festival.* When Jesus was twelve years old, he went along with them. On the way home, Joseph and Mary had already been traveling a day when they realized they hadn't seen Jesus since they left. Surely, they thought, he was with one of the relatives. They searched among their friends and family in the caravan, asking, "Have you seen Jesus?" When the answer was repeatedly, "No," they were beside themselves with worry. Where could he be?

When they didn't find him, they went back to Jerusalem to continue the search. After three long days, they finally found him in the last place they expected: sitting among the teachers in the temple courts! He was listening to them intently, asking questions and even answering them. And everyone there was astounded at his understanding and answers.

When his parents saw him, they were shocked. Mary asked, "Son, why have you treated us like this? Look, your father and I have been very worried, searching for you."

He responded, "Why were you looking for me? Didn't you know I had to be in my Father's house?"

But they didn't understand what he meant. Then he went back to Nazareth with them, and he obeyed them. And Jesus grew in wisdom, maturity, and favor with God and men.

---

* The Passover Festival was a seven-day celebration in Jerusalem to commemorate God's deliverance of Israel from Egyptian bondage, how he passed over their homes on the night he slew all the firstborn of Egypt. (See Exodus 12:1–30.) The story was retold on the first night at a ritual dinner known as a seder. Passover was immediately followed by the seven-day Festival of Unleavened Bread. All Jewish men were required to go to Jerusalem for the festival.

Over seven hundred years earlier, Isaiah, looking into the future, said, "He grew up like a tender green shoot before God, like a root from the dry ground. He had no attractive form, no splendor that we should be drawn to him, and no beautiful appearance that we should desire him."[6]

Part 2

First Year
of Ministry

Chapter 4

Public Ministry Begins

John watched the sun peek through the outcropping of rocks in the distance and took a deep breath of the early morning air. He routinely got up before sunrise. It gave him time to commune with God before his many disciples surrounded him. He lived in a wilderness that most people avoided, but he enjoyed the seclusion. He lived a simple life with no means of income, existing on the locusts and wild honey he found in the region. He fasted regularly. People who visited from the city had offered to support him many times, some bringing new robes, but he was content to wear his camel hair tunic held together with a leather belt. The pleasures of this world had never appealed to him. They only distracted him from his purpose, what God had revealed to him. He was to prepare for the Lord Jesus' arrival. His location in the Judean wilderness near the Jordan River was perfectly suited for that purpose, as it gave him easy access to water for baptisms. He traveled all around the region, telling people the kingdom of heaven was near and urging them to repent and be forgiven. As they confessed their sins, he baptized them in the river. For this reason, they called him John the Baptist.

Day after day people came from Jerusalem, Judea, and all around the Jordan. John knew his work was divinely ordained; no human could orchestrate such a following for a prophet like him. Sometimes his calling was too deep to fathom. They told him he was the one God spoke of more than seven hundred years earlier, when the prophet Isaiah said, "I will send my messenger ahead of the Messiah to prepare his way."

༄

One day John looked toward Jerusalem and saw a group of Pharisees and Sadducees, members from the two leading Jewish sects, coming his way. The Pharisees were popular among the lower-ranking priests and middle-class merchants and tradesmen. They considered the oral law, which they believed could be traced back to Moses, to be as binding as the written Scripture. Their zeal for obeying the law led to the development of detailed religious legal interpretations that ruled their lives, and which they lived out in closed communities with strictly regulated admission policies. Each community was led by a scribe (a person who was skilled in the law).

The other sect, the Sadducees, was the most popular among the higher-ranking priests and the aristocracy. Both religious and political in nature, its members embraced Greek culture. They held a strong hand in the Sanhedrin, the Jewish ruling council, and actively participated in secular political affairs because Rome gave them governing authority over Israel. They were responsible for keeping peace in Israel, and they meted out severe punishment to anyone who disturbed that peace or challenged Roman authority. Sadducees considered only the written Scripture as authoritative and binding.

Of everyone who came to hear John preach, these religious leaders were the most difficult to get through to. They just wouldn't listen because they thought they knew all there was to know about God and the Scriptures. His frustration rose as they approached. "You brood of snakes!" he shouted. "Didn't I warn you to flee from God's anger? Your actions show no sign you've repented."

As he turned to walk away, they challenged him, "How can you speak to us like this? We're respected teachers and the sons of Abraham!" They, like many, thought their family heritage and religious rituals were adequate for their salvation. John knew otherwise.

He faced them and said, "Hear this! God can raise up children of Abraham from stones. The ax is already aimed at the root of the trees, and every tree that does not produce good fruit will be cut down and thrown into the fire."

By then a crowd had formed, and people were deeply concerned about what he said. They asked, "Then what should we do?"

John told them, "The person with two tunics should share with whoever has none, and whoever has food should do the same."

John noticed some tax collectors in the group. They were hated among the Jews because they worked for Rome and were seen as traitors. Most of them collected more than was required and pocketed the rest. Even they were coming to be baptized and asking, "Teacher, what should we do?"

He told them, "Don't collect a penny more than you're ordered."

When some Roman soldiers asked, "And what should we do?" he replied, "Stop falsely accusing people of crimes so you can extort money from them. Be content with what you're paid."

He could hear some in the crowd saying he was the Messiah, so he set them straight right away. "I baptize you in water on account of your repentance. But someone who's more powerful than I am is coming. I am not worthy to carry his sandals or even to stoop down to untie them. I'm baptizing you in water, but he will baptize you with the Holy Spirit and with fire."

Some of the people looked awestruck and others confused, so he continued. "His winnowing fork, the fork he uses to throw the wheat up into the air so the chaff is blown away from the grains, is in his hand. He won't just separate the grain from the chaff. He'll clean the floor where it falls, gather the wheat into his barn, and burn up the chaff with unquenchable fire."

Many gasped. Some walked away shaking their heads, while others stepped forward to be baptized.

John stepped into the Jordan and continued baptizing people most of the day. Suddenly, he sensed in his spirit the culmination of his ministry had finally arrived. He saw Jesus the Messiah approaching! John cried out, "This is the person I was talking about when I said, 'He who comes after me is greater than me because he existed before me.'"

John fell at Jesus' feet when he reached the river, but Jesus urged him to get up and said he wanted to be baptized. John protested and said, "No, my Lord! I need to be baptized by you, and you're coming to me?"

But Jesus gently laid his hand on John's shoulder and answered, "Let it be this way for now, cousin. It's right to do all that God requires." So John baptized him.

When Jesus was coming up out of the water, the heavens opened, and he saw the Spirit of God descending as a dove and coming to rest on him. And a voice from heaven said, "This is my Son whom I love and with whom I am well pleased."

John was in awe and stood there praising God. This was a man he'd known all his life and had grown up with. He knew he was special even then, but today he saw him in a whole new light. In fact, he was the light. To think, he'd been in such close contact with the Messiah and didn't even know it!

&

While still in the river, Jesus was filled with the Holy Spirit. As he stepped onto the riverbank, he was compelled by the Spirit to go deep into the wilderness and eat no food for forty days. At the end of that time, he was hungry and had little energy left. He sat down on a rock and wiped the sweat from his brow. The heat was unbearable.

"Well, what have we here?" Satan circled around him, laughing at his weakened state. Here, at his weakest point, his supreme adversary, none other than the devil himself, came to taunt him. They'd had a long history together before Jesus came to earth. He first knew him as the guardian cherub, a mighty angel clothed in jewels, walking in the presence of God in heaven. He lost his position, however, when he was found to be evil. He became an outcast in heaven and became prince of this world, of the earth. As one who hates God and whoever serves him, it's no surprise he came to mock Jesus and try to lure him into his service.

Jesus stood up to face his enemy. "I saw you fall like lightning from heaven."

"You've come a long way from when we last met," he sneered. "The King of heaven is now the servant of earth. Don't think Daddy is going to help you now. You're in my territory." He pointed to the numerous rocks that surrounded them. "If you truly are the Son of God, let's see you change these stones into bread."

Jesus was shaking from hunger. He could almost taste the bread on his lips. But he knew the devil was a liar, and in fact, the father of lies, so he knew not to fall into his trap. He answered, "The Scriptures say: 'Man shall not live by bread alone, but by every word that comes from the mouth of God.'"[7]

Suddenly, Satan took Jesus to the holy city, Jerusalem. He had him stand on the highest point of the temple and said, "If you are the Son of God, go ahead and jump! Don't the Scriptures say, 'God will command his angels concerning you,' and, 'They will lift you up in their hands, so you don't strike your foot against a stone'?"[8]

Jesus looked down at the big drop from the top of the wall, to the Kidron Ravine below, but wise to his schemes replied, "The Scriptures also say: 'Do not test the Lord your God.'"[9]

Next the devil took him to a high mountain, and in a moment, showed him all the kingdoms of the world and all their glory. Then he said, "If you bow down and worship me, I'll give you authority over all this and all its splendor. It's been handed over to me, and I can give it to whomever I wish."

As God's archrival, what a victory it would be for Satan if the Son of God were to come over to his camp. But Jesus had had enough of his deceptive devices. "Go away, Satan!" he said. "The Scripture also says: 'You shall worship the Lord your God and serve him only.'"[10]

When the devil had finished every temptation, he said, "This isn't over!" and he left Jesus alone. But Jesus knew he'd be back when he found the opportunity. Jesus sat back down on the rock, exhausted, among the wild animals of the wilderness. They roamed freely around him but made no threats. Then angels appeared and brought him food and water.

℘

Meanwhile, back at the Jordan River near Bethany, some priests and Levites sent by the Jewish leaders were grilling John the Baptist. "Who are you?" they demanded.

"I'm not the Messiah," John responded. "I'm a witness called to testify about the light, but I'm not the light."

"Then who are you?" they asked. "Elijah?" Devout Jews had been looking for the return of the great ninth-century BC prophet ever since the fifth-century BC prophet Malachi had prophesied that Elijah would return before the Messiah appeared.[11]

John replied, "No."

"Are you the Prophet?"

He again answered, "No."

They continued probing him. "Tell us something about yourself. Tell us who you are, so we can give an answer to those who sent us."

They were trying his patience with all their questions, so John quoted Isaiah the prophet: "I am the voice of one calling out in the wilderness, 'Make straight the way for the Lord.'"[12]

"Why then do you baptize if you're not the Messiah or Elijah or the Prophet?" they asked.

"I baptize in water," John replied, "but a man you don't yet know is coming after me and is already here among you. I'm not even worthy to untie the strap of his sandal."

When they couldn't get an answer that satisfied them, the men left and returned to Jerusalem.

❧

The next day John was with his disciples baptizing again. He saw Jesus coming toward him and called out in a loud voice within everyone's hearing, "Look, the Lamb of God who takes away the sins of the world! This is the one I told you about when I said, 'A man who is coming after me is greater than me.' This is the Son of God, God's chosen one!"

When he saw he had the crowd's attention, he explained further: "He's greater than me because he existed before me. Even though I've spent all this time baptizing people, I didn't recognize him at first. But

God told me, 'The one on whom you see the Holy Spirit descend is the one who will baptize people with the Holy Spirit.' Then I saw the Holy Spirit come down from heaven like a dove and remain on him."

જ્જ

The next day when John saw Jesus passing by in the distance, he called out, "Look, there's the Lamb of God!" When two of his disciples heard him say this, they immediately left him to follow Jesus. At first John was taken aback, but then he realized this was meant to be.

On his trip back to Capernaum, Jesus sensed someone following him. He turned around and saw the two disciples of John the Baptist, Andrew and John, trailing behind him. "What do you want?" he asked.

They replied, "Rabbi, where are you staying?"

He replied, "Come and I'll show you." So they went with him and followed him to Capernaum.

When they approached the town, Andrew rushed home to find his brother, Simon, who was getting ready for work. The two of them were fishermen who regularly worked at night. He burst inside and said, "We've found the Messiah!"

Simon shook his head, finished what he was doing, and headed out the door. He knew Andrew had been following John the Baptist and wondered if he'd now replaced him with some new prophet. Of course, being single, Andrew had more time on his hands. Simon was kept busy trying to earn a living for his wife and mother-in-law.

They walked side by side to the shore of the Sea of Galilee. Simon didn't want to destroy Andrew's enthusiasm about this new "prophet," yet he wasn't falling for it himself. After enduring the Romans all these years, he had long ago given up hope of ever seeing the Messiah.

When they reached the sea, they pushed their boat out from shore and climbed into it. Their partners, John and his brother James, were doing the same with their boat a short distance down the shore. The night dragged on, eerily silent, with the lapping of the water against the boat the only sound. Hours passed, but every time they checked their nets, they came up empty. As the sun started to rise, they decided to give up and head back to shore. When they got closer, Simon heard a commotion and looked to see what was going on. A short distance down the beach, a crowd was clamoring to get close to a man who appeared to be teaching them. It was none of his business, so he helped Andrew pull the boat onto the sand and started washing the nets.

Andrew stood up in the boat to get a better view. "That's the man I told you about—his name is Jesus!" Let's go down and see him.

After he took a quick glance at the man, Simon said, "We've got work to do." He threw the nets back into the boat and began to prepare them for the next day. After about ten minutes, he sensed someone watching him. He looked up into the piercing eyes of the teacher named Jesus. He felt uneasy, exposed somehow. It was like the man was seeing into his very soul! The crowd had followed him down the beach and surrounded their boat. Simon was shocked when Jesus got into it and asked him to push it out from the shore. He complied, speechless. Jesus sat down and began teaching the people from there, speaking knowledgeably—and with authority! Simon hadn't had a lot of schooling in the law of Moses, so most of what Jesus said was lost on him.

When Jesus finished speaking, he turned to Simon, and said, "Go out into the deep water and let down your nets for a catch."

Jesus' appearance was quite ordinary. No one gave him a second look, until they heard him speak, that is. Once he started talking, there was something remarkable about him. So Simon addressed him with respect. "Master, we worked hard all night and haven't caught a thing, but because you say to, we'll go back out and lower the nets."

Once he lowered the nets, the water started churning around them. They caught so many fish they had a hard time pulling up the nets without tearing them. They signaled James and John in the other boat, and they came to help. When they finished, both boats were filled to the point of sinking. The four fishermen just stood there, shocked by this miraculous catch.

Simon knew then and there this teacher Jesus was no ordinary person—he was a holy man of God! Just standing next to him made him feel like the most sinful man on earth, as if he were clothed in mud next to someone dressed in pure white. He fell to his knees in front of Jesus and said, "Leave me, Lord. I'm a sinful man."

"Don't be afraid," Jesus said. "From now on you'll be catching people. You are Simon the son of John. You will be called Peter, which means 'rock.'"

Meanwhile, John and James had gone back to their boat and started mending their nets with their father, Zebedee.

Jesus called out to them, "Follow me and I'll make you fishers of people."

They left their nets and their father then followed Jesus, along with Andrew and Peter (as Jesus was now calling Simon).

ↄↄ

The next day, Peter went to the meeting place Jesus had designated. Andrew was already there. He'd left the house earlier than necessary in his eagerness to get started. Peter, however, had a lot of explaining to do to his wife about his new calling. He'd never been overly religious, so it came as a bit of a shock to her that he was now following a holy man. But frankly no one was more shocked than he was. He always had the tendency to be impulsive; everyone knew that about him, but to leave his work with no means of support, well it was just crazy. He had no idea why Jesus called him anyway. He was just an ordinary fisherman. There was nothing special about him. Why didn't he call a Pharisee? They were the most religious people he knew, always quoting Scripture and praying in the streets where everyone could see them. You'd never catch him doing that.

Peter arrived just as Jesus did, and he told the group they were going to travel around Galilee. After a while, they stopped in Bethsaida, Peter and Andrew's hometown, where the two brothers had first learned the fishing business. Peter sat down to rest on a bench under a tree while he watched Jesus approach a man named Philip. Peter had seen him around town when he lived there but lost touch after their family had moved to Capernaum.

He heard Jesus call out to him, "Come and be my disciple."

Philip responded immediately, stopped what he was doing, and followed Jesus. When he saw this, Peter wished his own faith were stronger. Who was this man who had the power to influence others to follow him?

Philip asked Jesus if he could go tell someone else too. When he found his friend Nathanael, he rushed up to him and shouted, "We've found him! We've found the one Moses and the prophets wrote about! He pointed toward Jesus. "He's Jesus, the son of Joseph from Nazareth."

Nathanael looked unconvinced. "Nazareth? Can anything good come out of Nazareth?"

Philip motioned toward their group. "Come with us and see for yourself."

Jesus approached Nathanael and said, "I can see you're a true Israelite in whom there's no deceit."

"How do you know about me?" Nathanael asked.

"I saw you before Philip called you—while you were sitting under the fig tree," Jesus replied.

Nathanael's surprise was evident. "Rabbi, you truly are the Son of God and the king of Israel!"

Jesus said, "You believe just because I told you I saw you under the fig tree? You'll see greater things than that. I'm telling you the truth; you'll see heaven opened and the angels of God ascending and descending on the Son of Man."

Peter watched and listened. He could not help but wonder, "Just who is this who calls himself the Son of Man?"

❧

Three days later, Jesus informed Peter and the other disciples they'd been invited to a wedding in Cana. It wasn't far from Jesus' hometown of Nazareth, and he said his mother would be there because she knew the family. As they made their way there, Peter was somewhat surprised that Jesus was going at all. It hardly seemed like the work of God to be enjoying a celebration. Weren't they supposed to be denying themselves by fasting and praying like the Pharisees or John's disciples?

When they arrived, the area was packed with guests. In fact, it looked like the entire village had turned up. The feast was in full swing and appeared to have been going on for several days already. Jesus' mother, Mary, greeted them all as they came in, looking pleased to see them—but especially Jesus. Looking concerned, she turned to him and said, "They're out of wine."

Jesus sighed. "Mother, what does this have to do with me? My time hasn't come yet."

But Mary wasn't deterred. She told the servants, "Do whatever he says."

Jesus looked around and saw six stone water containers used for ceremonial hand washing. Each could hold anywhere from twenty to thirty gallons. He told the servants to fill them with water, and they filled them to the brim. Then he said, "Now take some to the head-waiter and have him taste it."

Curious, Peter followed the servants. When they located the head-waiter, they asked him to taste the liquid inside the containers. He ladled out a cup, and his eyes lit up when he tasted it. He even called the bridegroom away from the dancing and exclaimed, "Everyone brings out the choice wine first, and then, after the guests have drunk a lot, serves the cheaper wine. But you've saved the best till now!"

Peter wouldn't have believed it if he hadn't seen it for himself. Jesus had changed the water into wine—and not just any wine, but the finest wine, which would normally need to be aged for years! He sat down to catch his breath. He knew Jesus was special after the incident with the fish, but people could have explained that more easily. There was no explanation for this except it was a miracle of God. He felt exhilarated and afraid at the same time.

After the miracle at the wedding, the disciples began to believe in Jesus. He went to Capernaum with his mother, brother, and disciples and stayed for a few days.

Part 3

Second Year
of Ministry

<u>Chapter 5</u>

Controversy

That spring, when the Passover holiday was approaching, like all obedient Jews, Jesus went up to Jerusalem.* The Scriptures required every male Jew to go to Jerusalem to celebrate the festival. He didn't exclude himself, as he was living his life on earth in every way as an ordinary human being, experiencing all that they did. When he and his disciples entered the temple's outer courts, he was shocked to see tables set up with merchants selling cattle, sheep, and doves for sacrifices at exorbitant prices. At other tables were money changers exchanging foreign coins for temple currency to pay the tax, profiting big time off the foreign worshipers.

Outraged to see these greedy people degrading his Father's house and cheating the poor, he made a whip out of cords and drove them out of the courts with their sheep and cattle. "Get these things out of here!" he shouted. He overturned the money changers' tables, scattering their coins all over the ground. He told those selling doves, "Stop turning my Father's house into a marketplace!"

His disciples observed his actions from a distance. They remembered what King David had written about the Messiah a thousand years ago in one of his psalms, "Zeal for your house will consume me," and how more than seven hundred years ago, God had said through the prophet Isaiah, "My house will be called a house of prayer."

The Jews in the temple were indignant, demanding, "What gives you the right to do these things? Show us a miracle to prove your authority."

---

* There are three festivals (often referred to as Pilgrimage Festivals or Pilgrim Festivals) for which all Jews who were able were to go to Jerusalem to celebrate: Passover, Weeks (a.k.a. Pentecost), and Tabernacles (a.k.a. Booths).

Jesus wasn't about to give them what they asked for. Instead, he said, "Destroy this temple and in three days I'll raise it up!"

"That's preposterous!" they argued. "It's taken forty-six years to build this temple, and you're going to rebuild it in three days?"

Jesus had purposely said something they wouldn't understand. He wasn't going to give them the satisfaction of teaching them clearly. They were too proud to learn. Actually, he was speaking of another temple—his body. After he was raised from the dead, his true disciples would recall his words. Then they would believe the Scriptures and what Jesus told them.

❧

Jesus remained in Jerusalem for the Passover and the six-day Festival of Unleavened Bread that followed, performing many miracles. Many people believed in him after they saw the miracles, but he didn't allow himself to trust any of them. He didn't need anyone to tell him about people—what was in their hearts. After sundown on most nights, he went to the Mount of Olives to escape the crowds and pray to his Father. He would light a fire and set up camp for the night before meeting his disciples in the morning.

Nicodemus, one of the Jewish religious leaders, watched Jesus leave the temple grounds. He followed him in secret because he didn't want the other Pharisees to see him. Jesus had become quite controversial among his sect, and he wanted to find out more about him without their interference. He had heard about all the miracles he'd been performing and had to meet him for himself. Though Nicodemus had studied the Scriptures and taught the people the law of God for many years, he'd always felt there was something missing. He wondered, "Could Jesus fill the void?"

As he climbed the steep path up the Mount of Olives, he had to stop several times to catch his breath. His position required little in the way of athletics, and the exertion drained him. By now, dusk had turned to complete darkness. Thankfully, he'd brought a torch to light the way. As he drew closer to the top of the hill, he saw a fire flickering in a clearing. When he reached it, there was no sign of Jesus. Looking around, he saw a lone man standing in the distance. He must have sensed Nicodemus was there. He turned around, walked toward him, extended his hand, and invited him to sit with him by the fire.

Nicodemus grabbed Jesus' hand and felt a sense of peace wash over him. He stood near the fire but didn't sit down. He wasn't planning to stay long. He had to get back to the city before his absence was noticed. He came right to the point. "Rabbi, we know you're a teacher who has come from God. No one could perform the miracles you do unless God is with him."

Jesus also remained standing. He picked up a long branch and stirred the fire, not answering immediately. "I tell you the truth," he finally said. "Unless a person is born again, they can't see the kingdom of God."

Incredulous, Nicodemus looked Jesus straight in the eye. "How can a man be born when he's old? He can't enter his mother's womb a second time to be born again, can he?"

Jesus' eyes reflected the firelight as he looked intently at him. "Unless you are born of both water and the Spirit, you cannot enter the kingdom of God. What's born of the flesh is flesh, and what's born of the Spirit is Spirit. So don't be surprised I told you that you must be born again. The wind blows wherever it pleases, and you hear the sound it makes, but you can't tell where it comes from or where it's going. So it is with everyone who's born of the Spirit."

Nicodemus looked away and stared at the ground. He was embarrassed that he couldn't understand what Jesus was saying. "How can this be?" he asked.

"You claim to be a teacher of Israel," Jesus replied, "and you don't understand these things? We speak about what we know, and we testify about what we've seen, but you people still don't accept our testimony. I've spoken to you about earthly things, and you don't believe! How then will you believe if I speak about heavenly things?"

Nicodemus didn't know how to answer him. Though he was a respected teacher in Israel, he'd never heard of such concepts.

Jesus continued. "No one has ever ascended into heaven except the one who descended from heaven, the Son of Man. Just as Moses lifted the snake in the wilderness, the Son of Man must be lifted up so that everyone who believes in him may have eternal life."

Nicodemus wasn't sure who this "Son of Man" was, let alone what it meant for him to be "lifted up." Afraid to show his ignorance, he remained silent.

Jesus appeared to be deep in prayer, mouthing silent words with bowed head. He wiped his eyes. Had he been crying? He looked up at him with such compassion that Nicodemus felt disarmed. Speaking in a soft yet authoritative voice, he said, "God so loved the world that he gave his one and only Son so that whoever believes in him will not perish but have eternal life. God did not send his Son into the world to condemn the world but to save the world through him. Whoever believes in him is not condemned, but whoever does not believe has been condemned already because they haven't believed in the name of God's one and only Son."

Nicodemus felt drawn to him and wanted to believe what he was saying, but his religious upbringing was so ingrained in him, he found it difficult to admit—with all his knowledge—he'd somehow missed the truth.

Jesus was watching him, and he was sure he sensed his inner struggle. Coming closer, Jesus said, "This is God's judgment: Light has come into the world, but people loved darkness rather than the light because their deeds were evil. Everyone who does evil hates the light and will not come to the light for fear their deeds will be exposed. But those who live by the truth come to the light so that it may be revealed that their deeds have been done in God."

Nicodemus wondered, "Is he referring to himself as light? Wasn't God the only light? And how did one come to God?" His life had been founded on religious practices. Wasn't that enough? Based on what Jesus said, it appeared it wasn't. He sensed a need to give this some serious thought. He mumbled a few words thanking him. Then he made his way back down the path. He could tell Jesus was disappointed, but he wasn't yet ready to throw away all he thought he knew about God to embrace these new teachings.

ↁ

The next day Jesus and his disciples traveled into the Judean countryside where he taught them. Even there the crowds found them, and
the disciples baptized many people.

Up north near Salim John the Baptist was also baptizing, and
many people were coming to him. But then a dispute arose between
John's disciples and another Jew over whether to go to John or Jesus
for purification. John's disciples came to him and said, "Rabbi, the
man who was with you on the other side of the Jordan, the one you
testified about, is baptizing, and now everyone's going to him."

John waded out of the water onto the shore, disappointed his own
disciples hadn't yet understood his calling. He said to them, "No one
can receive anything unless it's been given to him from heaven. I told
you before I'm not the Messiah but only a man who's been sent ahead
of him. The bride goes where the groom is. The groom's best man
waits and listens for him, and he's filled with happiness when he hears
his voice. That's how I feel about Jesus. He must become greater, and
I must become less."

His disciples protested, worried he might be leaving them soon.
"But master, you're a great man of God too!"

John motioned them closer and explained, "The one who comes
from above is above everyone else. Those of us on earth belong to the
earth, and we speak as those from earth. The one who comes from
heaven is above everyone who comes from earth. He attests to what
he's seen and heard, yet hardly anyone on earth accepts his testimony.
But anyone who does accept it agrees that God is truthful."

"But we've accepted your testimony," they said.

"I'm not the one you need to accept," John said. "I'm talking
about the Son of God. Can't you see the Father loves the Son and has
placed all things under his authority? Whoever believes in the Son has
eternal life, but those who reject the Son will not see life because God's
wrath remains on them."

A few seemed to understand, but his words appeared to go over
the heads of most of them. Sadly, that would be the case for most of

Israel. John knew he'd done all he could to get through to them. God himself must do the rest to reveal the truth. He resumed preaching the good news of repentance and forgiveness of sin to all who would listen, pleading with them to repent.

ℰↃ

Surprisingly, the governor, Herod Antipas, wanted to hear what John had to say, so he summoned him to speak at his fortress. He enjoyed listening to him, but what he said about the need to repent troubled him because he was doing so many sinful things. And John had repeatedly chastised him for marrying Herodias, his brother Philip's former wife, for it was forbidden by Jewish law to marry a brother's former wife while the brother was still alive.[13] So John kept telling Herod, "You're breaking God's law." Eventually Herod became angry and wished him dead, but he feared the crowd because they considered John a prophet. Under pressure from his wife, he arrested John and threw him into prison, adding another sin to his long list.

ℰↃ

When Jesus learned John had been arrested, his heart sank. Knowing what John would have to suffer, part of him longed to help him, but he knew this had to occur to fulfill God's plan. He said a silent prayer for John to have strength.

Now the Pharisees had learned that Jesus was baptizing more disciples than John (though actually his disciples did the baptizing). Since he couldn't risk getting arrested before completing his work, he called his disciples together and told them they needed to withdraw from Judea for a while and go back north to Galilee.

Jesus chose an unorthodox route to Galilee. Rather than going to the east side of the Jordan River to avoid walking in Samaria as most Jews did, he decided to go through it. Most, if not all his disciples, had probably never set foot in there. The Jews hated the Samaritans because they held to a different form of Israelite religion the Jews viewed as heretical. As the group walked deeper into Samaria, Jesus could see his disciples were uncomfortable with his decision.

40

Jesus suddenly stopped walking, turned around, and said, "Stop debating among yourselves. Soon you'll see that God does not show favoritism the way humans do."

At noon the next day they came to a Samaritan town called Sychar, near Jacob's well and the field Jacob had given to his son Joseph. Jesus, tired from the long, hot journey, sat down by the well, and his disciples went into town to buy food. When a Samaritan woman came to draw water, Jesus asked her, "May I have a drink?"

She seemed taken aback by his accent and distinctive clothing. "How is it that you, a Jew, ask me, a Samaritan woman, for a drink— since you Jews don't associate with Samaritans?"

Jesus replied, "If you knew what the gift of God is and who's asking you for a drink, you would have asked me for a drink, and I would have given you living water."

"Sir," the woman said, "you don't have a rope or a bucket to draw water, and the well is deep. How do you propose to get this living water? You're not greater than our father Jacob, are you? He gave us the well and drank from it himself, as did his sons and his livestock."

Jesus answered, "Everyone who drinks this water will become thirsty again, but whoever drinks the water I'll give them will never be thirsty again. The water I give them will become a fountain of water springing up to eternal life in them."

The woman's face lit up. "Yes! Please give me this water, so I won't be thirsty and have to keep coming here to get more," she pleaded.

He told her, "Go call your husband and come back."

She averted her eyes. "I have no husband."

Jesus said, "You've spoken honestly when you say you have no husband. I know you've had five husbands, and the man you're living with is not your husband."

She looked up at him in shock. "Sir, I can see that you're a prophet! There's something I've wondered about. Since the time of our ancestors, we've worshiped on Mount Gerizim, but you Jews claim Jerusalem is the place where people must worship. What do you say?"

"Woman," Jesus replied, "believe me, a time is coming when you'll worship the Father neither on this mountain nor in Jerusalem. You

Samaritans worship what you don't know, and we Jews worship what we know to be true. You see, salvation is from the Jews. Yet a time is coming, and has just now arrived, when true worshipers will worship the Father in spirit and in truth. The Father is looking for people who will worship him that way. God is spirit, and those who worship him must worship in spirit and truth."

She nodded. "I know the Messiah is coming, and he'll explain everything to us when he comes."

Jesus perceived that she had the faith to believe. If only he could find such faith in Israel! He decided to reveal who he really was to her: "I, the one who is speaking to you, am he."

Looking stunned, she exclaimed, "I must go back to town immediately and tell the people about you! I'll say, 'Come and meet this man who knew all about me and told me everything I ever did. Could he be the Messiah?'" She rushed away, leaving her water jar behind.

As she was leaving, his disciples returned and were surprised he'd been talking with a Samaritan woman. But none of them dared ask, "What did you want with her?" or, "Why were you talking with her?" They urged Jesus to eat something, but he told them, "I have food to eat that you know nothing about."

So the disciples asked each other, "No one brought him anything to eat, did they?"

Jesus explained, "My food is to do the will of him who sent me and to complete his work. Don't you have a saying: 'Four months more and then the harvest'? I'm telling you, look at the fields around you. They're ripe for harvest now, and those who reap are receiving their reward and gathering fruit for eternal life. The saying is true: 'One reaps and another sows' so that the one who sows and the one who reaps may rejoice together. I sent you to reap what you haven't worked for. Others have worked, and you've received the benefit of their labor."

His disciples looked around and didn't see any ripe fields. Not wanting to appear foolish, they let the conversation end. They distributed the food among themselves and had their midday meal while

Jesus started talking to the arriving townspeople. The woman's message had already reached them.

Many of the Samaritans from that town believed in him because the woman said, "He told me everything I ever did." Some asked him, to stay so he remained two more days. Many more put their faith in him. They told the woman, "It's no longer just because of what you said that we believe. We've now heard it for ourselves and know this man really is the Savior of the world!"

෴

Jesus returned to Galilee in the power of the Spirit and taught in the synagogues. News about him spread throughout the region, and everyone praised him.

Then he decided it was time to visit Nazareth, his hometown, where he knew people would have a different attitude. Though he had many happy memories growing up there, he was not looking forward to the rejection he'd surely encounter. People knew him as "the carpenter's son," and it would be difficult for them to accept him as more than that.

At first, he received a warm welcome because many had seen what he'd done in Jerusalem at the Passover Festival. As usual, he went into the synagogue on the Sabbath. When he stood up to read, the attendant handed him a scroll of the prophet Isaiah. He unrolled it and came to the place where it says:

After reading, he rolled up the scroll, gave it back to the attendant, and sat down. The eyes of everyone in the synagogue were fastened on him, waiting for the lesson from the

"The Spirit of the Lord is on me, because he has anointed me to preach the good news to the poor, sent me to heal the brokenhearted, and sent me to proclaim release for the prisoners, recovery of sight for the blind, release for the oppressed, and that the year of the Lord's favor has arrived."

reading. Instead, he told them, "Today this Scripture has been ful-filled in your hearing."

Up to then everyone had been amazed by the words of grace that came from his lips. They'd been remembering his childhood and speaking well of him, often asking, "Isn't this Joseph's son?" But just as Jesus expected, the tide began turning when he started attending to his Father's business.

He responded, "Surely you want me to prove who I am just as you expect a physician to heal himself. And I imagine you'll tell me to do here in Nazareth what I did in Capernaum. But here's a truth: No prophet is accepted in his hometown. There were many Israelite widows during the famine in Elijah's time when it didn't rain for three and a half years. Yet Elijah was only sent to provide for a Gentile, the widow of Zarephath, in the Gentile region of Sidon."[14]

Agitated, the people began stirring in their seats, but Jesus continued: "In the days of the prophet Elisha, there were many Israelites with leprosy, yet not one of them was cleansed—only Naaman, a Syrian Gentile."[15]

Rather than understanding his call to repentance, they took it as an insult. A cacophony of outrage filled the synagogue. "Get out!" the people shouted. Suddenly they surrounded Jesus, shoving him outside to drive him out of town. He saw some men his family had known. They looked on in horror but did nothing. The crowd grabbed him and took him toward the hill on which the town was built. They dragged him by the arms, churning up dust and stones behind him. When they reached the top of the hill, they pushed him to the edge of the cliff to throw him off. Fighting back emotions ranging from anger to sorrow that the people who had known him all these years could turn on him this way, he escaped their hold and passed through them. Shaking out his clothes and refastening his sandal straps, he promptly set out on the road to Cana.

Chapter 6

Conflicts Begin

When Jesus reached Cana, the town where he'd turned water into wine, he sat down under a fig tree to rest. He draped his cloak partially over his head to block the sun and hopefully avoid recognition. He realized his effort had failed when he saw one of Capernaum's royal officials approaching him at a brisk pace. He smoothed out his disheveled clothes and stood up.

The man rushed up to him and said, "Sir, my son is very sick and close to death! Can you come heal him?"

Discouraged by the lack of faith he'd been encountering among his own people, Jesus said, "Unless you people see signs and wonders, you just won't believe."

The royal official continued to beg him, "Sir, just come down to Capernaum before my child dies."

Jesus was pleased by his faith, especially after what had happened to him in Nazareth. Compassion rose within him, and he said, "Go home. Your son will live."

The man took Jesus at his word and started on the twenty-mile journey home.

A little later Jesus set out for his home in Capernaum. He had decided to live there near the Sea of Galilee in the region of the tribes of Zebulun and Naphtali so that what Isaiah the prophet said would be fulfilled: "Land of Zebulun and land of Naphtali, beyond the Jordan River on the road to the sea, in Galilee of the Gentiles, the people living in darkness have seen a great light. A light has dawned on those living in the land of the shadow of death."[16]

When Jesus arrived in town, he sat down on the wall overlooking the harbor. He enjoyed watching the boats dock after returning from the lake. A short time later, he heard footsteps behind him. It was the royal official he met in Cana.

The man was beaming and said, "While I was still on the way here, my servants met me and told me my boy was getting better and was going to live! When I asked them what time he began to improve, they said, 'The fever left him yesterday at 1:00 p.m.' I realized that was the very moment when you said, 'Your son will live.' I told my family about you, and now we all believe!"

Jesus smiled, and his spirits were lifted. From that time on, he began to preach, "Repent, for the kingdom of heaven has drawn near."

❧

On the Sabbath day, Jesus went to a large synagogue. This building was much more impressive than many others he'd seen. People were sitting on all sides of the square structure on stone steps rising several levels. The leaders motioned for him to enter the main floor in the center. He looked up from there at the hundreds of pairs of eyes on him and felt as if he were in a stadium. It looked filled to capacity, and he could only surmise word had spread about his arrival.

When he sat down and began to teach, the people seemed enthralled because, rather than teach by constantly referring to the opinions of scholars, he taught with real authority from God. Their reactions varied from enraptured silence to expressions of awe. Suddenly, in the middle of his message, a man jumped up and disrupted the assembly. He shouted, "What do you want with us, Jesus of Nazareth? Have you come to destroy us? I know who you are—God's Holy One!"

Jesus stopped speaking and focused on him. He could tell the man was possessed by a demon, a fallen angel who followed Satan into sin and was cast out of heaven to earth. These evil spirits knew who Jesus was. He also knew they were roaming about trying to deceive as many people as possible, whoever was open to their evil influence, so they could take them down to hell with them. This spirit had taken control of the man and was speaking through him. Jesus, having higher authority than demons, commanded, "Be quiet! Come out of him!"

The man was thrown into convulsions, and the people around him backed away. Then the evil spirit came out of him with a shriek but without injuring him. Everyone was astounded and asked each other, "What kind of words are these—that with authority and power he gives orders to evil spirits, and they come out?" And the news about him spread to every place in the surrounding region.

When Jesus left the synagogue, Andrew and Peter were waiting outside for him. "Master," Peter said, "my mother-in-law has a high fever. We're beside ourselves with worry. Will you come and heal her?"

"Of course," Jesus said and followed them, along with James and John, to their home near the shore.

When they entered the house, Peter's wife—he could see she'd been crying—ran up to him. "Thank you for coming, Rabbi," she said. She led Jesus across the inner courtyard to her mother's room where the older woman was in bed.

Jesus felt her forehead, and she was burning up. As he touched her, she clasped his hand and held him tightly. She tried to lift her head but was too weak. He leaned over her and spoke with power: "I rebuke you, fever!" Instantly it left her. He took her hand and helped her stand. She immediately got up and started chopping up some vegetables for a stew. She invited them all to stay for the evening meal. Peter, his wife, and the other disciples just stood there awestruck.

After sunset, Jesus was eating with the others. He had just scooped up the last bit of lentil stew with his bread and was savoring the meal when he heard voices outside—in fact many voices. Peter cracked opened the door and looked out to see a long line of people snaking down the narrow street. It looked like the whole town had brought their sick and demon-possessed relatives and friends to Jesus for healing! They started to press against the door trying to get in, so Jesus stepped outside with his disciples.

Jesus cast out the evil spirits simply by ordering them to come out of the person. He laid his hands on each one and healed them.

Demons came out of many people, crying, "You are the Son of God!" But he rebuked them and would not let them speak because they knew he was the Messiah. This was to fulfill the prophecy of Isaiah: "He took our infirmities and bore our diseases."[17] This went on most of the night.

∾

In the early morning, while it was still dark, Jesus left the house and went off to a solitary place to pray. He was tired but pleased to have helped so many people. He could only hope some would believe in him and see their need for repentance. Sadly, most were only concerned with this world, and once they were healed, they went back to living as they always did.

When the light came up, Peter and the other disciples found him and said, "Everyone is looking for you."

Jesus knew he had to reach many more areas to fulfill his Father's will, so he responded, "Let's go to the nearby towns and villages, so I can preach there too. That's what I came to do." As he left town, people were begging him to stay. He wished he could heal everyone's illnesses, but he knew his time here was limited.

He traveled throughout Galilee and Judea, teaching and preaching the good news of the kingdom of heaven in the synagogues, healing every disease and sickness, and driving out demons. The news about him spread hundreds of miles to the north and northeast, even throughout Syria. People were bringing him all their sick family and friends, people with all kinds of diseases (including severe pain, demon possession, seizures, and paralysis). And he healed them all. Large crowds gathered around him wherever he went—people from Galilee, the ten cities of the Decapolis, Jerusalem, and Judea (including the region of Perea east of the Jordan).

Jesus went back up to the Sea of Galilee, and crowds were coming to hear him teach. As he walked down the street, he saw a tax collector named Matthew (also known as Levi, the son of Alphaeus) sitting at the tax collector's booth. He watched from a distance as people came to the booth to pay their taxes. He knew befriending this man would be controversial. Even he was surprised when in prayer he received the directive from his Father concerning Matthew. Tax collectors were outcasts among the Jews, being seen as traitors because of their service to Rome. They were also seen as the worst kind of sinners. People hated paying taxes to Rome to begin with, let alone being overcharged so the tax collector could make a profit.

Jesus approached the booth and looked inside. Matthew was counting money then pulled out his tax register book without looking up and said, "Name?"

"Jesus," he said. Matthew's head shot up, and Jesus said, "Follow me."

Matthew's surprise was evident. But he got up from his chair, left everything behind in the booth, and followed Jesus. The other disciples were standing a ways down the street and saw Matthew coming with Jesus. They started debating among themselves and making expressive gestures. But when Jesus and Matthew reached them, there was complete silence.

Matthew introduced himself to the group. In his line of work, he was used to talking to a lot of people. "Hello, I'm Matthew." He turned to Jesus. "I'd like to hold a dinner in your honor. Would you come?" He turned to the disciples and said, "Of course, you're all invited." Jesus nodded his agreement, and the disciples hesitantly followed his lead, not knowing what to make of this turn of events.

When Jesus arrived at Matthew's house on the night of the banquet, Matthew's steward ushered him inside to where servants were washing the feet of the arriving guests. This home was one of the most opulent he'd seen in Capernaum, but that was to be expected, given Matthew's income. Wearing a purple tunic made of the finest cloth, Matthew greeted Jesus and ushered him into the main room where the food was being served. The steward led him to a couch at the head of the table and promptly filled his wine glass. Jesus observed that the guests were mainly tax collectors and those of questionable moral character. Though Matthew appeared to have few, if any, friends among the common Jews, he seemed to be quite popular in these circles. He looked at Jesus from the other end of the table and raised his glass to toast him.

Just then Jesus' disciples arrived, and the servant seated them next to him. He could tell they were out of their element as course after course was served. Cucumbers, leeks, olives, bread, lamb, dates, figs, and so much more. Being simple fishermen, their diets consisted mainly of bread and fish. But Jesus didn't come for the food; he came for the conversation. Soon he had the whole table engaged in discussion as he taught about the kingdom of heaven. After dinner, several of the guests followed him outside to hear more.

The disciples were outside as well, waiting to see where Jesus would head next. Some Pharisees and their religious teachers were standing nearby, observing Jesus and the dinner guests. They asked, "Why does your teacher eat and drink with tax collectors and sinners?"

Overhearing them, Jesus walked over to them and said, "It's not the healthy who need a doctor, but the sick. Go and learn what the prophet Hosea meant when he said: 'I desire mercy, not sacrifice.'[18] I haven't come to call the righteous but sinners to repentance."

Some of John's disciples had gathered there, too, and asked, "How is it that we and the Pharisees fast and pray often, but your disciples go on eating and drinking." And the Pharisees asked the same thing.

Jesus replied, "How can the groomsmen fast and mourn while the bridegroom is still with them? The time is coming when the bridegroom will be taken from them. Then they'll fast. No one sews a patch made from new cloth on a tear in an old garment. If they do, the new piece won't match the old material. And when it's washed, the new piece will pull away and tear the old garment, making the original tear worse."

They looked confused. Few understood what he was saying through these metaphors. He purposely used them to confound those who were too closed-minded to accept the truth. He continued, "Does anyone pour unaged wine into old wineskins? No. If he does, when the grape juice ferments and gives off gas, the skin will burst. The wine will pour out, and the skins will be ruined. Rather, they put new wine into new, pliable wineskins, so both the skin and the wine are preserved. No one wants unaged wine after drinking aged wine, for they say, 'The old is better.'"

As Jesus started to walk away with his disciples, he could hear both groups calling after him, saying, "But you didn't answer!" But Jesus kept walking.

☙

After this there was a Jewish festival, so Jesus went up to Jerusalem. He stopped near the Sheep Gate at the Pool of Bethesda. There, along its five covered walkways, a great number of sick, blind, lame, and paralyzed people were lying. They were waiting for an angel of the Lord to come down into the pool and stir up the waters. It was said that whoever stepped in first after the water was stirred was healed from whatever disease afflicted them.

Jesus saw a man who couldn't walk lying there. He perceived he'd been waiting for quite a long time. He said to the man, "How long have you been here?"

"Thirty-eight years," the man answered.

Jesus asked him, "Do you want to get well?"

The man replied, "Sir, I have no one to put me into the pool when the water is stirred. While I'm trying to get in, someone else steps down ahead of me."

Then Jesus said to him, "Get up! Pick up your mat and walk." Immediately the man was healed. He picked up his mat and began to walk.

Now that day was a Sabbath, so the Jewish leaders said to the man, "It's the Sabbath! You aren't permitted to carry your mat."

But he replied, "The man who made me well told me, 'Pick up your mat and walk.'"

So they asked him, "What man told you to pick it up and walk?"

Jesus heard the exchange but didn't want the man he healed to reveal who he was, so he slipped away into the crowd. Later Jesus found him at the temple and said to him, "Now that you're healed, don't sin anymore so that nothing worse will happen to you." The man went away, and Jesus heard him telling the Jewish leaders who had healed him. Then Jesus returned to the temple's Court of the Gentiles. He had hoped to avoid the Jewish leaders there, but they still found him. All they'd had to do was follow the crowds.

The leaders' chief spokesman challenged him. "We have evidence you've been disobeying the law of Moses by working on the Sabbath. We talked to the man who was healed at the Pool of Bethesda, and he pointed you out as the one who did it. What do you have to say for yourself?"

Amazing! Jesus had healed a man who couldn't walk for thirty-eight years, an event that would lead most people to praise God, yet the one thing they thought about was that he healed someone on the Sabbath. So he told them, "My Father is still working, and I am working too."

This enraged them further. "So now you're not only breaking the Sabbath but claiming equality with God by calling him your Father? Outrageous!"

Jesus knew his life was in danger but continued to answer their objections. "I'm telling you the truth: The Son can do nothing by himself unless he sees his Father doing it; for whatever the Father does, the Son also does. The Father loves the Son and shows him everything he does, and the Father will show me even greater works than these so that you'll be amazed. For just as the Father raises the dead and gives them life, even so the Son also gives life to whomever he wishes."

The Jewish leaders huddled to plan their strategy. The head of the group stepped forward and said, "So let me get this straight. You are referring to yourself as the Son of God and saying that you have power over life and death?"

Jesus was aware they were using his answers to build a case against him. But he continued, "The Father does not pass final judgment on anyone but has given the responsibility for all such judgment to the Son so that all people will honor the Son just as they should honor the Father. Whoever does not honor the Son does not honor the Father who sent him. I'm telling you the truth: Whoever hears what I say and believes him who sent me will have eternal life and not be condemned. They have crossed over from death to life."

The leaders exclaimed, "We will have eternal life because we follow God! We don't have to listen to you."

Jesus responded, "A time is coming, and is here now, when the dead will hear the voice of the Son of God, and those who hear will live. For just as the Father has life in himself, he's also given the Son life in himself and the authority to execute judgment because he's the Son of Man."

"Who is this 'Son of Man'?" someone yelled out. "Is he the Messiah?"

Jesus said, "I am he, and you've spoken correctly."

By now a large crowd had gathered. Jesus spoke louder, so they could all hear him. He wanted as many as possible to know the truth. "Don't be amazed at this, for a time is coming when all who are in their graves will hear the Son's voice and come out. Those who have done what's moral and honorable will rise to a resurrection of life, and those who have practiced what's evil will rise only to be condemned."

The crowd reacted with alarm, and Jesus could see some people leaving. Others remained to hear more, so Jesus said, "By myself I can do nothing, so I judge only as I hear. My judgment is just because I don't seek to please myself but to obey the will of him who sent me. If I alone testify about myself, my testimony isn't valid. There's another who testifies about me, and I know that his testimony about me is true." Jesus turned to the Jewish leaders and said, "You have asked John the Baptist about me, and he's testified to the truth—not that I accept human testimony—but I mention it that you may be saved. He was a lamp that burned and gave light, and you chose to rejoice for a while in his light."

The religious leaders feared saying anything negative about John because he was considered a great prophet among the people, so they remained silent. Jesus continued: "My testimony is beyond John's, for the works that the Father has given me to accomplish, which I'm doing, make it obvious that the Father sent me. And the Father who sent me has testified about me. You've never heard his voice nor seen his form. You don't have his word living in you because you don't believe the person he sent."

The religious leaders had a quick answer: "The Scriptures don't say anything about God having a son. This is blasphemy!"

Jesus' response was even quicker: "You diligently study the Scriptures because you think that in reading and practicing them you possess eternal life, yet they are what testify about me. But you refuse to come to me, so you can have eternal life!"

Jesus knew their hearts were closed to the truth, and further discussion was pointless. He got up to leave, but the people pleaded, "Please stay! We know that you're a great man of God."

"I don't accept praise and honor from people," Jesus said.

"Just where do you think you're going?" the Jewish leaders protested. "We have more questions."

Jesus turned to face them after he'd gathered his things. "I know you—that you don't have the love of God in your hearts. I've come in my Father's name, and you refuse to let me into your lives. But if someone else comes in his own name, you'll receive them without question. How can you believe when you accept praise and honor from one another but don't seek it from the only true God?"

"We are pleasing to God," they argued. "We follow the law of Moses to the letter."

"Then don't think that I'll be the one to accuse you before the Father. The one who will accuse you is Moses himself—the very person on whom you've set your hope. If you really believed Moses, you'd believe me because he wrote about me."

"You're lying! Moses never wrote about you," they retorted.

As he was walking away, he asked them one last question: "Since you don't believe what Moses wrote, how are you going to believe what I say?"

As Jesus left the temple, many people followed, trying to grab hold of him. He increased his pace until he was clear of the crowded area then took a circuitous route through the marketplace, weaving in and out of the empty stalls that were closed for the Sabbath. When he reached the foot of the Mount of Olives where he'd set up camp, he breathed a sigh of relief. Some of his disciples were staying there with him while in town for the festival, and others were staying with friends or family in the city. Jesus, too, had been invited to people's homes, but he preferred the solitude here.

Peter called out to him as he approached. "Master, come and eat." Jesus could smell the fish cooking and sat down near the fire with the group. It was good to be among friends again—at least for now.

☙

On another Sabbath day Jesus and his disciples were walking through some grain fields. Now the law permitted anyone to pick grain when going by fields, but you weren't allowed to do it on the Sabbath. But since his disciples were hungry, they began picking heads of grain, rubbing off the husks in their hands, and eating the kernels.

When the Pharisees saw this, they said, "Look! What they're doing is unlawful on the Sabbath."

Jesus replied, "Haven't you read what David and his companions did when they were hungry? In the days of the high priest Abiathar, he entered the house of God and ate the special bread kept in the temple, even though, according to the law, only the priests were permitted to eat it. And David also gave some to those with him. If you understood what God the Father meant when he said through Hosea, 'I desire mercy, not sacrifice,'[19] you wouldn't have condemned the innocent. The Sabbath was made for the benefit of people, not people for the benefit of the Sabbath."

"So now you're making yourself equal in authority to King David?" the Pharisees asked.

"No," Jesus responded. "My authority is greater. The Son of Man is Lord of the Sabbath."

Indignant, perhaps even horrified, that a man would say his authority was greater than King David's, the Pharisees turned their backs on him and walked away.

On another Sabbath, when Jesus went into the synagogue to teach, a man with a crippled right hand was there. Some Pharisees and scribes were there too. Hoping to find a reason to accuse him of violating the law of Moses, they were watching to see if Jesus would heal the man even though it was the Sabbath.

But Jesus knew what they were thinking and said to the man, "Stand up and come forward." When he did, Jesus turned to the Pharisees and said, "I ask you, is it lawful on the Sabbath to do good or to do evil, to save a life or to destroy it?"

They remained silent.

Grieved by their hard hearts, he gave them a stern look and answered the question himself: "If one of you has a sheep, and it falls into a pit on the Sabbath, wouldn't you lift it out? How much more valuable is a man than a sheep? So it is lawful to do good on the Sabbath."

Then Jesus said to the man, "Hold out your hand." So he held it out, and it was fully restored.

Jesus watched the Pharisees leave in a rage. He knew they and the followers of Herod were plotting to destroy or even kill him. In light of this, he and his disciples left Jerusalem and went north to the Sea of Galilee. A large crowd followed—people from Jerusalem, Judea, Idumea, from beyond the Jordan, and from Tyre and Sidon. Jesus had healed so many that those who still had afflictions pressed forward trying to touch him. Power was coming out from him and healing everyone.

Whenever the evil spirits saw him, the possessed people fell before him, and the evil spirits cried out, "You are the Son of God!"

But he ordered them, "Don't say who I am!"

❧

Jesus went up a nearby mountain and spent the night in prayer to God. At daybreak he called all his disciples, and they gathered around him. He chose twelve to be apostles, men who were to spend time with him, go out and preach, and be given authority to cast out demons:

Simon, whom Jesus named Peter
Andrew, Peter's brother
James, son of Zebedee, brother of John

John, son of Zebedee, brother of James
Philip
Bartholomew (a.k.a. Nathanael)
Matthew
Thomas
James, son of Alphaeus
Thaddaeus
Simon the Zealot
Judas Iscariot, who betrayed him

Then Jesus went home, and again such a large crowd gathered that he and his disciples couldn't even eat a meal. When his family heard about all that was happening, they tried to restrain him, saying, "He's out of his mind."

When some people brought Jesus a demon-possessed man who was both blind and mute. Jesus healed him so that he could talk and see. All the crowds were amazed and asked, "Can this be the Son of David?"

Some scribes and Pharisees who had come down from Jerusalem said, "He's possessed by Beelzebul, the ruler of demons. This man casts out demons by his power."

Knowing their thoughts, Jesus said to them, "Any kingdom divided against itself will be destroyed, and every city or family divided against itself will not stand. If Satan casts out Satan, he's divided against himself. How then can his kingdom stand? And if I cast out demons by Beelzebul, by whom do your followers cast them out? So they'll be your judges. But if I cast out demons by the Spirit of God, then the kingdom of God has come upon you."

They were speechless so Jesus continued: "When a strong, fully armed man guards his own house, his possessions are safe. But when someone stronger attacks and overpowers him, he takes away the armor in which the man trusted and distributes the plunder. So how can anyone enter a strong man's house and carry off his property unless he first ties up the strong man? Then he can plunder his house."

The apostles gathered around Jesus and said, "Lord, we don't understand what you meant about the strong man."

Jesus said, "The strong man represents Satan, also referred to as Beelzebul. What I'm telling them is that I couldn't be casting out the demons who serve Satan without first restraining their leader. That's why it couldn't be by Satan I cast out demons. He would never cast out his own workers. Do you get it now?"

"Yes, Lord," they said.

Jesus then said to the crowd, "Whoever is not with me is against me, and whoever doesn't gather with me scatters. Those of you who accused me of casting out demons by Beelzebul, when in fact it was the Spirit of God, hear this truth! People will be forgiven for every sin, even blasphemy, but blasphemy against the Holy Spirit won't be forgiven. Anyone who speaks a word against the Son of Man will be forgiven, but anyone who speaks against the Holy Spirit won't be forgiven, either in this age or in the age to come." He said this because they were saying, 'He has an evil spirit.'"

"That's an outrageous thing to say about us!" the scribes shouted. "We're more righteous than 99 percent of these common people here, yourself included!"

Jesus said to them, "A tree is known by its fruit. Either make a tree good and its fruit will be good or make a tree bad and its fruit will be bad." He then faced the Pharisees and scribes and said, "You brood of vipers! How can you, being evil, say anything good? The mouth speaks out of the abundance of the heart. A good person brings good out of the good stored up in them, and an evil person brings evil out of the evil stored up in them. But I'm telling you, on the day of judgment everyone will have to give account for every careless word they've spoken. By your words you'll be acquitted, and by your words you'll be condemned."

Then some of the scribes and Pharisees said, "Just show us a miraculous sign, and we'll be satisfied."

Jesus replied, "This is a wicked generation that asks for a miraculous sign. Only an evil and adulterous generation does that. But no sign will be given except the sign of the prophet Jonah. Just as Jonah was a sign to the Ninevites, so will the Son of Man be to this generation. Just as Jonah was 'three days and three nights in the belly of a huge fish,'[20] the Son of Man will be three days and three nights in the heart of the earth. The men of Nineveh will stand up at the judgment with this generation and condemn it because they repented at the preaching of Jonah. And look, someone greater than Jonah is here!"

Jesus continued, "The Queen of the South will rise up at the judgment with this generation and condemn it because she came from the ends of the earth to hear Solomon's wisdom.* And look, someone greater than Solomon is here!

"When an evil spirit comes out of someone, it passes through dry places seeking rest, and not finding any, it says, 'I'll return to the house I left.' When it comes back, it finds it empty, swept clean, and put in order. Then it goes and brings back seven other spirits more wicked than itself. And they go in and live there, and the last state of that person becomes worse than the first. That's how it will be with this wicked generation."

As Jesus was saying these things, a woman in the crowd called out, "Blessed is the womb that bore you and the breasts that nursed you."

He replied, "More than that, blessed are those who hear the word of God and obey it."

While Jesus was still talking to the crowds, someone told him, "Your mother and brothers are standing outside wanting to speak to you."

Jesus replied to the one telling him, "Who's my mother, and who are my brothers?" Pointing to his disciples, he said, "Here are my mother and my brothers. Whoever does the will of my Father in heaven, that person is my brother and sister and mother."

Then Philip asked, "Master, what did the story about the seven evil spirits mean?"

Jesus answered, "It means that those who reject my teaching and refuse to believe in me are in a worse state than they were before they met me."

---

* Jesus may have been referring to the queen of Sheba, who visited Solomon and blessed the Lord upon seeing how God had blessed Solomon.

"How could that be?" Peter asked. "They were unbelieving before, and they are still unbelieving."

"Before they were ignorant," Jesus explained, "but now they have no such excuse for rejecting God's Son."

Part 4

Third Year
of Ministry

Chapter 7

How to Live Life

O ne day when Jesus saw the crowds following him, he went up a mountain to spend time with his apostles. He saw people from the crowd coming behind him, but he didn't stop them. The apostles gathered near him, and he began to teach them about the characteristics and blessings of those who believed in him:*

"Blessed are the poor in spirit,
  for theirs is the kingdom of heaven.
Blessed are those who mourn,
  for they will be comforted.
Blessed are the humble,
  for they will inherit the earth.
Blessed are those who hunger and thirst for righteousness,
  for they will be satisfied.
Blessed are the merciful,
  for they will receive mercy.
Blessed are the pure in heart,
  for they will see God.
Blessed are the peacemakers,
  for they will be called children of God.
Blessed are those who are persecuted for the sake of righteousness,
  for theirs is the kingdom of heaven.

---

* This chapter contains material from two famous sermons of Jesus, the Sermon on the Mount and the Sermon on the Plain. Because they contain so much similar material, we have combined the two as one event.

Blessed are you when people hate you, exclude you, insult
you, and reject your name as evil because of the Son of Man.
Rejoice in that day and leap for joy!
    Listen! Your reward in heaven is great,
        for that is the way their ancestors treated the prophets.
But woe to you who are rich,
        for you have already received your comfort.
Woe to you who are well-fed now,
        for you will go hungry.
Woe to you who laugh now,
        for you will mourn and weep.
Woe to you when all people speak well of you,
        for that is how their ancestors treated the false prophets!"

Jesus continued, "While you're here on earth, these attributes will
help you reflect God to the people. You are the salt of the earth. But if
the salt becomes tasteless, how can it become salty again? It's no longer
good for anything except to be thrown out and trampled by people."

Matthew asked, "So now we're to be a preservative and flavor
enhancer?" The others laughed.

Jesus smiled. "Yes, and that's not all. You are the light of the world.
A city on a hill can't be hidden; no one lights a lamp and puts it under
a basket. They put it on a stand, and it gives light to everyone in the
house. Let your light shine before everyone so that they may see your
good works and praise your Father in heaven. You see, there's nothing hidden except that which will be revealed and nothing secret that
won't come into the open."

"I've never seen myself as a light," Andrew said. "But I do my best
to follow the law of Moses. How does all you are saying relate to the
law?"

Jesus responded, "I didn't come here to abolish the law or the
prophets but to fulfill them. Until heaven and earth pass away, not the
smallest requirement will disappear from the law until all is accomplished. Anyone who breaks one of the least of these commandments
and teaches others to do so will be least in the kingdom of heaven, but

whoever obeys and teaches them will be called great in the kingdom of heaven. Unless your righteousness surpasses that of the scribes and Pharisees, you'll never enter the kingdom of heaven."

"That will be difficult," John said. "The Pharisees follow all the rules."

"Yes, they follow the rules and regulations, but I don't judge on outward appearances alone," Jesus said. "What I've taught you today will ensure that your inner selves are as pure as your outer selves. Remember, God looks at the heart."

Peter was alarmed. "So God is judging our thoughts too?"

Jesus nodded. "You've heard it said, 'Do not murder,' and, 'Whoever murders will be subject to judgment.' But I say that anyone who's angry with their brother will be subject to judgment. Whoever insults his brother will be brought before the highest court."

Then he said, "And whoever calls another, 'Fool!' will be in danger of hell's fire."*

The apostles gasped. "We're all guilty of thinking badly of others at times," James said. "What hope is there for us?"

"My true followers will receive the power to overcome these things—if they're willing," Jesus said. "If you are presenting your offering at the altar, and while there you remember your brother or sister has something against you, leave your offering in front of the altar. First go and be reconciled to your brother or sister, then come back and make your offering."

"But what if the other person is in the wrong?" Peter objected.

Jesus answered, "Make friends with your adversary on the way to court, so he doesn't hand you over to the judge, and the judge hand you over to the officer, and you get thrown into prison. I'm telling you the truth—you won't get out until you've paid the last cent."

"These are hard lessons," James said. "You're pretty much saying we have to make peace with people even if they're wrong."

"Maybe that's why the peacemakers are so blessed," Matthew interjected. "I know I'll need forgiveness from a lot of people."

---

* Some people believe he was forbidding certain expressions here (a literal interpretation of what he said). Others argue he was condemning the attitude of disrespect for another human being, a being God created on purpose and for a purpose.

"Well at least I never was unfaithful to my wife," Peter said. "I have that going for me."

Jesus looked at him and said, "You've heard it said, 'Do not commit adultery.' But I say that anyone who looks at a woman with lust for her has already committed adultery with her in his heart."

Some of them averted their eyes.

Jesus continued, "If your right eye causes you to sin, tear it out and throw it away. It's better to lose one part of your body than for your whole body to be thrown into hell. And if your right hand causes you to sin, cut it off, and throw it away. It's better for you to lose one part of your body than for your whole body to go into hell."*

Regardless, Jesus sensed he'd given them too much to take in all at once. "Let's eat," he said. The apostles laid out the bread, cheese, and olives they'd brought, relieved to take a break. Jesus walked out to the woods to confer with his Father. He would need his help in delivering the rest of the teaching.

∽

After the apostles had eaten and were refreshed, they returned to their places. Jesus came back and continued instructing them: "It's been said, 'Anyone who divorces his wife must give her a certificate of divorce.' But I say that everyone who divorces his wife for any reason except on the grounds of sexual immorality causes her to commit adultery. And anyone who marries a divorced woman commits adultery."

"It would be better not to get married!" a few observed.

"It would be difficult to do so anyway with the life we've chosen," John said.

Jesus didn't refute him. He knew many would leave their families, homes, jobs, and much more to follow him. He resumed the lesson: "You've heard it said, 'Do not swear an oath falsely but fulfill the vows you've made to the Lord.' But I say,

---

* Since Scripture teaches that a person's body is sacred, it appears that Jesus was speaking metaphorically, telling believers to cut out of their lives every source of temptation.

"Do not swear an oath at all:
  Neither 'By heaven,' for it is God's throne;
  Nor 'By earth,' for it is his footstool;

Nor 'By Jerusalem,' for it is the city of the great King;
  Nor 'By my head,' for you cannot make even one hair
  on your head black or white.

"Whenever you speak, simply let your 'Yes' truly mean 'Yes' and your 'No' truly mean 'No.' Anything other than that is from the evil one."

Jesus paused to let his words sink in, taking a long, hard look at Peter, knowing he'd struggle with this. He knew how unreliable human promises were and didn't want his disciples to fall into sin by making them—especially to God. He knew his next teaching would be controversial, so he took a deep breath before saying, "You've also heard it said, 'An eye for an eye, and a tooth for a tooth.' But I say, don't even resist an evil person. If anyone slaps you on the right cheek, turn the other to him too. If someone takes your outer garment, don't stop them from taking your inner garment too. If a Roman soldier forces you to carry his pack a mile, carry it for two. Give to anyone who asks, and don't turn away from anyone who wants to borrow from you."

The apostles let out a collective sigh. "Really?" Peter challenged. "Do we really have to be kind to soldiers, too, when they've oppressed us all these years?" The others murmured their agreement.

"Yes," Jesus elaborated. "Though Scripture says, 'Love your neighbor,' and many of your teachers tell you to hate your enemy, I say love your enemies. Do good to those who hate you, bless those who curse you, and pray for those who mistreat you. If you love those who love you, what reward will you have? Don't even the tax collectors, those who work to prosper themselves and Rome, and the worst sinners do that? And if you greet only your family and friends, what are you doing more than anyone else? Don't even Gentiles do that? And if you lend to those from whom you expect repayment, what credit is that to you? Even sinners lend to sinners to get back the same amount. Be perfect just as your heavenly Father is perfect."

Simon the Zealot said, "So if we love our enemies, do good, and lend, expecting nothing in return, we will be rewarded?"

"Yes," Jesus said. "Your reward will be great, and you'll be children of the Most High because he, too, is kind to the ungrateful and even to the wicked. The Father causes his sun to rise on the evil and the good and sends rain on the righteous and the unrighteous."

Matthew understood. "It's true," he said. "When I was a tax collector, we only helped people we liked. But now we must be different: salt and light in a bland, dark world. But how will people know I've changed?"

"Beware of practicing your righteousness before men to be seen by them," Jesus warned. "Otherwise, you have no reward from your Father in heaven."

"So are you saying the Pharisees won't get a reward for their good deeds because they do them publicly?" John asked.

"It's their motive that counts with God," Jesus answered. "Are they really doing those things to help people, or are they only doing them to be seen? For instance, when you give money to a needy person, don't blow your horn as the hypocrites do, so you'll be honored by men in the synagogues and streets. I'm telling you the truth: the horn blowers received their reward in full."

Judas Iscariot didn't seem pleased with this teaching at all. Jesus watched him closely as he stood up and paced around and argued, "I don't see how we can display God to people without doing these things publicly. As our treasurer, I suggest we find ways to let people know all the good we're doing. I mean, you gave me the position for a reason, knowing I was the most qualified."

Matthew cleared his throat. "I have no idea why you were given the position, as some of us have more experience handling money. Suffice it to say, I trust our Lord to do what's best."

Jesus didn't like the direction the conversation was taking, so he interrupted them and continued teaching: "When you give, don't let your left hand know what your right hand is doing so that your giving may be in secret. And then your Father, who sees what you've done in secret, will reward you openly."

Judas was not finished making his views known. "We need some reward here, too, when making such sacrifices," he protested. "I for one don't want to wait until heaven to get mine."

Jesus kept silent, knowing what was in his heart. A few of the others appeared to as well. He felt it best to change the subject away from money for the moment. He said, "Some of you have wondered why I go off by myself to a mountain or the wilderness."

"We know you like to be alone to rest sometimes," Peter said. "You must be tired after talking to so many people and meeting their needs."

"That's part of the reason," Jesus conceded, "but it's mainly so I can pray to my Father."

"We pray in synagogue," John said, "but you pray much more than that, even daily, like the Pharisees do."

"I'm glad you brought them up," Jesus replied, "because they're a perfect example of how you shouldn't pray. Don't be like those hypocrites who love to pray while standing in synagogues and on street corners to be seen by people. I'm telling you the truth: They've received their reward in full."

"Then how should we do it?" Andrew asked.

"When you pray, go into your inner room, close the door, and pray to your Father who is unseen," Jesus answered. "And he who sees what you do secretly will reward you.

"And when you pray, don't use meaningless repetitions like the pagans. They think they'll be heard because of their many words. Don't be like them! For your Father knows what you need before you ask him. This is how you should pray:

'Our Father who is in heaven,
    hallowed be your name.*
    May your kingdom come, and
    may your will be done,
        on earth as it is in heaven.

---

* "Hallowed": set apart as sacred, highly venerated.

> Give us today our daily bread, and
> forgive us our debts,
> > as we also have forgiven our debtors.* And
> do not lead us into temptation, but
> deliver us from evil.'**

"Forgive and you'll be forgiven. If you forgive others for their sins, your heavenly Father will also forgive your sins. But if you don't forgive others for their sins against you, your Father won't forgive your sins against him."

"It's definitely to our benefit to forgive!" John exclaimed.

Jesus continued: "Ask and it will be given to you. Seek and you will find. Knock and the door will be opened for you. For everyone who asks receives. Those who seek find. And the door will be opened to those who knock. Which of you, when his child asks for bread, will give him a stone? Or if he asks for a fish, will give him a snake? Or if he asks for an egg, will give him a scorpion? If you, being evil, know how to give good gifts to your children, how much more will your Father in heaven give good things, and the Holy Spirit, to those who ask him?

"Here's an example of what I mean: Suppose one of you has a friend and you go to him at midnight and say, 'Friend, lend me three loaves of bread. A friend of mine has dropped in after a journey, and I have nothing to serve him.' And he answers from inside, 'Don't bother me. The door is already locked, and my children and I are in bed. I can't get up and give you anything.' I'm telling you, even though he won't get up and give him the bread because he's his friend, because of the man's persistence, he'll get up and give him as much as he needs."

"This part I like!" Peter said. "But what about all the fasting the Pharisees and John's disciples do? Will we need to do that too?"

---

* "Debts" and "debtors": terms that refer to an unfulfilled obligation, not a contractual debt.

** The Greek construction of this sentence also allows, "Deliver us from the evil one" (as opposed to "from evil"). The early Christian church added, "For yours is the kingdom, and the power, and the glory forever. Amen."

"A time will come when you will want to fast," Jesus answered. He knew after his death they would want to fast and pray, but he would tell them that another time. "But when you fast, don't look gloomy like the hypocrites do. They make their faces unattractive, so people will know they're fasting. I'm telling you the truth: They've received their reward in full. Instead, comb your hair and wash your face so that it won't be obvious you're fasting, except to your Father. He sees what's done in secret and will reward you."

***

Jesus looked toward Jerusalem, longing for his people to believe in him. Yet he knew most would not. He looked at the apostles, pleased in his knowledge that they would carry his message throughout the civilized world after he was gone. That's why it was so important to build up their faith through lessons and healings.

Matthew approached him and said, "Lord, I saw a nice piece of property in Capernaum with plenty of room for you to teach. Would you like me to look into it for you? This way, you wouldn't have to be outdoors so much. We could also add some nice furniture."

Jesus answered, "Sell your possessions and give to the poor. Don't store up for yourselves treasures on earth, where moth and rust destroy, and where thieves break in and steal. Provide purses for yourselves that won't wear out—treasure in heaven that won't run out, where neither moth nor rust destroy, and where thieves don't break in and steal. For where your treasure is, there your heart will be also."

The apostles were talking among themselves, obviously disturbed. Finally, James spoke up. "Are you saying we need to take a vow of poverty and live similarly to John the Baptist?"

Jesus explained. "It's a matter of the heart. Someone could give away all they own but be far from God. Another could be wealthy and love God with all their heart. The point is that no one can serve two masters. Either you'll hate one and love the other, or you'll be devoted to one and despise the other. You can't serve both God and possessions."

"This is difficult to understand," Thaddaeus said. "How do you know if you love possessions too much?"

Jesus responded, "The eye is the lamp of the body. So if your eyes are healthy, your whole body will be full of light. But if your eyes are evil, your whole body will be full of darkness. Therefore, watch out that the light within you is not darkness. For if your whole body is full of light, with no dark part, it will be completely lit—just like when lamplight shines on you."

Judas shook his head. "It's not practical to give up your possessions," he said. "I have to pay my debts. If I give everything away, what will I live on?"

Jesus responded, "Don't worry about your life, what you'll eat or drink, or your body, what you'll wear. Isn't life more than food, and the body more than clothing? Look at the birds. They don't sow or reap or store food in barns, yet your heavenly Father feeds them. Aren't you more valuable to God than they are? And it is more blessed to give than to receive."

"I'd like to believe that," Peter said. "But after struggling to support my family for so long, I don't know how to stop worrying about where my income will come from."

"Which one of you can add a single hour to his life by worrying?" Jesus said. "And why do you worry about clothing? Consider how the lilies of the field grow. They don't labor or spin cloth. Yet I'm telling you that not even Solomon in all his glory was clothed like one of these. If God so clothes the grass of the field, which is here today and thrown into the fire tomorrow, won't he take even better care of you, O you of little faith! So don't worry, saying, 'What will we eat?' or 'What will we drink?' or 'What will we wear?' For the unbelievers strive for all these things, and your heavenly Father knows you need them. But seek first his kingdom and his righteousness, and all these things will be given to you. Don't be afraid, little flock, for your Father delights to give you the kingdom."

"Please pray for us to have faith like this, Lord!" Peter said. "I'm not sure what tomorrow will bring."

Jesus put his hand on Peter's shoulder and said gently, "Don't worry about tomorrow, for tomorrow will worry about itself. Each day has enough trouble of its own."

Jesus knew these lessons were difficult for them and for anyone who was used to living in this troublesome world. He prayed silently to his Father to give them the faith they needed then continued: "Give, and it will be given to you; the full measure pressed down, shaken together, and flowing over will be poured in your lap. By your standard of measure, it will be measured back to you."

"I have a question," Andrew said. "If we're this generous in giving to others, won't we eventually run out ourselves?"

Jesus said, "He who supplies seed to the sower and bread for food will also supply and multiply your seed for sowing and will also increase the harvest of your righteousness. You'll be enriched in every way, to be generous to all, and this will produce thanksgiving to God."

გა

Jesus stepped away to get a drink of water. His throat was getting dry after teaching so long. As he was pouring it into a cup, he heard a heated exchange between Matthew and Judas. Those two had not gotten along well from the beginning. He walked up behind them.

"You don't belong here with the rest of us," Judas said to Matthew.

"I have as much right to be here as you do," Matthew retorted. "What gives you the right to judge me?"

"How do we know we can trust you after all you stole from people?" Judas shot back. Just then they both saw Jesus and stopped speaking.

"Be merciful just as your Father is merciful," Jesus said. "Don't judge, and you won't be judged. Don't condemn, and you won't be condemned. In the same way you judge others, you'll be judged, and with the standard you use, you'll be measured."

"But, Lord," Judas protested, "how can you ignore all he's done?"

Jesus answered, "Can the blind lead the blind? Won't they both fall into a pit? Why do you look at the tiny speck of dust in your brother's eye, but don't notice the board in your own eye? How can you say, 'Let me take the speck out of your eye,' while the board is still in your own eye? You hypocrite! First take the board out of your eye. Then you'll see clearly to remove the speck from your brother's eye."

Judas got up in a huff and went to sit by himself.

Jesus sat back down to teach: "Don't give what's holy to dogs, and don't throw your pearls to pigs, or they'll trample them under their feet and then turn and tear you to pieces."

The apostles looked toward Judas then back at Jesus. No one said a word.

Jesus continued: "Beware of false prophets who come to you in sheep's clothing but inwardly are ravenous wolves. You'll know them by their fruit. Do people pick grapes from thornbushes or figs from thistles? In the same way, every good tree bears good fruit, but every bad tree bears bad fruit. A good tree can't bear bad fruit, nor can a bad tree bear good fruit. Every tree that doesn't bear good fruit is cut down and thrown into the fire. So you'll know them by their fruit. The good person produces good out of the good treasure stored up in their heart, and an evil person produces evil out of the evil stored up in their heart. For the mouth speaks out of whatever fills a person's heart.

"Not everyone who says to me, 'Lord, Lord,' will enter the kingdom of heaven, but only those who do the will of my Father in heaven. Many will say to me on that day of judgment, 'Lord, Lord, didn't we prophesy and drive out demons and perform many miracles in your name?' Then I'll declare to them, 'I never knew you. Depart from me, you who do evil! Why do you call me, "Lord, Lord," and not do what I say?

"Everyone who hears these words of mine and does them will be like a wise man who built his house on the rock. The rain fell, the rivers rose, and the winds blew and beat against the house, but it didn't fall because it had been founded on the rock. But everyone who hears these words of mine and doesn't do them is like a foolish man who built his house on sand. The rain fell, the rivers rose, and the winds blew and beat against the house, and it fell. And great was its fall."

As Jesus had been speaking, more and more people had found them, and by now a large crowd was surrounding them. Noticing all the people, John said, "Master, you've taught us a lot today. What would you say is the most important thing from all we've learned?"

Jesus stood up and spoke in a loud voice so that everyone could hear him: "In everything, do to others as you'd have them do to you. This is what's required by the Law and the Prophets. Be sure to enter through the narrow gate, for small is the gate and narrow is the road that leads to life—and only a few find it. The way that leads to destruction is easy, for the gate is wide—and many enter through it."

With that, Jesus called his apostles and started down the mountain. The crowd went down with them, and when they reached the bottom, more of Jesus' disciples were waiting for him, along with others who had come from all over the area. Suddenly, a leper came out of nowhere and knelt before Jesus. People backed away and put their cloaks over their faces, not wanting to catch the dreaded disease. They were shocked when Jesus didn't flinch or move back.

The leper begged, "Lord, if you're willing, you can make me clean."

The crowd gasped when Jesus touched him. Moved with compassion, he said, "I'm willing. Be clean!" Immediately, the leprosy was gone. Then Jesus told him, "See that you don't tell anyone. Instead, go show yourself to the priest and offer the offering Moses wrote of in the law as proof of your healing to them."

But instead the man ran out and told everyone. He spread the news so wide Jesus could no longer enter a town openly because of the large crowds that gathered to hear his teaching and be healed. Even when he stayed in unpopulated places, people came to him from everywhere.

Chapter 8

Opposition Develops

After the time spent teaching on the mountain, Jesus went back to Capernaum. He preferred this quiet lakeside town to the crowded Jerusalem, and he didn't miss his encounters with the Pharisees and their accusations. He was passing by the lake on his way home when some Jewish elders came up to him. He recognized them from the synagogue.

"Rabbi," they said, "one of the centurions sent us to find you. His beloved servant is terribly sick, lying at home paralyzed, suffering terribly, and close to death. He asked if you'd come and heal him. This man is worthy." They pleaded with him, "Please grant this wish because he loves our nation and has even built our synagogue."

Jesus was astounded a Roman military officer not only loved Israel but was seeking him out. He said, "I'll come with you and heal him."

Just before Jesus arrived at the house, the centurion sent some friends to tell him, "Lord, don't trouble yourself. I'm not worthy for you to come under my roof. I didn't even think about personally coming to you on account of my unworthiness. But just say the word, and I know my servant will be healed. I, too, am a man under authority with soldiers under me. I tell this one, 'Go,' and he goes, and I tell that one, 'Come,' and he comes. And I tell my servant, 'Do this,' and he does it."

When Jesus heard this, he marveled at the centurion's faith, turned to the crowd following him, and said, "I'm telling you the truth: I haven't found such great faith in anyone in all Israel. Many will come from the east and the west and will eat with Abraham, Isaac, and Jacob in the kingdom of heaven. But the sons of the kingdom will be cast into the darkest darkness where there will be weeping and gnashing of teeth."

Then Jesus said to the centurion's messengers, "Go! It will be done just as you have believed." And the servant was healed that same hour.

☙

Soon afterward, Jesus and his disciples, with a large crowd following, went to Nain, a village about thirty miles southwest of Capernaum. As they approached the town gate, a dead man was being carried out, followed by a typical funeral procession. They told Jesus the man was the only son of his widowed mother.

When Jesus saw the mother, he felt her sorrow and was moved with compassion for her. He said, "Don't cry." Then he walked up and touched the coffin, and the pallbearers stopped in their tracks and put it down. They were shocked he'd made himself ceremonially unclean by touching the vessel containing a dead body.

Jesus said, "Young man, I say to you, get up!" Jesus opened the lid, and the dead man immediately sat up and began to talk! Jesus presented him to his mother, alive! She was overjoyed and ran up to hug him.

Awestruck, the people started praising God, saying, "A great prophet has risen among us. God has visited his people." This news about Jesus continued to spread throughout Galilee, Judea, and the surrounding country.

☙

A Pharisee named Peter invited Jesus to dine with him, so he went to the man's house and ate. A woman of that town who lived an openly sinful life learned Jesus was eating at the Pharisee's house, so she brought an alabaster jar of perfume and stood quite close behind. She bowed at his feet, weeping. When her tears began to wet his feet, she wiped them with her hair, kissed them, and anointed them with perfume.

78

When the Pharisee who'd invited Jesus saw this, he thought, "If this man were really a prophet, he'd know who she is, what sort of person is touching him, that she's a sinner."

Knowing his thoughts, Jesus got his attention, saying, "Simon, I have something to tell you."

And he responded, "Tell me, Teacher."

Jesus said, "A moneylender had two debtors. One owed him almost two years' wages and the other about two months' wages. When they both were unable to pay, he graciously forgave them both. Now which one will love him more?"

Simon said, "I suppose the one who had the bigger debt canceled."

Jesus agreed, saying, "You've judged correctly."

Then he turned toward the woman and said to Simon, "See this woman? I came into your house, and you didn't give me any water to wash my feet, but she wet my feet with her tears and even wiped them with her hair. You didn't welcome me with a kiss, but she hasn't stopped kissing my feet since I entered your house! You didn't anoint my head with oil, but she's anointed my feet with perfume. Therefore I'm telling you, her sins, though many, have been forgiven because she loved me so much. But he who is forgiven little loves little."

He looked down at her and said, "Your sins are forgiven. Your faith has saved you. Go in peace." Her eyes lit up, and her expression changed from sorrow to joy. She left, rejoicing in God.

The other Pharisees reclining at the table began to ask each other, "Who is this who even claims he forgives sins?"

❧

Sometime later, when Jesus was teaching in the towns and rural areas on their route home, two of John the Baptist's disciples found him and said, "When we visited John in prison, we told him about all you've been doing. He sent us here to ask you, 'Are you the one who is to come, or should we look for someone else?'"

Jesus knew John would be wondering, with all the miracles Jesus had been performing, why he hadn't gotten him out of prison. In the previous hour alone, Jesus had cured many people with diseases, sicknesses, and evil spirits, and he'd also given sight to a lot of blind people. It grieved him that John had to suffer this way. But hard as it was for people to understand, his kingdom was not of this world. So Jesus replied, "Go back and report to John what you've seen and heard: The blind receive sight, lame people walk, lepers are cleansed, deaf people hear, the dead are raised, and the good news is preached to the poor. Blessed is anyone who takes no offense at me."

As John's disciples left, Jesus talked to the crowd about him: "When you went to see John the Baptist, what did you go out into the wilderness to see? A reed swayed by the wind? No, but if not that, what did you go out to see? A man dressed in soft clothes? No, those who wear soft clothing and live luxuriously are in kings' palaces. So what did you go to see? A prophet? Yes, I tell you—and more than a prophet. John is the one about whom it's written: 'I'm sending my messenger ahead of you who will prepare your way before you.'

"Let me tell you—among those born of women, there's no one greater than John. Yet the least in the kingdom of God is greater than he is. From the days of John until now, the kingdom of heaven has suffered violent opposition, and violent men continue to attack it. All the writings of the prophets and the law looked forward to this ministry of John. And, if you're willing to accept it, he is the "Elijah" who Malachi prophesied would come. If you can hear me, pay attention."

When all the people following Jesus (even the tax collectors) heard this, they acknowledged God's way was right. That's why they went to John to be baptized. But the Pharisees and other experts in the law didn't go to John. They rejected John's proclamation of God's way.

And Jesus said, "To what should I compare this generation? What are the people like? They're like children sitting in the marketplaces, always complaining, 'We played the flute for you, and you didn't dance like we wanted. We sang a sad song, and you didn't have sympathy for us.' John came neither eating bread nor drinking wine, and you accused him of having a demon. The Son of Man has come eating and drinking, and you accuse me of being a glutton and a drunk, a friend of tax collectors and sinners. But wait and see. My wisdom will be proven right by the life and deeds of those who follow it."

Then Jesus began to denounce the cities in which most of his miracles had been done because they didn't repent. "Woe to you, Chorazin! Woe to you, Bethsaida! If the miracles done in you had been done in Tyre and Sidon, they would have repented long ago in sackcloth and ashes. I'm telling you, it will be more bearable for Tyre and Sidon on the day of judgment than for you! And you, Capernaum, you think you'll be carried up to heaven? No, you'll be brought down to Hades. If the miracles done in you had been done in Sodom, they would have repented of their rampant immorality, and the city would still be here. I'm telling you, it will be more bearable for the people of Sodom on the day of judgment than for you."

Jesus prayed, "I praise you, Father, Lord of heaven and earth, because you've hidden these things from the wise and intelligent (those at the top of the social ladder) and revealed them to little children (ordinary people). Yes, Father, this was pleasing to you."

Then he told the crowd, "All things have been handed over to me by my Father. No one knows the Son except the Father, and no one knows the Father except the Son and those to whom the Son chooses to reveal him. Come to me, all you who are weary and heavily burdened, and I will give you rest. Take my yoke upon you and learn from me, for I am gentle and humble in heart, and 'you'll find rest for your souls.'[21] My yoke is easy, and my burden is light."

ᔕᔑ

After this, Jesus traveled through many other communities proclaiming the good news of the kingdom of God. He brought his twelve apostles, along with some women who had been cured of evil spirits and diseases, including Mary Magdalene, Joanna, Susanna, and many others who were providing support for Jesus and his disciples out of their own means. Because the group had grown too large to stay in people's houses, they usually stayed in rural areas.

As Jesus entered the camp, he saw Mary Magdalene cooking some fish over the fire while Joanna was putting out some bread. When Mary saw Jesus had returned, she called out, "Lord, come have something to eat."

Peter came over first and said, "I'm famished!" Some of the others broke off pieces of bread and ate them standing up.

Jesus accepted some food and sat down with the others. The disciples started sharing stories of the miracles Jesus performed that day while the women listened intently.

Mary looked over at Jesus then said to Joanna, "Before I met Jesus, my life was nothing but one dark day after another."

"I know what you mean," Joanna said. "You already know about the illness I endured for years before I met him. He healed me of it and brought new meaning to my life. I never felt good about my husband, Cuza, managing Herod's household. Herod is such a wicked man!"

"Yes," Mary agreed. "Were you aware that he cast seven demons out of me?"

"Seven! No, I didn't know that," Joanna admitted.

Mary continued, "Until I met Jesus, I didn't realize how deeply Satan had afflicted me. Oppressed and tormented, I was desperate to get help. One day I went to hear Jesus teach, and I knew he was sent from God. I begged him to heal me, and since then I've been a new person. It was the least I could do to serve him this way."

Susanna overheard their conversation and said, "I feel the same way. I enjoy supporting our Lord's work with my money much more than buying things for myself. I feel part of something important when I travel with you all."

Jesus was pleased with what they were saying and smiled. After finishing his meal, he called his apostles over so they could prepare to leave again. The women seemed surprised they were going back out so late in the evening, but Jesus knew the timing was perfect for what he had to do.

ↄ◌

As they were walking along the road toward the Sea of Galilee, a crowd started forming around them. Suddenly, a scribe ran up to him and said, "Teacher, I'll follow you wherever you go."

Jesus replied, "Foxes have holes, and birds have nests, but the Son of Man has no place to lay his head."

Then Jesus said to another disciple, "Follow me."

But the man answered, "Lord, first let me go and live with my father until he dies."

Jesus said, "Follow me now, and let the dead bury their own dead. As for you, it's time to proclaim the kingdom of God. Don't let anything keep you from following God now."

Yet another person said, "I'll follow you, Lord, but first let me go back and say good-bye to my family."

Jesus told him, "No one who puts their hand to the plow and looks back is fit for service in the kingdom of God." He knew some of their hearts were divided between following him and following the world. Some people would get caught up in the excitement of the moment and make a purely emotional decision without counting the long-term cost. Jesus needed disciples who would follow him wholeheartedly.

Then Jesus said, "Let's go over to the east side of the lake." When they reached the boat, Peter looked up at the sky and said, "It looks like a nice, clear night for sailing."

Jesus said nothing but got into the boat while one of the fishermen took the helm. Exhausted from the day, he rested on a cushion in the stern but fell into a deep sleep. After only about a half hour, Peter was shaking him awake. There was pandemonium on deck as a fierce storm descended upon them. The strong winds created waves that sent water breaking over the side of the boat, and it was quickly filling up. The disciples were frantically trying to bail out the water, but even these seasoned men of the sea were no match for the fury of this storm.

Panicking, they called out, "Teacher, don't you care that we're sinking? Save us, Lord! We're going to drown!"

Jesus shouted back to be heard over the howling winds, "You of little faith! Why are you so afraid?" Then he stood up, raised his hands in the air, and said, "I rebuke you, wind!" Turning to the raging waters, he cried, "Quiet! Be still!" All at once, the wind died down, and the sea became calm. This time he asked his disciples more quietly, "Why were you afraid? Do you still have no faith?"

Filled with fear and awe, they asked each other, "Who is this man? What kind of person is this? He commands even the winds and the water, and they obey him!"

⁑

When they reached the southeast side of the lake (the predominantly Gentile region), Jesus got out of the boat. This area outside the town was more remote, and the only people around were a couple of farmers. Suddenly, Jesus saw two men rushing toward him. One looked to be in a rage and appeared to be naked. Jesus perceived that the men were possessed by demons. The disciples backed away behind Jesus.

"Be careful!" one of the farmers warned, "That man is so violent no one can go near him." He motioned toward the naked one. "I've heard he used to live in town, but the demon in him kept driving him into the wilderness. Now he lives in the tombs. He had often been bound with chains and shackles and kept under guard, but he'd broken them off and escaped. Nobody was strong enough to subdue him or bind him anymore. Night and day among the tombs and in the mountains, he cries out, gashing himself with stones. He hasn't worn clothes or lived in a house for a long time."

When the demon-possessed men saw Jesus, they fell on their knees in front of him. They cried out, "Why bother us, Son of the Most High God? Have you come to torture us before the appointed time?"

Jesus commanded, "Come out of them, you evil spirits! What's your name?"

The answer came back, "Our name is Legion, for there are many of us. Please don't send us into the abyss!"

Now off in the distance on a nearby hill, a herd of about two thousand pigs was feeding, so the demons begged Jesus to let them go into them, "If you cast us out, send us into that herd of pigs."

Jesus gave them permission, saying, "Go!" The evil spirits came out of the men and went into the pigs. There was a thundering roar of a stampede as the whole herd rushed down the steep bank into the sea and drowned.

When the herdsmen saw what had happened, they ran off. A short time later, when Jesus saw the whole town coming out to meet him, he knew the men had reported everything to them. When they arrived, they found the formerly violent man who had been demon possessed sitting calmly at Jesus' feet, clothed and in his right mind. The witnesses told the people how the demon-possessed men had been restored and how the pigs had drowned. Once they saw for themselves what had happened, the people were gripped with fear and begged Jesus to leave their region.

Jesus had done what he came to do, so he started to get back into the boat to return home. Just then, the formerly violent man who had been demon possessed ran up to him and fell to his knees. "Please take me with you," he begged.

But Jesus sent him away, instructing him, "Go home to your people and tell them the great things the Lord has done for you, how he had mercy on you." The man agreed to go around the town and throughout the Decapolis to proclaim the great things Jesus had done for him.

ଏ୭

When Jesus had crossed back over the sea to Capernaum, a large crowd was waiting for him, expecting his return. So he stayed by the sea to minister to them.

As he was speaking, Jairus, the president of a synagogue, ran up to him and fell at his feet. "My twelve-year-old daughter is dying! Please come lay your hands on her so that she'll be healed and live. She's my only child!" he pleaded. He collapsed on the ground, sobbing.

Jesus felt his pain and helped him up, agreeing to go with him. They started on the way to his home with a large crowd close around them. Suddenly, Jesus sensed power going out from him. He turned around to the crowd and said, "Who touched my cloak?"

When everyone denied it, Peter said, "Master, the whole crowd is pressing in on you."

The other disciples agreed, "You see so many people pushing against you and yet you ask, 'Who touched me?'"

But Jesus insisted, "Someone touched me. I sensed that power went out from me." He continued looking around.

Finally a woman, trembling with fear, came up to him and fell in front of him. "It was me. I've been suffering from a bleeding disorder for twelve years and spent all I had on doctors, but my condition only got worse. I'd heard about you and thought to myself, 'If I just touch his cloak, I'll be healed.' And it happened! When I touched you, I immediately felt the blood stop flowing!" she said jubilantly.

Jesus said, "Take heart, daughter, your faith has healed you. Go in peace and be healed of your affliction."

While Jesus was speaking to her, some men came from Jairus' house and told him, "Your daughter is dead. Don't bother the teacher anymore."

Overhearing them, Jesus told the synagogue official, "Don't be afraid. Just believe and she will be healed."

Jesus didn't let anyone follow him any farther except Peter, James, and John. When they arrived at the home, people were weeping, wailing, and playing flutes.

Jesus said, "Why all this mourning? Stop it! She isn't dead but asleep."

Having already seen that she was dead, they began laughing at him.

So after putting them all out, he took the child's parents and the three disciples and went into the child's room. He took her by the hand and said, "Little girl, get up." Immediately her spirit returned, and she stood up and walked around. Her parents were awestruck! Then Jesus told them to give her something to eat. He also gave them strict orders not to tell anyone about this. But as always, he knew the news would travel fast.

After that, Jesus was heading back with the three disciples to meet the rest of the group. He sensed someone following them and heard a voice cry out, "Son of David, have mercy on us!"

Jesus turned around to see two blind men with wooden canes coming toward him. Clearly, they were coming in the hope of getting sight. So he asked them, "Do you believe I can give you sight?"

They replied, "Yes, Lord."

He touched their eyes and said, "It will be done to you according to your faith."

Instantly, their eyes were opened! At first, they shielded them from the bright light, then peeked out and looked around, amazed by their surroundings. They started praising God and jumping up and down with joy. The crowd was amazed.

Jesus sternly ordered the men, "See that no one knows about this."

Jesus walked a distance along the shore and sat down to rest, but people gathered around him, hoping to see a miracle. A short time later, a couple of men brought a demon-possessed man to him who couldn't speak. Jesus cast the demon out, and the man began speaking. People were saying, "Nothing like this has ever been seen in Israel."

But Jesus noticed some Pharisees standing nearby watching. He heard them say, "It's by the ruler of demons that he drives them out."

He stopped to rest at a house, but as always, he began teaching. The crowd surrounded him and the house where he was staying. Scribes and Pharisees came from every village of Galilee and Judea, even from as far away as Jerusalem, to hear him teach. So many people had gathered there was no room left, not even outside the door.

As he preached the Word of God to them, the power of the Lord was present to heal the sick. Suddenly Jesus heard a sound above him and looked up. He was astonished when he saw some men digging through the clay and straw roof. Soon they'd opened a hole big enough to lower a man on a cot through it right in front of Jesus in the middle of the crowd! They looked down at Jesus from the roof and said, "Rabbi, will you please heal him? He was paralyzed in an accident and can no longer walk. We couldn't get into the house due to the crowds, so we had no other choice but to come through the roof. We'll pay for the damage."

When Jesus saw their faith, he said to the paralyzed man, "Take heart, son, your sins are forgiven."

Some of the scribes and Pharisees were saying to each other, "Why does he speak like that?" and "This man blasphemes!" and "Only God can forgive sins."

Jesus knew right away what they were thinking, so he asked them, "Why do you think evil in your hearts? Why are you thinking this way about these things? Which is easier to say, 'Your sins are forgiven,' or 'Get up, take your cot and walk'? So that you may know the Son of Man has authority on earth to forgive sins, watch this."

Then he told the paralyzed man, "Get up, take your bed, and go home." Immediately the man got up, picked up his cot, and walked out in full view of everyone!

Filled with both fear and excitement, the crowd praised God, saying, "We've never seen anything like this!" and "We've seen extraordinary things today."

Jesus sent the crowd away in the early hours of the morning. They'd been coming to the house most of the night, and he knew his disciples would need their rest for the work ahead. As his popularity increased so would the opposition against him. He walked down the deserted streets to the beach and watched the waves lapping against the shore. This was a good place to be alone and speak to his Father.

Chapter 9

Parable after Parable

Just after sunrise, Jesus' disciples came to him, then the crowds of people found him too. He began to teach, and such a large crowd gathered around him he had to get into a boat and teach from it while they stayed on the shore. He told them this story:

> "A farmer went out to sow. As he scattered the seeds, some fell close beside the path, and the birds came and ate them up. Some fell on rocky ground, where they did not have much soil and sprang up quickly because the soil was not deep. But when the sun came up, the plants were scorched, and they dried up because they had no root. Other seeds fell among the thornbushes, and the thornbushes grew up and choked them out. But others fell on good soil and produced a crop—some a hundred, some sixty, and some thirty times greater than what was sown."

When he finished, he called out, "If you hear me, pay attention!"

Peter waded out to him and said, "Master, have you eaten? We weren't sure since you left the house so early. Come to shore and have something."

Jesus and Peter pushed the boat to shore, and Jesus and the apostles went down the beach to a quieter area. When they had all sat down, Peter said, "Look, my wife packed you some food." He opened his bag and handed Jesus some bread and honey.

"Thank her for me," Jesus said as he broke off a piece of the bread and poured honey on it.

John asked, "Lord, why are you telling the people stories instead of saying plainly what you mean? We have no idea what the sowing of seed has to do with the kingdom of God." The others agreed.

Jesus answered, "To you it's been granted to know the secrets of God's kingdom, but it hasn't been granted to them. Whoever has understanding will be given more, and they will have an abundance of it. But whoever doesn't have understanding, even what they have will be taken from them."

They looked confused, so Matthew asked, "But we don't understand them either, yet you say this knowledge has been given to us?"

Jesus replied, "You have me to explain them to you, and because you're my followers, you'll accept my teaching and take it to heart. Many in the crowd will not."

"Especially the Pharisees," Andrew chimed in.

Jesus nodded. "I speak to them in parables because though they see, they don't see, and though they hear, they don't hear or understand. The prophet Isaiah's words have come true in them: 'People will keep hearing but never understand, and they will keep seeing but never perceive.'"[22]

"What about us?" Peter asked. "How do you see us?"

Jesus answered, "Your eyes and ears are blessed because they see and hear. I'm telling you the truth: Many prophets and righteous people longed to see what you see but didn't see it and to hear what you hear but didn't hear it."

Peter passed food around to the others and looked toward the crowd gathered in the distance. "Why won't they listen to you, Lord? It's obvious you're speaking the truth."

"The hearts of those people have become hard," Jesus said. "They scarcely hear with their ears, and they've shut their eyes. Otherwise they'd see with their eyes, hear with their ears, understand with their hearts, and turn to me. And I would heal them."

One of the disciples asked, "Now that it's just us, will you tell us what the story of the sower means?"

Jesus explained, "The farmer sows the word of God. When anyone hears the message about the kingdom of God and doesn't understand it, Satan, the evil one, comes and snatches away what was sown in their hearts, so they won't believe and be saved. This is the seed sown beside the path."

"So this is someone who hears your message but doesn't believe it?" James asked.

"Correct," Jesus replied. He motioned to the crowd. "Many of those people like to see the miracles, but when I tell them they need to repent and believe in me to be saved, they don't accept it. Their hearts are closed to the truth."

"Which is what you mean by hard hearts," John said.

"I think their problem is they don't see themselves as sinners needing God's forgiveness," Peter interjected. "For instance, the Pharisees think their religious practices will save them."

"You're right," Jesus said. "Religious rituals alone have no power to change the heart."

"And they're not willing to learn because they think they already know everything," Andrew added.

"The sad thing about that," Jesus said, "is I've come to fulfill the very promises they've been waiting for."

"If only they could see that!" Thomas said. "But like you said, 'Even seeing they don't see.'"

"Master, why is it we can see but they can't?" Nathanael wondered.

Jesus answered, "These things are spiritually discerned but only by those who are born again through the Spirit of God. Those who don't believe in me are not able to understand them. Now hear what it means when the seed falls on rocky ground. These are the people who hear the word of God and receive it happily. They believe for a while, but since they have no root in themselves, their joy is only temporary. They immediately fall away when there's a time of testing, like when trouble or persecution comes because of the word."

There was a long moment of silence, then Matthew spoke up. "Master, how will we endure that if it comes?"

Jesus wanted to say, "You mean, 'When it comes,'" but kept it to himself. Instead, he said, "My true followers will be given the power to withstand it. But those who aren't really serious about following me will desert me and the faith."

"May we never be deserters!" Matthew exclaimed.

"I know who are my own," Jesus said. "And they will never leave me."

"So who are the thornbush people?" Andrew asked.

Jesus replied, "These are the people who hear the word, but it's choked out by the worries of the world, the deceitfulness of wealth, and the riches and pleasures of life. "

John spoke up. "So these are people who say they want to follow you, but then when they have problems or get distracted by wanting to make money or to live the good life, they fall away?"

Jesus nodded. "We've already encountered several in this category. You see them for a while and then you don't."

"Oh, here we go again," Judas said. "Needing to feel guilty for having a bit of money."

"It's about who your master is," Jesus said. "Who's yours, Judas?"

"You, of course," Judas answered. "I just don't see why we can't have both. I mean the more we have, the more we can help the poor."

"I can sort of see his point," Philip said. "Isn't doing good works what you mean by being fruitful in the faith?"

"As long as the good works are a result of true faith," Jesus said. "Again it's a matter of the heart. Are you following me with all of it, or is it divided among other interests and desires?"

"So is this undivided heart the 'good soil'? Peter asked.

"You're starting to get it," Jesus said. "These are the people with high ideals and moral character who have a good heart. They hear the word and understand it, retain it, and patiently bear fruit thirty, sixty, a hundred times what was sown."

Peter said, "That's the kind of heart I want—one that bears fruit a hundredfold. I assume that means through the work of the disciples I help bring into your kingdom."

Jesus kept his own counsel. He knew Peter would help bring many more than a hundred into the kingdom, but he also knew about the struggle he'd have to overcome first.

"The crowds are getting restless," Jesus said. "Let's head back to them."

They walked down the beach, and Jesus pushed the boat out from shore a bit, got back into it, and continued to teach: "Consider carefully what you hear. By the measure you use, it will be measured back to you—and more will be added to you! For whoever has will be given more, and whoever does not have, even what they have will be taken from them."

Jesus watched the crowd from his vantage point on the boat. He noticed some people staring intently in his direction while others looked confused. Then there were some who seemed to lose interest and were leaving. He decided to share another parable:

> The kingdom of God is like this: A man scatters seed on the soil. He sleeps at night and gets up every day, and the seed sprouts and grows, though he doesn't know how it happened. The soil produces the crop by itself—first a leaf, then a head, then mature grain in the head. And when the crop is ripe, he immediately sends for the sickle, because the harvest has come.

In the distance, Jesus saw a group of Pharisees conferring among themselves then looking back at him. He knew it wouldn't be long before they challenged him again. But this was normal. They truly were lost sheep. He continued teaching:

> The kingdom of heaven is like this. A man sowed good seed in his field. But while everybody slept, his enemy came and sowed cockles, false wheat, among the wheat. When the plants sprouted and formed heads, the weeds appeared.*
>
> The owner's servants asked him, "Sir, didn't you sow good seed? Why does the field have weeds?"
>
> He replied, "An enemy did this."

---

* "False wheat": a cockle that looks like wheat while growing, but its grain (the seed) is toxic. Because the false wheat was stronger at the base of its head than the wheat, it did not droop like the desirable wheat when it was ripe. So its presence did not become evident until the real wheat ripened and drooped.

So the servants asked, "Do you want us to pull them up?"

He replied, "No, you might uproot the wheat while you're pulling them out. Let them both grow together until the harvest. I'll tell the harvesters, 'First collect the weeds and tie them in bundles to be burned, then gather the wheat into my barn.'"

A few in the crowd looked shaken, apparently grasping the meaning of the parable. But the others showed no reaction, so Jesus continued:

The kingdom of heaven is like a mustard seed, which a man took and planted in his field. Though it's smaller than all the other seeds, it becomes larger than all the garden plants and develops big branches so that the birds of the air can come and perch and nest in the shade of its branches.

The kingdom of heaven is also like leaven that a woman took and mixed into a bowl of flour until all of it was leavened.

After receiving several blank stares from the crowd, Jesus rowed to shore, and he and his disciples headed back to the house. He saw some from the crowd trying to follow but raised his hand to stop them. He needed some time to teach the men he'd chosen to carry out his work.

Once inside, they went into the courtyard, and the apostles sat around Jesus. He could tell they were anxious to get the meaning of the parables.

"Rabbi, the last two parables about the mustard seed and the leaven seem to mean the kingdom of heaven will start out small then keep growing until it overcomes everything around it. Is this right?" Andrew asked.

"Yes, you've understood correctly," Jesus said.

"It doesn't sound like anyone will be able to stop it," John observed.

"Yes, again," Jesus said with a smile. "And you apostles will have a big part in that."

They seemed pleased, then asked, "Would you explain the story about the weeds in the field?"

"Of course," he answered. "The one who sows the good seed is the Son of Man. The field is the world. The good seed are the children of the kingdom. The weeds are the children of the evil one. And the enemy who sows them is the devil. The harvest is the end of the age, and the harvesters are angels. As the weeds are pulled up and burned in fire, it will be at the end of the age. The Son of Man will send out his angels, and they'll weed out of his kingdom all the things that cause sin as well as those who practice lawlessness. They'll throw them into the furnace of fire, where there will be weeping and gnashing of teeth. Then the righteous will shine like the sun in the kingdom of their Father. If you hear me, pay attention."

"The kingdom of heaven sounds like a wonderful place," John said. "But I don't want to be anywhere near the furnace of fire!" The others murmured their agreement.

"This is why I've come," Jesus said. "To warn people about it and to give them a way of escape. Sadly, most people won't accept it."

John asked Jesus, "Will you tell us more about the kingdom of heaven? We want to learn all we can."

Jesus answered, "The kingdom of heaven is like treasure hidden in a field, which a man found and then hid. Rejoicing, he sold all he had then bought the field." He was making it clear that when a person finds something as valuable as salvation, they should give up whatever it takes to obtain it. He reinforced the idea with his next sentence: "The kingdom of heaven is also like a merchant looking for beautiful pearls. When he found one of great value, he sold everything he had and bought it."

Jesus was aware that many pretend to be believers but in reality are living life for themselves without trusting God for salvation and provision. So he warned them: "The kingdom of heaven is like a net that was cast into the sea and caught all kinds of fish. When it was full, they pulled it ashore. Then the fishermen sat down and collected the good fish, but they threw away the bad fish. So it will be at the end of the age. The angels will come and separate the evil from the righteous and throw them into the furnace of fire where there will be weeping and gnashing of teeth."

"Just like the weeds being separated from the wheat!" Thomas observed.

Jesus nodded then asked them, "Have you understood all these things?"

They answered, "Yes."

Then he told them, "Every teacher of the law who has been instructed about the kingdom of heaven is like a homeowner who brings new and old things out of his treasure room. Both have value."

"So we need to teach people both the new and the old," James said. The others agreed.

From then on, Jesus spoke the word of God to the crowd in parables, as much as they could grasp. His parables fulfilled Asaph's prophecy: "I will open my mouth in parables. I will utter things hidden since the creation of the world."[23] But he did explain all the parables to his disciples when he was alone with them.

C/O

Jesus and his disciples left Capernaum and visited all the surrounding communities, teaching in their synagogues, preaching the good news of the kingdom, and healing every disease and sickness. When he saw the crowds, he felt compassion for them because they were bewildered and helpless, like sheep without a shepherd. The sheer number of people meant he could no longer do it all alone. He looked at the twelve apostles and knew it was time. They were ready.

That evening, after a long day of teaching, he led them into an unsettled area outside of town, and they set up camp. Once they had gathered around the fire to share a meal, he said to them, "The harvest is plentiful, but the workers are few. So ask the Lord of the harvest to send workers into his harvest fields."

"Are we those workers, Lord?" Peter asked.

"Yes, and many more will come after you," Jesus said. "But you've been bystanders long enough. It's time for you to do the same things you've seen me doing."

He could see a mixture of joy and fear on their faces as he laid hands on each one of them and gave them power and authority to cast out every kind of demon and to heal every kind of disease and sickness. Then he instructed them:

> "Take nothing for the journey except a walking stick and sandals. Don't take food, a travel bag, or even an extra tunic. Stay in the first house you enter until you leave town. Go to the lost sheep of Israel, not the Gentiles or the Samaritans. I've given you all this counsel freely, so you do the same to others. Preach that the kingdom of heaven is near. Heal the sick, raise the dead, cleanse the lepers, and cast out demons. Don't take any gold or silver or copper in your belts. When any place won't take you in or listen to you, shake the dust off your feet as a testimony against them. I'm telling you the truth: It will be more bearable for the people who lived in Sodom and Gomorrah on the day of judgment than for that town!"

The camp was buzzing with excitement after this, and the men weren't even touching their food. Peter, looking quite pleased with himself, sauntered around the fire and said, "I'm sure people will be more than happy to give us lodging after they see what we can do."

Jesus had to bring him back down to earth. "Yes, some will be happy to see you. But others . . . ." He let his words trail off. "The truth is—I'm sending you out as sheep among wolves. So be as wise as snakes and as innocent as doves. Beware of people—they'll hand you over to the councils and flog you in their synagogues. You'll be brought before governors and kings because of me. So you'll testify about me to them and the Gentiles."

Peter sat back down and said, "It doesn't matter. I'm with you to the end, Lord."

Jesus knew his time of testing would come soon enough, so he said nothing.

James looked worried and said, "What could I possibly say in front of such high officials? I haven't had a lot of schooling. I'm sure I'd be speechless from fear."

Jesus consoled him. "Whenever they arrest you, don't worry about what you're to say or how you're to say it. The Holy Spirit will teach you in that very hour what you should say. It won't be you speaking, but the Spirit of your Father speaking through you."

John said, "I like the sound of that: 'The Spirit of my Father!' So God is my Father like he's your Father!"

"Yes, he is," Jesus said. "He's the Father of all who believe in me."

"So this makes us all brothers!" Andrew blurted out, just making the connection.

Jesus noticed most of them smiling then cautioned them, "Sibling will betray sibling, even to death, and a father will betray his child. Children will rebel against their parents and have them put to death. And everyone will hate you because of my name. But whoever endures to the end will be saved. Whenever you're persecuted in one city, flee to another. I'm telling you the truth: You won't finish going through the cities of Israel before the Son of Man comes."

"But Master, you call yourself the Son of Man, and you're already here," Peter pointed out.

"That's very astute of you," Jesus said, "but this refers to when I come again."

"Where are you going that you need to come again?" Peter put his head in his hands and said, "This is too much to take in."

Philip broke into the conversation. "Getting back to the persecution and people turning on us—surely, they won't see us the same way they do you. We're only your followers."

Jesus answered, "A disciple is not above his teacher nor a servant above his master. It's enough for the disciple to become like his teacher and the servant like his master. If the Pharisees called me, as the head of the house, the devil, how much more will they defame you, the members of my household?"

Simon the Zealot spoke up. "I'm used to conflict. Before I followed you, I was bent on revolution against Rome. Yet I must admit, even I'm feeling some fear about what's ahead of us."

"You don't need to fear them, Simon," Jesus said gently. "Nothing is concealed that won't be revealed or hidden that won't be made known. What I tell you in the dark, speak in the daylight. What you hear whispered in your ear, proclaim from the housetops. Don't fear those who kill the body but can't kill the soul. Rather, fear the one who can destroy both soul and body in hell."

"That's easier said than done," James admitted. "I don't have the courage the rest of you do. I'm shaking in my sandals even thinking about it."

Jesus placed his hand on his shoulder to calm him and said, "Aren't two sparrows sold for a cent? Yet not one of them will fall to the ground without the agreement of your Father. And even the very hairs of your head are all numbered. So don't be afraid. You're worth more than many sparrows. Whoever acknowledges me before men, I will acknowledge before my Father in heaven. And whoever disowns me before men, I'll disown them before my Father in heaven.

"But don't suppose I've come to bring about peace on earth. I didn't come to bring peace but a sword. As Scripture says, I've come to turn, 'A man against his father, a daughter against her mother, and a daughter-in-law against her mother-in-law. A person's enemies will be the members of their own household.'"[24]

"And here I thought I was done with conflict!" Simon said. "But it looks like I'm heading right into it, and it could be right in my own household."

"You've spoken correctly," Jesus said. "The truth is—whoever loves their father or mother or son or daughter more than me is not worthy of me. Whoever does not take up their cross and follow me is not worthy of me. Whoever finds their life will lose it, but whoever gives up their life for my sake will find it."

Jesus knew they wouldn't yet understand what taking up their cross or giving up their life meant, but soon enough they would. He looked at their faces. The earlier lightheartedness had been replaced by the weight of worry. To encourage them he said, "Whoever receives you receives me, and whoever receives me receives the one who sent me. Anyone who receives a prophet because they're a prophet will receive a prophet's reward. And anyone who receives a righteous person because they're a righteous person will receive a righteous person's reward."

This appeared to cheer them up. "So there will be rewards?" Andrew asked.

Jesus nodded. "Hear this truth: Anyone who gives even a cup of cold water to one of the least of my followers will never lose their reward."

This seemed to calm them, and they started eating their meal.

ℰᴓ

After Jesus had finished instructing them, he went to teach and preach in towns in Galilee. Then he sent them out in pairs to proclaim the kingdom of God and to heal the sick. They went out and preached that people should repent. They cast out many demons and anointed many sick people with oil and healed them.

Meanwhile, Herod Antipas was keeping John the Baptist in prison. His wife Herodias held a grudge against John and wanted to kill him because he kept telling Herod their marriage was unlawful, that Scripture forbade his marriage to her, the ex-wife of his brother Philip.[25] But Herod refused to execute John because he was not only afraid of him but the many people who thought he was a prophet. Herod himself believed John was a righteous and holy man, so he'd been protecting him.

But Herod was a weak man, perhaps even cowardly. He had a banquet to celebrate his birthday and invited his court officials, the military commanders, and the leading men of Galilee. When Herodias' daughter Salome danced for them, she pleased Herod and his dinner guests so much that he promised with an oath to give her anything she asked for. He said, "Ask me for anything you want, and I'll give it to you." He even swore, "Whatever you ask, I'll give you, up to half my kingdom."

She asked her mother, "What should I ask for?"

And she answered, "The head of John the Baptist."

So the girl said to Herod, "I want you to give me the head of John the Baptist on a platter."

Herod gasped in shock. What had he done? He was deeply grieved, but he was weak. Because of his oaths in front of his dinner guests, he was unwilling to refuse her. Immediately he sent an executioner and ordered him to bring John's head. The executioner went and beheaded John in the prison and brought back his head on a platter. He gave it to the girl, and she gave it to her mother.

When John's disciples heard, they came and took his body and laid it in a tomb.

Sometime later, when Herod heard about Jesus and all the miracles he was doing, he didn't know what to think. Some people were saying John the Baptist had risen from the dead. Others were saying Elijah had appeared. And still others said one of the prophets of long ago had risen again. Herod even told his attendants, "This must be John the Baptist, the man I beheaded. He's risen from the dead! That's why miraculous powers are at work in him." But privately he wondered, "I had John beheaded, so who is this man I hear such things about?" And he wanted to go see him.

Part 5

Fourth Year
of Ministry

Chapter 10

Looking toward the Sacrifice

A round the time of the Passover Festival, Jesus was weary from teaching in the towns near the Sea of Galilee. He sat down by the shore and reached in his bag to retrieve the figs he'd packed for the journey. The people had been coming to him nonstop for healings, and without the apostles there to help him manage the crowds, he needed some rest. He missed them. They weren't only his students but his friends. He was happy when he looked down the shore to see them walking toward him, returning from their preaching, teaching, and healing mission.

When they reached Jesus, being overjoyed to be back with him, they each hugged him. Peter embraced him so tightly that he almost couldn't breathe. Appointing himself as the group spokesman, he said, "Lord, you should have seen all we did! We healed the blind, the sick, and even lepers. And we told people about the kingdom of God."

"You did well," Jesus said with a smile. "Did you encounter any opposition?"

"Yes, in some places," Peter said. "We were even run out of town a couple of times, just like you were run out of Nazareth."

"It's a good thing we weren't carrying a lot with us," John added, "or we couldn't have gone back for it."

"Andrew and James were even put in jail overnight!" Peter said.

"It's true, Lord!" Andrew exclaimed. "James and I were working together, and the Pharisees didn't like what we were doing, so they had us arrested. Thankfully, Matthew knew the town officials, who were able to get us out."

Judas glared at Matthew. "You have a nerve lecturing me about wanting to take coins on the journey! How were you able to bribe them unless you took some yourself?"

Matthew gave him a sharp look and explained. "I didn't have to bribe anyone. They couldn't understand why I was no longer a tax collector and wanted to learn more. They even came to one of our meetings. In truth, they were more open to our message than the Pharisees."

Jesus was not surprised by that news. "I'm pleased with all you've accomplished for the kingdom," he said.

Turning somber, John said, "We were so sorry to hear about John the Baptist. We met some of his disciples on the road, and they gave us the news."

"It's horrible what Herod did to him!" Andrew exclaimed. "I got to know him well. I even lived out in the wilderness with him."

"I, too, knew him well. We grew up together. We've lost a great man of God," Jesus said.

"All the more reason to watch out for Herod," Peter warned. "John's disciples told me he was looking for you."

"He's heard about all you've been doing and wants to meet you," Nathanael added.

"I wouldn't trust him, Lord, especially after what happened to John," Peter said.

Jesus agreed, knowing full well what was in Herod's heart. He said to the disciples, "Come away with me to a quiet place to get some rest."

C/O

They went to the shore and found a boat heading to Bethsaida. There they hoped to find a quiet place in Philip the Tetrarch's territory, out of the reach of Herod Antipas.

When they arrived, they traveled to a secluded area on a mountainside. As they climbed the hill, they heard thousands of voices. They couldn't believe it when they reached the top and saw a huge crowd of people gathered there. After seeing the miraculous healings

Jesus had performed and recognizing him leaving by boat, they had followed on foot from all the villages and got there ahead of them. When he saw them caring for their sick relatives and friends, he felt sympathy for them. They were like sheep without a shepherd, so he welcomed them and began teaching them about the kingdom of God and healing their sick.

That evening the disciples came to him and said, "This is a desolate place, and it's already quite late. Send the crowds away, so they can go to the surrounding farms and villages and find lodging and buy themselves something to eat."

When Jesus looked up and saw the size of the crowd, he asked Philip, "Where can we buy bread so that these people can eat?" He asked this only to test him because he already knew what he was planning to do.

Philip answered, "Half a year's wages wouldn't be enough to feed all these people!"

But Jesus said, "They don't need to go away. You give them something to eat."

Then Andrew said, "Here's a boy who has five loaves of barley bread and two fish, but what good are these among so many people?"

Jesus said, "Bring them to me," and he ordered the crowd to sit in groups of about fifty. And because there was lots of grass, they sat in groups of fifties and hundreds.

Jesus took the five loaves and the two fish, and looking up to heaven, he said a blessing, broke the loaves, and kept giving them to the disciples to set before the people—as much as they wanted. He also divided the two fish among them all. Everyone ate until they were full—about five thousand men, plus women and children.

Jesus told his disciples, "Gather the leftover pieces so that nothing's wasted." They gathered them up and filled twelve baskets.

After the people saw the miraculous sign he'd performed, they marveled and said, "Truly this is the prophet who is to come into the world!"

☙

Jesus knew they were about to take him by force and make him king. So he sent the crowds away and instructed the disciples to sail ahead of him to Capernaum. He withdrew to a mountainside, spread his cloak on the ground near a clearing and spoke to his Father. With all that had been going on, he hadn't had time to properly mourn John the Baptist's death. When he first heard about it from John's disciples shortly before his own disciples had returned from their journey, he wasn't prepared for the intensity of sorrow that gripped him. Even though he knew what was coming, he hadn't anticipated how deeply he'd feel the loss. They had bonded as children, and his loss left a deep void. When evening came, he wiped the tears from his eyes and went to the shore to check his disciples' progress.

He saw their boat, now some distance from land, being tossed around by the waves. The men were straining at the oars because of the strong winds. Even still, he wasn't ready to join them just yet. What he planned to do next would show them who he really was.

At about four o'clock in the morning, after the disciples had rowed more than three miles, Jesus stepped off the shore and walked on top of the water until he reached them. He intended to pass right by them, but the disciples saw him.

Terrified, they cried out in fear, "It's a ghost!"

Immediately he calmed them, "Take courage. It's me! Don't be afraid."

Peter called out, "Lord, if it's you, tell me to come to you on the water."

"Come," he said.

So Peter got out of the boat, walked on the water, and went toward Jesus. But when Peter felt the strong winds and waves, he became afraid and began to sink. He cried out, "Lord, save me!"

Jesus reached out his hand, caught him, and said, "You of little faith. Why did you doubt?"

When the two of them had climbed into the boat, the wind instantly stopped, and the apostles were astonished. (For they hadn't yet understood about the loaves because their hearts were still not open to the full truth about Jesus.) But now they worshiped him, saying, "Truly you are the Son of God!" And immediately the boat was at the shore where they were heading.

When they landed on the other side of the lake, they moored their boat at Gennesaret, just down the shore from their home base in Capernaum. When Jesus came ashore, people there immediately recognized him. So they ran and sent word throughout the region. People carried the sick on pallets to wherever they heard Jesus was. They laid them down wherever he went, whether in a village or town, the countryside, or a marketplace. And they begged him to just let the sick touch the edge of his cloak. And all who touched it were healed.

⁂

The next day, the crowd that had witnessed Jesus feeding the five thousand realized the disciples had gone away. And Jesus was gone too. But only one boat had been there, and Jesus had not entered it with his disciples, so they didn't know where he had gone. Frustrated, they got into some boats that had arrived from Tiberias and went to Capernaum in search of Jesus. Upon finding him teaching in the synagogue, they asked him, "Rabbi, when did you get here? How?"

Jesus answered, "I'm telling you the truth: You're not looking for me because you saw the miraculous signs I performed, but because you ate all that you wanted. You shouldn't work for food that spoils, but for food that endures to eternal life, which the Son of Man will give you. God the Father has placed his seal of approval on him."

So they asked, "What must we do to do the works of God?"

Jesus said, "This is the work of God: to believe in him he has sent."

Then they demanded to know, "What miraculous sign will you do that we may see it and believe in you? What are you going to do to convince us? For instance, our ancestors ate the manna in the wilderness (as it is written, 'It's the bread the Lord has given you to eat')."[26]

Jesus replied, "Here's the truth: Moses didn't give you the bread from heaven, but my Father did. He gives you the true bread from heaven. The bread of God is he who comes down from heaven and gives life to the world."

Then they said, "Sir, give us this bread!"

Jesus declared, "I am the bread of life. Whoever comes to me will never hunger, and whoever believes in me will never thirst. But I have spoken to you, you have seen me, and still you don't believe me. Everyone the Father gives me will come to me, and whoever comes to me I will never cast out. I've come down from heaven to do the will of him who sent me, not to do whatever I want. And this is the will of him who sent me: that I lose none of those he's given me but raise them up on the last day. This is the will of my Father, that everyone who looks on the Son and believes in him will have eternal life, and I will raise them up on the last day."

Then the skeptical Jews began to grumble about him because he claimed, "I am the bread that came down from heaven." They said, "Isn't this Jesus, the son of Joseph, whose father and mother we know? How can he now claim, 'I came down from heaven'?"

But Jesus replied, "It's written in the Prophets: 'They will all be taught by God.'"

"We already know God and are taught by him," they said. "You, we don't recognize."

Jesus continued, "Stop grumbling among yourselves. No one can come to me unless the Father who sent me draws them. And I will raise each one of them up on the last day. Everyone who's heard and learned from the Father comes to me. But no one here has seen the Father except the one who is from God. Only he has seen the Father."

"Everyone knows that no one can see God and live, which shows you're lying," they countered.

"I'm telling you the truth! Whoever believes in me has eternal life," Jesus replied.

"We believe in God. We don't need to believe in you," they said.

Jesus was grieved by their hard hearts. There was no getting through to them. He continued: "I truly am the bread of life. You mentioned that your ancestors ate the manna in the wilderness. Well, they still died. But here is the bread that's come down from heaven so that anyone may eat from it and not die. I am the living bread that came down from heaven. Whoever eats this bread will live forever. And the bread that I give, my flesh, is for the life of the world."

The Jews began to argue among themselves, "How can this person give us his flesh to eat?"

And Jesus continued, "Believe this truth: Unless you eat the flesh of the Son of Man and drink his blood, you have no life in you. Whoever eats my flesh and drinks my blood has eternal life, and I will raise them up on the last day. For my flesh is genuine food, and my blood is genuine drink. Whoever eats my flesh and drinks my blood remains in me and I in them. Just as the living Father sent me, and I live because of the Father, so the one who gets nourishment from me will live because of me. This is the bread that came down from heaven. Unlike your ancestors who ate manna and died, whoever gets their nourishment from this bread will live forever."

After saying these things, Jesus stood up and went outside where several of his disciples were waiting. Many of them complained to him, "This is a difficult teaching. Who can accept it?"

But Jesus, aware of their grumbling, said, "Does this offend you? Then what if you see the Son of Man ascend to where he was before?"

"Well, if we see a miracle like that then maybe we can believe in you," they answered.

"That's unlikely," Jesus said. "As I mentioned earlier, no one can come to me unless the Father has granted it to them."

A few responded, "Though we have doubts, we can try harder to believe."

Jesus answered, "It's the Spirit who gives life. Human effort counts for nothing. The words I've spoken to you are words of Spirit and life. Yet there are some of you who still don't believe." Jesus had known from the beginning who wouldn't believe and who would betray him.

As a result of this teaching, many of his disciples turned back and no longer walked with him. He turned to his twelve apostles standing nearby and asked, "You don't want to leave, too, do you?"

Peter answered, "Lord, to whom would we go? You have the words of eternal life, and we've believed and come to know that you're the Holy One of God."

Then Jesus replied, "Haven't I chosen you twelve? Yet one of you is a devil!" He meant Judas, the son of Simon Iscariot, for he, one of the twelve apostles, was going to betray him.

By now a large group had gathered outside. Because Jesus, the main attraction, had left the building, people were filing out to the street. Many were curiosity seekers, and few had open hearts. Jesus noticed a group of Pharisees and scribes from Jerusalem looking in his direction. He'd seen them in the synagogue and knew they were here to stir up trouble for him, so he started walking away.

They caught up to him and, walking alongside him, asked, "Why do your disciples break the tradition of the elders? They don't wash their hands before they eat."

Jesus replied, "Really? You're talking to me about handwashing! Let me ask you this—why do you break the command of God for the sake of your tradition? Didn't God say, 'Honor your father and mother'? and 'Anyone who speaks evil of his father or mother must be put to death'?[27] But you say that whoever tells their father or mother, 'Whatever I have that could help you is already promised as an offering to God,' doesn't have to honor their father or mother with what they have. You're a bunch of hypocrites!"

"How dare you," they said, "when we're the ones following the law and you're not!"

"Which law?" Jesus responded. "If you mean your own made-up rules, then you're right. Isaiah was speaking about you when he said, 'These people honor me with their lips, but their hearts are far from me. They worship me meaninglessly, and they teach the rules invented by humans as doctrine.'[28] You nullify the word of God for the sake of your man-made laws.

"We follow all God's commands!" they insisted.

"That's not true," Jesus said. "You've become experts at setting aside God's commandments—just to keep your own traditions."

"We don't have to listen to this," they said indignantly. "Wait until our superiors hear about this!" Then they turned their backs on him and left.

He turned to the crowd that had been following him and called out, "Listen to me, everyone, and understand. It's not what goes into a mouth that makes a person unclean but what comes out of the mouth. Nothing outside a person can make them unclean by going into them. It's what comes out of a person that makes them unclean."

When he reached the house, his disciples asked, "Don't you know that the Pharisees were offended by what you said?"

Jesus replied, "Leave them. They're blind guides. Every plant that my heavenly Father did not plant will be uprooted."

Peter then asked, "Could you explain the parable to us?"

Jesus answered, "Don't you understand that what goes into a person from the outside can't make them unclean because it doesn't go into the heart? Whatever enters the mouth goes into the stomach and then goes out into the sewer. What comes out of a person's heart is what makes them unclean, like

evil thoughts,	adultery,	sensuality,
sexual immorality,	greed,	envy,
theft,	wickedness,	slander,
murder,	deceit,	arrogance, and foolishness.

"These are what defile a person, not eating with unwashed hands," Jesus said.

They were astounded, then Matthew spoke up. "Are you saying that all foods are clean?"

Jesus replied, "I see you're finally beginning to understand."

The others were amazed by this teaching and kept discussing it long after Jesus had gone to bed.

ლ

The next day Jesus took the disciples to the vicinity of Tyre, an important Phoenician city on the coast about forty miles northwest of Capernaum. He entered a house and tried to remain unseen, but he couldn't escape notice.

Surprisingly, a Canaanite woman came to him and cried out, "Have mercy on me, Lord, Son of David! My daughter is cruelly demon possessed." Even though the woman was a Gentile, she kept asking Jesus to drive the demon out of her daughter.

But Jesus didn't say a word to answer her, so his disciples came to him and urged, "Send her away because she keeps crying out after us."

Jesus turned to the woman and said, "I was sent only to the lost sheep of Israel."

But she came and bowed down before him and said, "Lord, please help me."

He replied, "It's not right to take the children of Israel's bread and throw it to the dogs."

"Yes, Lord," she said, "but even the dogs eat the crumbs that fall from their master's table."

Then Jesus said to her, "Woman, your faith is great. Let it be done to you as you wish." And her daughter was healed at that very moment. When she went home, she found her child lying on the bed and the demon gone.

Jesus then went ten miles north to another important Phoenician city, Sidon, then down to the Sea of Galilee and into the region of the Decapolis.

Some people brought him a deaf man who also had difficulty speaking. When they begged Jesus to heal him, Jesus took the man away from the crowd and put his fingers into the man's ears. Then he spit into his own hands, touched the man's tongue, looked up to heaven, sighed deeply, and said, "Be opened!" Immediately, the man's ears were opened, his tongue was loosened, and he spoke plainly! Jesus commanded the people not to tell anyone, but the more he ordered them to be quiet, the more they proclaimed it.

People were absolutely astounded, saying, "He's done everything perfectly. He even made the deaf hear and the mute speak!"

❧

Jesus returned home to Capernaum and walked along the Sea of Galilee. Then he went up a mountain and sat down. Large crowds came to him, bringing the lame, the blind, the crippled, the mute, and many others. They laid them at his feet, and he healed them. The crowd was amazed when they saw the mute speaking, the crippled restored, the lame walking, and the blind seeing. And they praised the God of Israel.

Jesus called the disciples over and said, "I'm concerned about these people. They've been with me three days now and have nothing to eat. I don't want to send them away hungry. Some could collapse on the way home."

The disciples asked, "Where can we get enough bread in this desolate place to feed such a crowd?"

Jesus asked, "How many loaves do you have?"

"Seven," they replied, "and a few small fish. But that's nowhere near enough."

Jesus ignored that comment and directed the crowd to sit on the ground. He took the seven loaves, gave thanks, broke them, and gave them to his disciples to serve the people; and they set them before the crowd. Because they had a few small fish, too, he blessed them and instructed the disciples to serve them. Everyone ate all they wanted. The disciples picked up seven baskets of leftover pieces, even though there were about four thousand men, plus women and children. Then Jesus sent the crowd away.

❧

Jesus and his disciples went back across the Sea of Galilee to the region of Magadan, not far from Magdala, Mary Magdalene's hometown. She was traveling with them on this journey, so he said to her before they docked, "Do you want to visit any family while you're in the area? We could stop for a few days."

Mary's face fell. "I'd rather not," she said and motioned to Jesus and the apostles, "You're my family now. The memories there would only remind me of what I once was. Plus, as you saw in your own hometown, the people wouldn't listen to me."

115

"I do understand, all too well," Jesus said.

When they arrived at the port, they disembarked. Jesus hadn't walked far from the dock when some Pharisees and Sadducees came to test him, as if they'd been waiting for him. They walked right up to him and demanded, "Show us a miraculous sign from heaven so we can believe in you."

Sighing deeply in his spirit, he said to them, "Why does this generation demand a miraculous sign? When evening comes, you say, 'It will be fair weather tomorrow, for the sky is red.' In the morning you say, 'It will be stormy today, for the sky is red and cloudy.' You understand the face of the sky, but you can't understand the signs of the times.

With that, Jesus turned around and stamped his sandals on the dock to dislodge the dust. Then he went back to the boat and got in. The disciples were confused but followed him.

"Lord, we only just arrived," Peter said.

Jesus instructed the helmsman to head across the lake and said, "I told you twelve that if a town won't receive you, you're to shake the dust from your feet and leave."

Peter then said to Andrew, "Do you have any bread? I'm so hungry!"

Andrew shot back, "I thought you were bringing it!" He looked at the others. "Does anyone have something to eat?"

They were rummaging in their sacks and found only a half a loaf. They realized they'd forgotten to take food.

"Lord, there's not enough bread for us all," Andrew said.

"Watch out!" Jesus warned. "Beware of the leaven of the Pharisees and Sadducees, and even the leaven of Herod."

They deliberated about this, saying, "It's because we didn't bring any bread."

Aware of their discussion, Jesus said, "You of little faith, why do you reason among yourselves about having no bread? Don't you see or understand yet? Do you have hardened hearts? You have eyes—don't you see? You have ears—don't you hear? Don't you remember when I broke the five loaves for the five thousand? How many basketfuls did you pick up?"

"Twelve," they replied.

"And when I broke the seven loaves for the four thousand, how many basketfuls did you pick up?"

"Seven," they answered.

Jesus shook his head. "And you still don't understand? How is it you don't know that I wasn't talking to you about bread but to beware of the leaven of the Pharisees and Sadducees?"

Then they understood that he was not telling them to be on guard against leaven, but it was a metaphor against the teaching of the Pharisees and Sadducees—that just as a little bit of good (a few loaves and fish) can lead to a lot of good (baskets full of fish), a little bit of evil (the teaching of the Pharisees, leaven in a clump of dough) can lead to a lot of evil (a large bowl of raised dough).

☙

They crossed back over the lake and landed at Bethsaida. While Jesus was sitting there enjoying the sunny day and watching the townspeople come and go from the food stalls in the market, a couple of men were leading a blind man to Jesus.

They kneeled in front of him and said, "Rabbi, will you touch him so he can see?"

Jesus got up and took the blind man by the hand and led him out of the village. He spit on the man's eyes, put his hands on him, and asked, "Do you see anything?"

The man looked up and said, "I see people, but they look like walking trees."

Again Jesus put his hands on the man's eyes. The man stared hard and shouted, "I can see! I can see!" His sight was fully restored, and he now saw everything clearly.

Jesus sent him home, telling him, "Don't go into the village."

Then Jesus and his disciples walked about twenty-five miles north to the towns and villages around Caesarea Philippi. He told his disciples, "They need to hear my message too."

When they reached their destination, Jesus asked his disciples, "Who do the people say the Son of Man is?"

They replied, "Some say John the Baptist, others say Elijah, and others, Jeremiah, or one of the other great prophets."

Then he asked them, "Who do you say I am?"

Peter answered, "You are the Messiah, the Son of the living God."

Jesus replied, "Blessed are you, Simon son of Jonah, for flesh and blood did not reveal this to you, but my Father in heaven. And I tell you that you are Peter, and on this rock I will build my church, and the gates of Hades will not prevail against it. I will give you the keys of the kingdom of heaven. Whatever you forbid on earth will be forbidden in heaven, and whatever you permit on earth will be permitted in heaven." Then he warned his disciples not to tell anyone that he was the Messiah.

Peter was astounded by Jesus' words and asked the others if they knew what he meant.

"Rock is not what comes to mind when I think of you, brother," Andrew said. The others laughed.

"With God all things are possible," Jesus said.

∽

They found a clearing on the outskirts of town where they could set up camp, and Jesus went off by himself. He spent some time praying for his disciples, knowing they'd need strength for what was ahead. He looked at them in the distance, talking and laughing. They'd become quite close during these past few years. Jesus was no exception. He cared for them deeply. He was almost surprised by the depth of human emotion within him. He hated to steal their joy by telling them what was coming, but they needed to be prepared.

Jesus came back to the group and found them sitting around the fire while Mary and Johanna were distributing the bread, olives, and dates they'd bought at the market. He sat down, and the apostles looked in his direction, no doubt sensing his somber mood.

"What is it, Lord?" James asked. "You look troubled."

Jesus answered, "What I have to tell you won't be easy to hear."

"Tell us," Peter said. "You know we're here for you no matter what."

They all put down their food and leaned in toward Jesus.

"We've had many good times together on this journey," Jesus said. "I've come to love you not only as my disciples but as my friends. That's why what I have to say now is difficult."

"We feel the same about you," John said.

"Up to now we've avoided going to Jerusalem except at festival times," Jesus said.

"It was for our own safety," Philip added, "and for yours, since the elders, chief priests, and scribes would love to throw you in jail."

Jesus hesitated, then he continued. "I must go to Jerusalem. There I will be rejected by and suffer many things at the hands of the elders and chief priests and scribes. And they are going to kill me. But then I will be raised to life on the third day."

Peter was appalled and rebuked him, "Heaven forbid, Lord! This will not happen to you!"

But Jesus looked at his other disciples then rebuked Peter and said, "Get behind me, Satan! You're a stumbling block to me. You're not seeking the things of God, but the things of men."

Peter turned away in shame and said, "I don't get it. One minute he's praising me, and the next he's telling me the devil is speaking through me!" Andrew put his hand on his shoulder to console him.

"Take heart," Jesus said to the others. "After three days, I will be raised from the dead."

Their faces reflected shocked disbelief, yet Jesus continued, "If anyone wants to come after me, they must deny themselves, take up their cross, and follow me. Whoever wants to save their life will lose it, but whoever loses their life for my sake will find it. How does a person benefit if they gain the whole world yet lose their soul? What can a person give to God in exchange for their soul? The Son of Man will come in his Father's glory with his angels, then he will reward each person according to their deeds. I'm telling you the truth: Some who are standing here will certainly not taste death until they see the Son of Man coming in his kingdom."

The apostles commiserated among themselves, not knowing what to make of Jesus' astounding statements. But they understood a little better about a week later when they had a mountaintop experience.

જી

Jesus led James, Peter, and John up Mount Hermon to pray. But after a while, the three of them fell into a deep sleep. They were awakened suddenly when Jesus' appearance started to transform right in front of them. His face shone like the sun, and his clothes became white as light. Suddenly, Moses and Elijah appeared in glorious splendor and were talking with him about his death, which he was about to accomplish at Jerusalem. Fully awake now, the three apostles saw his glory and the two men standing with him.

Peter, as terrified as the rest of the disciples, was speechless. Finally, not even knowing what he was saying, he blurted out, "Lord, it's good for us to be here. Let's put up temporary shelters: one for you, one for Moses, and one for Elijah."

While he was speaking, a bright cloud formed and came over them. Fear gripped them as it enveloped them. A voice came out from it, saying, "This is my beloved Son, whom I've chosen and with whom I'm very pleased. Listen to him!"

When the disciples heard this, they fell on their faces. Jesus came over and touched them and said, "Get up. Don't be afraid."

When they looked around, they no longer saw anyone with them except Jesus. Later, when they were coming down the mountain, Jesus ordered them not to tell anyone about what they'd seen until he had risen from the dead. They kept what he said to themselves, discussing what "risen from the dead" could mean.

Then they asked Jesus, "Why do the scribes say that Elijah must come first?"

Jesus replied, "Elijah is coming first, and he will restore all things. But I tell you, Elijah has already come, and they didn't recognize him as a prophet but did to him whatever they wished. In the same way, the Son of Man is going to suffer at their hands."

Then the disciples understood that when referring to Elijah he meant John the Baptist. They shook their heads in confusion.

જી

The next day, when they reached the bottom of the mountain, they saw the other disciples standing within a large crowd, and some scribes were arguing with them. When the crowd saw Jesus, they were excited and ran to greet him. He asked the disciples, "What are you discussing with the scribes?"

Suddenly, a man spoke up from the crowd. "Lord, have mercy on my son, my only child. He has seizures and suffers terribly. Whenever the evil spirit seizes him, he screams, then he convulses, foams at the mouth, grinds his teeth, and becomes rigid. It rarely leaves him, and it mauls him when it does. I asked your disciples to drive it out, but they couldn't."

Jesus responded, "O faithless and perverse generation! How long will I be with you? How long will I put up with you? Bring him here to me."

As the boy was coming, when the spirit saw Jesus, it immediately threw the boy into a convulsion. He fell to the ground, writhed in pain, and was foaming at the mouth. Jesus asked the father, "How long has this been happening?"

He replied, "Since childhood. Many times it has attempted to kill him, throwing him into fire or water. If you can do anything, please take pity, and help us."

"If I can?" Jesus said. "Anything is possible for those who believe."

Immediately the boy's father cried out, "I do believe! Help me overcome my unbelief."

Now when Jesus saw that a crowd was rapidly gathering, he rebuked the evil spirit. "You deaf and mute spirit, I command you, 'Come out of him, and do not enter him again.'"

After crying out and violently convulsing the boy, it came out, and the child was healed from that very moment. The boy looked so much like a corpse that many said, "He's dead." But Jesus took him by the hand and lifted him. He stood up, and Jesus gave him back to his father. They were all amazed at the greatness of God.

Later, after Jesus had gone into a house in Capernaum, the disciples came to him privately and asked, "Why couldn't we cast it out?"

He replied, "Because you have little faith! I'm telling you the truth: If you have faith as small as a mustard seed, you can say to this mountain, 'Move from here to here,' and it will move. Nothing will be impossible for you. But this kind does not go out but by prayer and fasting."

☙

They left Capernaum by separate routes and reassembled in Galilee. Jesus didn't want anyone to know where they were because he was teaching his disciples privately. One of the things he told them was, "The Son of Man is going to be betrayed into the hands of men. They will kill him, and three days after being killed, he will rise."

They didn't understand what he was saying because its meaning was hidden from them, so they couldn't grasp it. They were greatly distressed by what he said, but they were afraid to ask him about it.

Later, back in Capernaum, Peter burst into Jesus' house. Trying to catch his breath, he blurted, "Lord, while I was in town, the collectors of the two-drachma temple tax came to me and asked, 'Does your teacher pay the temple tax?' Caught off guard, I answered yes then ran here as fast as I could."

"So what's your question?" Jesus asked. "Are you wondering whether I obey the laws of men and pay the tax?"

Peter hesitated then said, "Well, yes."

Jesus responded, "What do you think, Peter? From whom do the kings of the earth collect duty and taxes—from their own citizens or from foreigners?"

Peter answered, "From foreigners."

"Then the sons of God are exempt," Jesus said. "But so that we don't offend them, go to the lake and throw out your hook. Take the first fish you catch, and when you open its mouth, you'll find a Greek coin. Take it and give it to them for my tax and yours."

On another day in Capernaum, the disciples walked in debating among themselves.

"What are you arguing about?" Jesus asked.

They were silent at first. Then Peter said, "We wanted to know: who's the greatest in the kingdom of heaven?"

Sitting down, Jesus called the Twelve over and said, "If anyone wants to be first, they must be last of all and the servant of all." Then, knowing their innermost thoughts, he took a child and put him in the midst of them. And then, taking him in his arms, he said to them, "I'm telling you the truth: Unless you're converted and become like little children, you will never enter the kingdom of heaven. Whoever humbles themselves like this child is the greatest in the kingdom of heaven. And whoever welcomes one of these little children in my name, welcomes me. And whoever welcomes me, does not just welcome me but the one who sent me.

"But if anyone entices one of these little ones who believe in me to sin, it would be better for them to have a heavy millstone hung around their neck and to be drowned in the deep sea. Woe to the world because of its enticements to sin. It's inevitable that temptations to sin will come, but woe to the person through whom they come!"

He motioned to the child. "So see that you don't look down on one of these little ones. For I'm telling you that their angels in heaven always see the face of my Father in heaven. For the Son of Man has come to save that which was lost." And he sent the child off to play.

The disciples looked a bit embarrassed they'd asked who was the greatest. Then John changed the subject. "Teacher, earlier today when we were near the synagogue, we saw someone casting out demons in your name. We tried to stop him because he doesn't follow you along with us."

Jesus replied, "Don't stop him. No one who does a mighty work in my name will be able to speak evil about me afterward, for whoever is not against us is for us. Anyone who gives you a drink of water because you belong to Christ—I'm telling you the truth—will certainly not lose their reward."

John answered, "Well, I'm glad you don't find anything wrong with what that man was doing because he absolutely refused to comply with our request. My question is—what if he had been doing something wrong and wouldn't listen to us? I know we want peace and unity, but some things just shouldn't be done."

"You ask a good question," Jesus responded. "If your fellow believer sins against you, go and show them their fault privately. If the person listens to you, you've gained your fellow believer. But if they won't listen, take one or two others with you so that 'by the testimony of two or three witnesses every spoken matter may be confirmed.'²⁹ If the person refuses to listen to them, tell it to the church. And if the person refuses to listen even to the church, treat the person as you would a pagan or a tax collector."

"Maybe you'd have the authority to do this," Andrew said. "But we don't have that kind of power."

Jesus said, "Here's the truth: Whatever you bind on earth will be bound in heaven, and whatever you loose on earth will be loosed in heaven. If two of you on earth agree about anything you ask, it will be done for you by my Father in heaven. Where two or three come together in my name, I'm there in the midst of them."

While the disciples were loudly debating what he could have meant, Jesus went to get a cup of water. Peter found him and asked, "How many times can someone sin against me and I continue to forgive them? Up to seven times?"

Jesus answered, "Not just up to seven times but countless times. He pulled out a stool for Peter and told him to sit down. "Let me tell you a story to illustrate what the kingdom of heaven is like: A king wanted to settle accounts with his servants. As he began to settle, one who owed him several million dollars was brought to him, but he was unable to pay it. So the lord ordered that the servant, his wife, his children, and all his possessions be sold and repayment made.

"The servant fell to his knees and pleaded, 'Be patient with me, and I'll pay back everything.' The servant's master, moved by compassion, forgave him the debt and let him go. But the servant went out and found one of his fellow servants who owed him about four months' wages. And he grabbed him and started choking him and said, 'Pay back what you owe me!'

"His fellow servant fell to his knees and begged him, 'Be patient with me, and I'll repay you.' But he refused. Instead, he went and put him in prison until he repaid the debt.

"When his fellow servants saw what had happened, they were very upset, and they went and told their master everything that had happened. Then he called the servant in and said, 'You wicked servant! I canceled all that debt because you begged me. Shouldn't you have had mercy on your fellow servant, just as I had mercy on you?' And in anger, his lord turned him over to the jailers to be tortured until he paid back all he owed."

By this time, the other apostles were standing by Peter, not wanting to miss any valuable lessons from their master.

Jesus turned to them all and concluded: "So, too, will my heavenly Father treat each of you if you don't forgive your fellow believer from your heart."

&

The next day, Jesus left Capernaum and went south, traveling the customary route east of the Jordan River down as far as Jericho. Large crowds gathered around him again, and as was his custom, he taught and healed them.

As usual, some Pharisees came to test Jesus. They asked him, "Is it lawful for a man to divorce his wife for any reason at all?"

Jesus answered, "Haven't you read that he who created them 'made them male and female' at the beginning and said, 'For this reason a man will leave his father and mother and hold tightly to his wife, and the two will become one flesh'? So they're no longer two but one flesh. Therefore what God has joined together, let no person separate."

So the Pharisees asked him, "Why then did Moses direct us that a man could give a certificate of divorce to his wife and send her away?"

Jesus replied, "Because of your hardness of heart! That's why Moses permitted you to divorce your wives. But from the beginning, it wasn't meant to be this way. I tell you that anyone who divorces his wife, except for sexual immorality, and marries another woman commits adultery."

His disciples said, "If the situation of a man and his wife is like this, it's better not to marry."

Jesus replied, "Not everyone can accept this statement but only those to whom it's been given. There are eunuchs who are eunuchs from birth; and there are eunuchs who were made eunuchs by others; and there are eunuchs who have made themselves like eunuchs, not marrying for the sake of the kingdom of heaven. Those who are able to accept this, let them accept it."

Later Jesus took a walk and stood looking at the sea. When he turned around, he saw that people were bringing their babies and small children to him, hoping he'd lay his hands on them and pray for them. When the disciples reached him, they began rebuking those who brought them, thinking they were watching out for him.

When Jesus saw this, he was indignant. He called the children to himself and said, "Let the little children come to me. Don't prevent them. The kingdom of God belongs to ones like these. I'm telling you the truth: Anyone who refuses to receive the kingdom of God like a little child will never enter it." And he took the children in his arms, put his hands on them and blessed them, and went on from there.

Chapter 11

Stirring Up the Festivals

"Why are you staying out here in the back of beyond?" Jesus' half brothers said as they hiked up to Jesus' campsite on the outskirts of Nazareth.

"I guess you haven't heard he was literally dragged out of town last time he was there," Peter retorted.

"We were traveling throughout Galilee," Jesus said, "and this seemed as good a place as any to stop. I'm happy to see you. Rest a while and have a bite to eat."

"Sorry, but we can't stop," they said. "We're on the way to Jerusalem for the Shelters Festival and need to make some progress before nightfall." They surveyed the state of the camp and said, "Speaking of which—why aren't you preparing to leave yourselves?"

"It's not the right time," Jesus said.

Despite this, his own brothers suggested, "You should go to Judea, so your followers there may see the works you're doing. No one acts in secret if he wants to be well known. If you are going to do the things you speak of, prove yourself to the world!"

Jesus responded, "The opportune time for me to go hasn't come yet, but anytime is good for you. The world can't hate you, but it hates me because I accuse it of evil deeds. So you go to the festival yourselves. I'm not going yet because my time has not yet fully come."

They, who didn't believe in him yet, sighed, then turned and left. Jesus and his disciples remained in Galilee a little longer. Eventually they headed for Jerusalem, not openly, but in secret.

When they approached a Samaritan village, he sent messengers ahead to prepare for his arrival. He hoped they'd remember when he was last there, when they received him with open arms because of the testimony of the Samaritan woman. But when the villagers heard he was heading for Jerusalem, they refused to welcome him. Their enmity with the Jews was too deep and went too far back.

When James and John heard this, they were incredulous. "After all you did for them too! Lord, do you want us to call fire down from heaven to destroy them?"

Jesus turned and rebuked them: "You sons of thunder don't know what kind of spirit you're of! The Son of Man didn't come to destroy people's lives but to save them."

After stopping in another village, they finally reached the outskirts of Jerusalem. Jesus observed all the people constructing their booths to celebrate the Festival of Shelters—a time when Jews were to come to Jerusalem and live in temporary shelters for a week to commemorate Israel's time in the wilderness after escaping from Egypt. His disciples looked around at all the activity and said, "Where do you want us to set up our shelters, Lord?"

He answered, "Somewhere a bit more remote. There will be enough engagement with the people in the city itself and at the temple. We will need a quiet space to pray and reflect."

Jesus went into Jerusalem to the temple area while the disciples were preparing. He kept hidden until it was time to make himself known. At the festivities, he overheard a lot of discussions about the controversy over him. His half brothers were right about that. Some were saying, "He's a good man." Others replied, "No, he deceives the crowd." But no one spoke about him openly for fear of the Jewish leaders, who were watching for him and asking, "Where is he?" Needing a break, he went to the camp.

ༀ

In the middle of the festival week he went back into the city and began to teach in the temple courts. The Jews there were astonished at his teaching and asked, "How does he know the Scriptures, though he hasn't studied under a rabbi?"

Jesus answered, "My teaching isn't mine but his who sent me. If anyone wants to do his will, they'll know whether the teaching is from God or whether I speak from myself. Whoever speaks from themselves seeks their own glory, but whoever seeks glory for the one who sent them is a truthful person. There's nothing false in them. Hasn't Moses given you the law? But not one of you keeps it, so why do you want to kill me?"

The crowd answered, "You have a demon! Who wants to kill you?"

Jesus answered, "I did just one miraculous work, and you're all upset. Yet because Moses gave you the rite of circumcision—not that it came from Moses but from the patriarchs—you circumcise a male child on the Sabbath. Now if a male child can be circumcised on the Sabbath so the law of Moses won't be broken, why are you angry with me for making a man entirely whole on the Sabbath? Don't judge only according to appearance, but think with righteous judgment."

Jesus was dismayed the religious leaders were still offended that he'd healed the disabled man at the pool of Bethesda on the Sabbath the last time he was in town. They were still talking about it!

One person looked over at Jesus and asked, "Isn't he the one they want to kill? But look, he's speaking in public, and they're doing nothing to him."

Someone else said, "The authorities haven't recognized this is the Messiah, and we know where he's from. When the Messiah comes, no one will know where he's from." But he was wrong. The Scriptures said the Messiah would be born in Bethlehem.[30]

Then Jesus, who was still teaching in the temple courts, cried out, "You all know me and where I'm from! But I haven't come on my own. He who sent me is true. You don't know him, but I know him because I'm from him, and he sent me."

They tried to arrest him, but no one laid a hand on him because his time hadn't yet come. Yet many in the crowd believed in him, asking, "When the Messiah comes, will he perform more miracles than this man?" When the Pharisees heard the crowd whispering these things about him, they and the chief priests sent temple officers to arrest him.

But Jesus continued teaching: "I'm going to be with you for only a little while longer, and then I'm going back to the one who sent me. You'll look for me, but you won't find me, and where I am, you cannot come."

The Jews asked each other, "Where does he intend to go that we won't find him? Does he plan to go to the Jews living outside of Israel and teach the God-fearing Gentiles and those who have become Jews? What did he mean by saying, 'You'll look for me, but you won't find me,' and 'Where I am, you can't come'?"

ç⁊

On the festival's last and greatest day, Jesus stood and cried out to the crowds, "If anyone is thirsty, come to me and drink. Whoever believes in me, as the Scripture says, 'Rivers of living water will flow from within them.'"[31] He was talking about the Holy Spirit, whom those who believed in him were going to receive. But the Spirit had not yet been given because Jesus had not yet been glorified.

When they heard these words, some of the people said, "This really is the Prophet."[32]

Others said, "He's the Messiah."

But others objected, "Surely the Messiah is not going to come out of Galilee? Doesn't Scripture say the Messiah will come from the line of David and from Bethlehem, the village where David lived?"

Jesus saw the temple officers who were sent to arrest him listening to his teaching. He said to them, "Why don't you do what you came to do?"

The officers answered, "Because no one has ever spoken the way you do."

Some of the Pharisees were standing there and said to the officers, "Have you also been deceived? Has even one of the authorities or the Pharisees believed in him? But this crowd, which knows nothing of the law, is under a curse."

So the people were divided because of Jesus. Though some wanted to apprehend him, no one did anything.

Just then, Jesus saw Nicodemus, the influential Pharisee who had met with him secretly to ask questions, step forward. He defended Jesus by saying, "Our law doesn't judge a man without our first hearing from him to find out what he's been doing." He'd left their last meeting on the precipice of belief. Jesus wondered if he'd since become one of his followers.

Others replied, "Are you from Galilee too? Search the Scriptures, and you'll find that no prophet arises from Galilee." Then they all went home, but Jesus went to Mount of Olives to pray before rejoining the disciples.

ℂℌ

At dawn he went to the temple courts again. All the people came to him, and he sat down to teach them. But to test him, the scribes and Pharisees brought a woman caught in adultery. Hoping to find a reason to arrest Jesus, they stood her in the midst of the group and said, "Teacher, this woman was caught in adultery—in the very act. In the law, Moses commanded us to stone such a woman to death. But what do you say?"

Jesus stooped down and wrote on the ground with his finger, but they kept on asking questions. So he straightened up and said, "The sinless one among you, let him be the first to throw a stone at her." Then he stooped down and wrote on the ground some more.

After hearing this, and having been convicted by their consciences, they left, one by one, beginning with the oldest, until Jesus was left alone with the woman still standing there. Jesus stood up and asked her, "Woman, where are your accusers? Has no one condemned you?"

She replied, "No one, sir."

"Then I don't condemn you either," Jesus declared. "Now go and sin no more."

Jesus spoke to the people again and said, "I am the light of the world. Whoever follows me will never walk in darkness but will have the light of life."

The Pharisees challenged him: "Your testimony isn't valid because you're appearing as your own witness."

131

Jesus replied, "Even if I testify about myself, my testimony is valid because I know where I came from and where I'm going. But you don't know where I came from or where I'm going. You judge by human standards. I pass judgment on no one. And even if I do pass judgment, my judgment is valid because it isn't I alone who judges but I and the Father who sent me. In your law it's written that the testimony of two witnesses is true. I am one witness, and I testify about myself, and the Father who sent me also testifies about me."

So they asked him, "Where is your Father?"

Jesus replied, "You don't know me or my Father. If you knew me, you'd know my Father too." Even though he taught these things openly in the temple courts in the area called "the treasury," no one seized him because his time had not yet come.

Later, Jesus told them again, "I'm going away, and you'll look for me, and you'll die in your sins. Where I'm going, you're not able to come."

So the Jewish leaders asked, "Will he kill himself because he says, 'You can't come where I'm going'?"

But he continued, "You're from below. I'm from above. You're of this world. I'm not of this world. That's why I told you that you'll die in your sins. Because unless you believe I am he, you'll die in your sins."

They asked him, "Who are you?"

Jesus replied, "What have I been telling you from the beginning? I have much to say about you and in judgment of you. But he who sent me is trustworthy, and I tell the world the things I've heard from him."

They didn't understand he was telling them about his Father, so he said, "When you lift up the Son of Man, then you'll know that I do nothing from within myself or on my own authority, but I speak only the things the Father has taught me. The one who sent me is with me. He hasn't left me here alone because I always do what pleases him."

As he said these things, many people believed in him.

Jesus spoke to the Jews who had believed what he was saying but had not put their trust in him: "If you live by my teaching, you are truly my disciples. Then you'll know the truth, and the truth will set you free."*

They answered him, "We're Abraham's descendants and have never been slaves of anyone. How can you say we'll be set free?"

Jesus replied, "I'm telling you the truth: Everyone who practices sin is the slave of sin. Now a slave does not remain in the household forever, but a son does remain a family member forever. So if the Son sets you free from slavery to sin, you'll be free indeed."

Their ignorance of their own sin exposed their true allegiance. "I realize you're Abraham's descendants," Jesus continued, "but you want to kill me because my words find no place in you. I'm telling you about the things I've seen when I've been with my Father in heaven, but you're doing the things you've heard from your father."

They responded, "Abraham is our father."

But Jesus said, "If you were Abraham's children, you'd be doing what Abraham did. But as it is, you're seeking a way to kill me, a man who's told you the truth I heard from God. Abraham didn't do things like this! You're doing the works of your father."

They objected, "We're not children of anyone but our legitimate father. We have only one Father: God."

Jesus replied, "If God were your Father, you'd love me, because I've come to you from God. I haven't come on my own. He sent me. Why don't you understand what I'm saying? Here's why: because you're not able to hear what I'm saying. You're children of your father, the devil, and you choose to do what your father wants. He was a murderer from the beginning and does not uphold the truth because there's no truth in him. Whenever he lies, he speaks from his own nature, for he's a liar and the father of lies.

"So because I tell the truth, you don't believe me! Can any of you convict me of sin? If I'm telling the truth, why don't you believe me?

---

* "The truth will set you free": When people realize that God is truly God, Creator and King of the universe and active in it today, they become free to break the traditions and cultural restraints of mankind and freely follow him. And when people read the truth presented in Scripture and believe it, they are likewise freed to follow it, regardless of the consequences, knowing that God's will is more important than all other considerations.

Whoever is a child of God hears and obeys what God says. That's why you don't hear—because you are not children of God."

The Jews responded, "Isn't what we said right, that you're a demon-possessed Samaritan?"

Jesus replied, "I'm not possessed by a demon. Rather, I honor my Father, and you dishonor me. I'm not seeking glory for myself, but there is one who's looking for it from you, and he's the judge. I'm telling you the truth: Whoever obeys my word will never see death."

At this they declared, "Now we know you're possessed by a demon. Both Abraham and the prophets died, yet you say, 'Whoever obeys my word will never see death.' Are you greater than our father Abraham who died? And the prophets who died too? Who do you think you are?"

Jesus explained, "If I glorify myself, my glory is nothing. But my Father glorifies me—the one of whom you say, 'He is our God.' Though you don't know him, I do know him. If I said I didn't know him, I would be a liar like you. But I do know him, and I obey his word. Your ancestral father Abraham rejoiced at the thought of seeing my day. He saw it and was glad."

The Jews responded, "You're not even fifty years old, and you've seen Abraham!"

"I'm telling you the truth," Jesus answered. "Before Abraham was born, I am!"* So they picked up stones to throw at him. But Jesus hid himself then left the temple, passing through the midst of them.

৬৯

He met up with his disciples a distance from the temple. As they walked along, they saw a blind man. Jesus pointed him out to them and said, "He's been blind from birth."

His disciples asked, "Rabbi, who committed the sin that caused him to be born blind, this man or his parents?"

Jesus answered, "Neither this man nor his parents sinned, but it happened so the works of God might be displayed by what happens

---

* Now in Hebrew and Aramaic "I Am" was the name of God. Thus, Jesus was declaring himself to be God, which was blasphemy in their eyes.

to him. We need to do the works of him who sent me as long as it's day. Night's coming, when no one can work. While I'm in the world, I am the light of the world."

Then he spit on the ground, made mud with the saliva, put it on the man's eyes, and told him, "Go wash in the Pool of Siloam." So the man went and washed and came back seeing!

Jesus observed the reaction of the people. The man's neighbors and those who'd previously seen him as a beggar asked, "Isn't this the man who used to sit and beg?" Some said, "Yes, it's him." Others said, "No, but he looks like him."

But he insisted, "I am the man."

So they asked him, "How were your eyes opened?"

He answered, "The man called Jesus made mud and put it on my eyes. Then he told me, 'Go to Siloam and wash.' I went and washed, and then I could see."

"Where is he?" they asked him.

He replied, "I don't know."

Jesus had hidden himself and followed unseen as they brought the man who'd been blind to the Pharisees at the synagogue. Today was the Sabbath, so they asked him exactly how he'd received his sight.

"He put mud on my eyes," the man replied, "and I washed, and now I see."

Some of the Pharisees said, "This man isn't from God. He doesn't keep the Sabbath day holy. He was working by performing the healing and making the mud—not to mention his healing of the lame man on yet another Sabbath!"

But others asked, "How could a sinner perform such miracles?" And there was division among them. Then they questioned the blind man some more: "What do you say about him because it was your eyes he opened?"

He replied, "He's a prophet."

The Jewish leaders didn't believe the man had been blind and had received his sight until they sent for his parents. They asked them, "Is this your son, who you say was born blind? How come he can see now?"

His parents answered, "We know this is our son, and he was born blind. But we don't know how it is he sees now or who opened his eyes. Ask him. He's of age. He'll speak for himself." Jesus knew his parents had said this because they were afraid of the Jewish leaders, who agreed that anyone who stated openly that Jesus was the Messiah would be put out of the synagogue.

They summoned the man a second time and said, "Give glory to God by telling the truth, and understand that we know Jesus is a sinner."

The man replied, "I don't know whether he's a sinner or not. I just know one thing: I was blind and now I see."

Then they asked, "What did he do to you? How did he open your eyes?"

He answered, "I've already told you, and you didn't listen. Why do you want to hear it again? Do you want to become his disciples too?"

Then they verbally abused him and defended themselves: "You're his disciple! We're disciples of Moses. We know God spoke to Moses. But as for this man, we don't know where he comes from."

The man answered, "Now isn't that remarkable? You don't know where he comes from, though he opened my eyes. We know God doesn't listen to sinners, but he hears whoever is God-fearing and does his will. Since the beginning of time, nobody has ever heard of someone opening the eyes of a man born blind. If this man were not from God, he could do nothing."

They said, "You were born entirely in sins. How dare you lecture us!" And they threw him out.

Jesus heard they had thrown him out of the synagogue, so when he found him, he asked, "Do you believe in the Son of Man?"

The man replied, "Who is he, sir? Tell me so I may believe in him."

Jesus said, "You've actually seen him. He's the one talking with you now."

Then the man recognized Jesus' holiness and said, "Lord, I believe," and he dropped to his knees to worship him.

Jesus said to the group that had surrounded them, "For judgment I have come into this world: so the blind will see and those who think they see, but don't, will be exposed as blind."

Some Pharisees who were standing nearby heard this and challenged him. "We aren't blind, too, are we?"

Jesus replied, "If you were blind, you wouldn't be guilty of sin. But since you claim that you can see, your guilt remains."

"How could we be guilty when we follow all 613 laws of God to the letter?" they shot back.

Jesus answered, "I'm telling you the truth: Anyone who doesn't enter the sheep pen by the gate but enters by climbing in another way is a thief and a robber. The one who enters by the gate is the shepherd of the sheep. The gatekeeper opens it for him, and the sheep listen to his voice. He calls his own sheep by name and leads them out. When he's brought out all his sheep, he walks ahead of them—and his sheep follow him because they know his voice. They won't follow a stranger but will flee from him because they don't know his voice."

"We have no idea what you're talking about," the Pharisees said. "What does this have to do with sheep?"

Because the Pharisees still didn't understand what he was telling them, he explained: "I'm telling you the truth: I am the gate for the sheep. All who came before me were thieves and robbers, but the sheep didn't listen to them. Anyone who enters through me will be saved. They will come in and go out and find pasture. The thief comes only to steal and kill and destroy, but I've come that they may have life and have it abundantly."

The Pharisees conferred among themselves, shaking their heads and gesturing wildly. Finally, they said, "If you refuse to speak plainly, we can't properly answer you."

Jesus continued with his parable, not only for their benefit but for the crowd that had gathered around them. "I am the good shepherd who lays down his life for the sheep. The hired hand isn't the shepherd and doesn't own the sheep. When he sees the wolf coming, he abandons the sheep and flees. Then the wolf snatches them and scatters them. He flees because he's a hired hand and doesn't care about the sheep. I know my own sheep, and my own know me. Just as the Father knows me, I also know the Father—and I lay down my life for the sheep. I have other sheep that are not of this sheep pen that I must also bring in. They will listen to my voice, and there will be one flock with one shepherd. I lay down my life, so I may take it up again. Because of this, my Father loves me. No one takes it from me, but I lay it down of my own free will. I have the authority to lay it down and the authority to take it up again. I received this command from my Father."

The Jewish leaders were divided again because of these words. Many of them said, "He's demon possessed and insane. Why do you listen to him?" But others said, "These aren't the sayings of someone who's possessed by a demon. Can a demon open the eyes of the blind?"

After this exchange, Jesus left the city to return to his disciples. There would be many more encounters like this, and the conflict would only grow worse until—he tried not to think about what awaited him.

ↀ

A month later, in November, Jesus was in Jerusalem for the Festival of Dedication, a time when Jews celebrated the reconstruction and dedication of the new temple almost two hundred years earlier. He went to the temple and was walking in Solomon's Colonnade in the court of the Gentiles. Some Jews gathered around him and asked, "How long will you keep us in suspense? If you're the Messiah, tell us plainly."

Jesus kept walking. "I did tell you, but you didn't believe me. The works I do in my Father's name testify about me, but you don't believe because you're not my sheep. My sheep listen to my voice. I know them, and they follow me. I give them eternal life, and they will never perish." He stopped and gave them a stern look. "No one . . . I said no one will snatch them out of my hand. My Father, who's given them to me, is greater than all, and no one can snatch them out of my Father's hand. I and the Father are one."

At this, yet another time Jesus claimed to be God, the Jews who heard this picked up rocks to stone him to death, but Jesus said to them, "I've shown you many good works from the Father. For which of them are you going to stone me?"

They replied, "We're not stoning you for any good work but for blasphemy because you, who are just a man, claim to be God."

Jesus responded, "Isn't it written in the Scripture, 'I said you are gods'?[33] If the psalmist called them to whom the word of God came 'gods,' and Scripture can't be broken, do you say that I, whom the Father set apart as his own and sent into the world, am blaspheming because I say, 'I am the Son of God'?"

They stopped picking up stones for a moment and said nothing, unable to come up with a suitable response.

Jesus continued, "If I don't do the works of my Father, don't believe me. But if I do them, even though I don't seem believable, believe the evidence provided by the works I've done, so you may know and understand the Father is in me, and I am in the Father."

They tried to grab him, but he escaped their grasp. He called his disciples together, and they left the city and headed back to Capernaum, stopping at Bethany for the night.

Part 6

Death and Resurrection

Chapter 12

Heading to His Last Passover

As usual, in the spring Jesus and his disciples headed to Jerusalem to celebrate the Passover. They stopped by Bethany to visit Lazarus and his sisters, Martha and Mary. Jesus had become good friends with the three after they'd become his followers. They readily opened their home to them whenever they came near Jerusalem. When they entered their house, Mary ran up to Jesus. "Lazarus will be so excited to see you when he gets home from work. He's heard about your miracles—we all have—and he has so many questions."

Martha put out water for them to wash with then showed Jesus to a seat at the head of the table. She then rushed out of the room to prepare the meal. Meanwhile, Mary sat at Jesus' feet and listened to him intently as he spoke about his Father and the kingdom of heaven.

Martha kept coming and going from the room and serving Jesus and his disciples. Suddenly, exasperated, she said to Jesus, "Lord, don't you care that my sister has left me to do the serving by myself? Tell her to help me!"

But Jesus answered and said to her, "Martha, Martha, you're worried and troubled about so many things, but only one thing is needed. Mary's chosen the better part, and it won't be taken away from her."

೧೦

After their stay in Bethany, Jesus and the disciples headed across the Jordan River to Perea, where John had first been baptizing. Many of John's disciples were still meeting together even after his death. They were elated to see Jesus, and he stayed to teach them and the many others who came to him. They said, "Though John didn't do miracles, all he said about this man was true." And many at that place believed in Jesus.

After this, Jesus appointed seventy-two others and sent them ahead in pairs to every city and village where he was about to go. He gave them the same instructions he gave the twelve apostles when he sent them out: "The harvest is plentiful, but the laborers are few. So ask the Lord of the harvest to send out workers into his harvest. Go! I'm sending you out like lambs among wolves. Don't take a purse, bag, or extra sandals, and don't stop to greet anyone on the road. Whatever house you enter, first say, 'Peace to this house.' If a peace-loving person is there, your peace will rest on them. If not, it will return to you. Stay in that house, eating and drinking whatever they give you, for the worker deserves their wages. Don't move from house to house.

"Whenever you enter a town and are welcomed, eat what's set before you. Heal the sick who are there and tell them, 'The kingdom of God has come near you.' But whenever you enter a town and are not welcomed, go into its streets and tell them, 'As our witness against you, we're wiping off even the dust of your town that clings to our feet. But know this: The kingdom of God came near your town.' I'm telling you, it will be more bearable on the day of judgment for the people who lived in Sodom than for that town."

He closed by reminding the disciples, "Whoever listens to you listens to me, and whoever rejects you rejects me, and whoever rejects me rejects him who sent me."

Several days later, the seventy-two returned. Elated, they said, "Lord, even the demons submit to us in your name!"

Jesus replied, "I saw Satan fall like lightning from heaven! Believe me, I've given you authority to trample on snakes and scorpions (Satan's demons) and upon all the power of the enemy, and nothing will harm you. However, don't rejoice that Satan's spirits submit to you, but rejoice that your names are written in heaven."

Then he told the seventy-two, "All things have been put under my authority by my Father. No one knows who the Son is except the Father. And no one knows who the Father is except the Son and anyone to whom the Son chooses to reveal him." Then Jesus turned to the twelve apostles and said privately, "Remember, you've been blessed that your eyes see what you see. As I've told you before, many prophets and kings longed to see what you see but didn't see it, and they wished to hear what you hear but didn't get to hear it."

ᥱᷓ

Later, Jesus was teaching in a synagogue, and an expert in the law stood up to test him. "Teacher," he said, "what must I do to inherit eternal life?"

Jesus replied, "What's written in the law? How do you understand it?"

He answered: "'You shall love the Lord your God with all your heart and with all your soul and with all your strength and with all your mind,'[34] and 'Love your neighbor as yourself.'[35]

Jesus nodded. "You've answered correctly. Do this and you'll live."

But wanting to justify himself, he asked Jesus, "And who is my neighbor?"

Jesus responded with a story:

"A man who was going down from Jerusalem to Jericho was attacked by thieves. They stripped him of his clothes, beat him, and went away, leaving him half dead. By chance, a priest happened to be going down the same road. When he saw the man, he passed by on the other side. Then a Jewish temple assistant came by and saw him and also passed by on the other side. But a traveling Samaritan came upon him and, when he saw him, had compassion. He went over to him, bandaged his wounds (even pouring oil and wine on them), put the man on his own donkey, took him to an inn, and stayed to take care of him. The next day he gave the innkeeper two denarii and said, 'Take care of him. If you spend more, I'll repay you when I return.'

"Which of these three do you think proved to be a neighbor to the man who fell into the hands of robbers?"

The expert in the law replied, "The one who showed him mercy." Jesus told him, "Go and do likewise."

☙

Then Jesus set out on his final journey to Jerusalem, teaching in towns and villages along the way and traveling along the border between Samaria and Galilee. He knew he was no longer welcome in Samaria because they had refused him permission to pass through on a previous trip.

"Jesus, Master, have mercy on us!" multiple voices cried out as Jesus and his disciples entered a village.

Jesus turned around and saw ten lepers standing at a distance. He felt for them and said, "Do as the law commands. Go, show yourselves to the priests."[36] And they were made clean as they went. One of them saw that he was healed and came back, praising God in a loud voice. He fell on his face at Jesus' feet and thanked him. And he was a Samaritan!

Jesus asked him, "Weren't ten cleansed? Where are the other nine? Didn't anyone else return to give praise to God except this foreigner?" Then he said to him, "Get up and go. Your faith has made you well."

☙

In the next town, after Jesus had been teaching in the synagogue, a Pharisee came up to him and said, "Rabbi, will you come to my home for a meal?"

The apostles looked indignant and surrounded Jesus as if to protect him. But Jesus said to them, "It's OK. I'll catch up with you later."

When he entered the home, it was filled with Pharisees and scribes. Jesus was shown a place at the table, though not at the head, as was the case when he dined with the tax collectors. This didn't surprise him, as he was hardly a guest of honor here. After the food was served, Jesus picked up a piece of bread, and suddenly the room became silent with all eyes on him.

The Pharisee who invited him said, "You'll forgive us if we're shocked that you didn't wash your hands before the meal, as that's the ritual we Jews follow."

Jesus addressed everyone at the table: "Now you Pharisees clean the outside of the cup and dish, but inside you're full of robbery and wickedness. You fools! Didn't he who made the outside make the inside also? Give what's inside you as charity to the poor, then everything will be clean."

"How dare you insult me in my own home!" the Pharisee responded.

Jesus got up to leave without even eating his meal.

Once outside, the scribes and the Pharisees began to oppose Jesus strongly and interrogate him with many questions, hoping to catch him in something he might say. A crowd formed around them, and someone yelled out, "Teacher, tell my brother to divide the inheritance with me."

Jesus replied, "Man, who appointed me a judge or an arbiter between you two?" And he warned him, "Watch out and be on your guard against every kind of greed. A person's life is not made up of the abundance of their possessions."

And he told them this parable: "The land of a certain rich man produced abundantly. He thought to himself, 'What should I do, since I have no place to store my crops?' Then he said, 'I know. I'll tear down my barns and build bigger ones to store all my grain and my goods there. Then I can tell myself, "You have enough saved to live for many years. Take it easy; eat, drink, and have fun."' But God said to him, 'You fool! Tonight your soul is demanded from you, so who will get what you prepared for yourself?' So it is with people who store up wealth for themselves but are not rich toward God."

The man who asked about the inheritance didn't seem pleased with Jesus' answer, nor did some of the more well dressed among the crowd. But he noticed his disciples and some of the Pharisees from the dinner party were listening intently.

Jesus continued: "Be dressed for service and keep your lamps burning, like people waiting for their master to return from a wedding dinner, so they can immediately open the door for him when he comes and knocks. Blessed are those servants whom the master finds watching when he comes. I'm telling you the truth: He will dress himself to serve, have them eat at the table, and come and wait on them. And if he comes in the middle of the night or early in the morning and finds them awake, happy are those servants. You, too, must always be ready because the Son of Man will come at an hour when you don't expect him."

Peter asked, "Lord, are you directing this parable just to us or to everyone else as well?"

"This message is to all my true followers," Jesus answered. "Who then is the faithful and wise manager whom the master puts in charge of his servants to give them their allowance of food at the proper time? Blessed is that servant whom the master finds fulfilling their responsibility when he returns. I'm telling you the truth: He'll put that servant in charge of all his possessions.

"But suppose the servant is evil and says in his heart, 'My master is delayed in coming back,' and he begins to beat the male and female servants, eat and drink and get drunk. The master of that servant will come on a day when he is not expected. He will shame the servant and assign him a place with the unbelieving hypocrites, where there will be weeping and gnashing of teeth. That servant, who knew his master's will and didn't get ready or do what his master wanted, will be beaten severely. But the one who didn't know his master's will and did things that deserve a beating will only be beaten a little.

"From everyone who's been given much, much will be required. And from anyone who's been entrusted with much, much more will be asked. I've come to bring fire to the earth, and how I wish it were already kindled! But I have a baptism of suffering to undergo, and how distressed I am until it's accomplished!

"When you see a cloud rising in the west, immediately you say, 'A shower's coming,' and it does. And when the south wind blows, you say, 'It'll be hot today,' and it is. You hypocrites! You know how to interpret the appearance of the earth and the sky, but why don't you know how to interpret this present time? Why don't you judge for yourselves what's right?"

Some present told Jesus about the Galileans whose blood Pilate had mixed with their sacrifices. Jesus asked them, "Do you think those Galileans were the worst sinners of all the other Galileans because they suffered this way? No! I'm telling you, unless you repent, you'll all perish likewise. Or do you think those eighteen who were killed when the tower of Siloam fell on them were worse sinners than all the other people living in Jerusalem? No! I'm telling you, unless you repent, you'll all perish likewise."

Then he told them another parable: "A man had a fig tree planted in his vineyard, and when he went to look for fruit on it, he didn't find any. So he told his vineyard keeper, 'Look, for three years I've been coming to look for fruit on this fig tree and haven't found any. Cut it down! Why should it use up the ground?' The man replied, 'Sir, leave it alone again this year, until I dig around it and fertilize it. If it bears fruit next year, great; if not, cut it down.'"

The disciples gathered around Jesus, and Philip asked, "Lord we don't understand the parable. What does the fig tree represent?"

Jesus motioned to the crowd. "The fig tree represents the people of Israel or any person who hears the message about the kingdom of God and doesn't repent. The people who haven't believed in me are being given a little more time. But their time is not unlimited."

Some of the Pharisees were standing outside their little circle waiting for Jesus to return to the crowd. When he did, they asked, "So tell us then when the kingdom of God is coming."

Jesus answered, "The kingdom of God is not coming with visible signs to be seen, so people won't be saying, 'Look, here it is!' or 'There it is!' For the kingdom of God is in your midst."

Then he told his disciples, "The time is coming when you'll long to see one of the days of the Son of Man's return, but you won't see it. People will tell you, 'Look, there he is! ' or 'Look, over here!' Don't go away to follow them. For the second coming of the Son of Man will be just like lightning, which flashes from one end of the sky to the other end of the sky. But first he must suffer many things and be rejected by this generation.

"The second coming of the Son of Man will happen just as in the days of Noah. People were eating and drinking, marrying and being given in marriage right up to the day Noah entered the ark. Then the flood came and destroyed them all.

"The same thing happened in the days of Lot.[37] People were eating and drinking, buying and selling, planting and building. But the day Lot left Sodom, fire and burning sulfur rained down from heaven and destroyed them all. The day the Son of Man is revealed a second time will be just like that.

"On that day, anyone on their housetop who has possessions inside better not waste time going down to get them. Likewise, anyone in the field shouldn't run back home. Remember Lot's wife who turned into a pillar of salt when she looked back at Sodom and Gomorrah![38] Whoever tries to keep their life safe will lose it, and whoever loses their life will preserve it. I'm telling you—on that night two people will be in one bed, and one will be taken and the other left. Two women will be grinding grain together, and one will be taken and the other left. Two men will be in the field; one will be taken and the other left."

The disciples asked, "Where will this be, Lord?"

He replied, "Just look where the vultures are gathering. As a carcass in a field tells you the vultures will be coming, the signs of the times will tell you the end of the age is coming."

Then Jesus told them a parable to show they should pray at all times and not lose heart: "In a certain city there was a judge who neither feared God nor gave respect to anyone. And there was a widow there who kept coming to him, pleading, 'Grant me justice against my opponent.' For a while he refused, but finally he thought, 'Even though I don't fear God or give respect to anyone, I'm going to give this widow justice because she keeps bothering me; otherwise she'll keep coming and wear me out!'"

And the Lord said, "Did you notice what the unjust judge said? Won't God bring about justice for his chosen ones who cry out to him day and night? Will he delay long over their prayers? I'm telling you, he'll bring about justice and quickly. But when the Son of Man comes, will he find faith on the earth?"

Jesus concluded his lesson by directing a final parable to those who trusted in their own righteousness and looked down on everyone else: "Two men, one a Pharisee and the other a tax collector, went up to the temple to pray. The Pharisee stood by himself and prayed this: 'God, I thank you that I'm not like other men—swindlers, evildoers, and adulterers—or even like this tax collector. I fast twice a week and give a tenth of everything I get.' But the tax collector stood at a distance, unwilling even to lift his eyes toward heaven, beating his breast and saying, 'God, be merciful to me, a sinner.'

"I'm telling you that this man, rather than the other, went home justified before God. Those who exalt themselves will be humbled, and those who humble themselves will be exalted."

ɛ⁄ɔ

After that, they moved on to the next town. Not only were people following Jesus as he walked, but more people were waiting at the town entrance. Right then, a man ran up to Jesus, fell on his knees, and asked, "Good Teacher, what must I do to inherit eternal life?"

Jesus answered, "Why do you call me good? No one is good except God alone. You know the commandments:

'Do not commit adultery.
Do not murder.
Do not steal.
Do not give false testimony.
Honor your father and mother.'"

The man replied, "I've kept all of them since I was young."

Jesus felt love for him. "You still lack one thing," he said. "If you want to be perfect, complete in every way, sell everything you have, give it to the poor, and you'll have treasure in heaven. Then come and follow me."

The man's face fell at these words, and he went away grieving because he was extremely wealthy with many possessions.

Sorrowful himself at the man's loss, Jesus looked around and said to his disciples, "How difficult it is for those who have wealth to enter the kingdom of God!" The disciples were amazed at his words, so Jesus told them again, "Children, how hard it is to enter the kingdom of God for those who trust in their wealth. It's easier for a camel to go through the eye of a needle than for a wealthy person to enter the kingdom of God."*

The disciples were even more astounded and asked among themselves, "Then who can be saved?"

Looking at them, Jesus said, "With people alone this is impossible but not with God. All things are possible with God."

Peter said, "Look, we've left everything to follow you. What will there be for us?"

Jesus replied, "I'm telling you the truth: Upon the renewal of all things, when the Son of Man sits on his glorious throne, you who have followed me will also sit on twelve thrones, judging the twelve tribes of Israel. And everyone who has left homes or brothers or sisters or father or mother or wife or children or lands on account of me and the good news of the kingdom of God will receive a hundred times as much in this present age, along with persecutions, and in the age to come, eternal life. But many who are first will be last, and the last will be first."

The disciples were pleased when they heard about the thrones, but they didn't understand his last statement. "Lord, what do you mean about the first being last and the last being first?" Andrew asked.

Jesus explained: "The kingdom of heaven is like this: A landowner went out early in the morning to hire workers for his vineyard. After agreeing with them to pay a denarius a day, he sent them to work. About 9:00 a.m. he went out and saw others standing idle in the marketplace. He told them, 'You also can go and work in my vineyard,

---

* "Eye of a needle": Many explanations have been given for this term, some more believable than others. But you do not have to understand the term to understand the point of what he said: we cannot get ourselves into heaven.

and I'll give you whatever is right.' So they went. He went out and did the same thing again around noon and yet again at 3:00 p.m. About 5:00 p.m. he went out and found others standing around. He asked them, 'Why have you been standing here idle all day long?'

"They replied, 'Because no one has hired us.'

"He told them, 'You can go and work in the vineyard too.'

"When evening came, the owner of the vineyard said to his manager, 'Call the workers and pay them their wages, starting with the last ones hired up to the first.'

"The workers who were hired at about 5:00 p.m. came and each received a denarius. When the first men hired came, they expected to receive more. But each one of them also received a denarius. When they received it, they grumbled against the landowner: 'These last men only worked an hour, yet you've made them equal to us who worked all day in the heat.'

"He answered one of them, 'Friend, I'm doing no wrong to you. Didn't you agree to work for a denarius? Take what you earned and go. I want to give the last man the same amount I gave you. Don't I have the right to do what I want with what's mine? Or are you envious because I'm generous?'"

Jesus concluded, "So, as I said, in the kingdom of God the last will be first, and the first will be last. It makes no difference which you are; all will be treated the same."

❧

Later they got back on the road, and Jesus spoke to the disciples as they walked behind him. "Listen, we're going up to Jerusalem, and the Son of Man will be handed over to the chief priests and scribes. They'll condemn him to death and hand him over to the Gentiles, who will mock him, spit on him, flog him, and then kill him. And after three days, he will rise." They still didn't understand any of these things. The meaning of "he will rise" was hidden from them.

They were debating among themselves when a woman emerged from the crowd behind them and came right up to Jesus. "Mother!" James and John said. "What are you doing here?"

She pulled her sons close beside her and had them kneel with her in front of Jesus. "We'd like to request a favor," she said.

"What is it you want?" Jesus asked.

Their mother replied, "Tell me these two sons of mine will be seated at your right and your left, at the places of highest honor in your kingdom."

Jesus was amazed at her boldness and responded, "You don't know what you're asking!" He turned to James and John and asked, "Can you drink the cup that I drink or be baptized into the baptism of suffering that I'm baptized into?"

"Yes, we can," they answered as one.

So Jesus told them, "You'll surely drink the cup that I drink and be baptized into the baptism that I'm being baptized into. But for you to sit on my right or left is not mine to give. Those places are reserved for those my Father has chosen."

When the other ten disciples heard about this, they were angry at James and John. "You have some nerve!" Judas said. "What gives you the right to exalt yourselves over the rest of us?"

Jesus called them all aside and said, "You know the rulers of the Gentiles lord it over them, and their superiors exercise their power over them. It's not to be this way among you. Instead, whoever wants to be great among you must be your servant, and whoever wants to be first among you must be a servant of everyone else. The Son of Man didn't come to be served but to serve and to give his life as a ransom for many lives."

This was such heavy teaching; the disciples kept quiet for a while after that.

❧

When they reached Jericho, Jesus looked up into a sycamore fig tree and shouted, "Zacchaeus, hurry down from there!"

The apostles couldn't believe it, but there was a man up in a tree! Then Matthew recognized him and said, "He's a wealthy, high-ranking tax collector! What in the world is he doing up there?"

Zacchaeus scrambled down from the tree in such a hurry he almost fell part of the way. He landed right in front of Jesus and had to look up at him because he was short. "Sorry for my less-than-eloquent entrance, Lord," he said. "The crowd was blocking my view."

"I need to stay at your house today," Jesus said.

The disciples and bystanders looked at one another in shock. But no one was more surprised than Zacchaeus himself. "I don't know what to say," he stammered. "Of course, you're welcome . . . but why do you want to stay with me?"

Everyone who saw this began muttering about Jesus: "He's going to be the guest of a sinful man."

But Zacchaeus said to the Lord, "Look, Lord, right now I'm giving half my possessions to the poor, and if I've cheated anyone, I'll pay back four times what I took."

Jesus said to him, "Today salvation has come to this house because this man, too, is a son of Abraham. The Son of Man came to seek and to save the lost."

When they left Jericho, a large crowd followed them. When two blind men who were sitting by the road begging heard that Jesus of Nazareth was going by, they began to cry out, "Lord, Son of David, have mercy on us!"

The crowd told them off and warned them to be quiet, but they cried out even louder, "Lord, Son of David, have mercy on us!"

Jesus stopped and said, "Call them here."

So they called to the blind men, "Have courage! Get up! He's calling for you."

One of them threw off his cloak, jumped up, and came to Jesus. The other man followed behind him.

Jesus said to the first one, "What's your name?"

"I'm Bartimaeus son of Timaeus."

"And what do you want me to do for you today, Bartimaeus son of Timaeus?" Jesus asked.

"Rabbi, I want to see again—we both do."

Moved with compassion, Jesus touched their eyes, and immediately they received their sight. Jesus told them, "Go, your faith has healed you."

Filled with gratitude, they joined the large crowd following Jesus. As they walked, Jesus told the people a parable because he knew as he neared Jerusalem they'd expect the kingdom of God was going to appear immediately when he arrived there. He said, "The kingdom of heaven is like this:

"A nobleman left his homeland and went to a distant country to be crowned king over his land by the emperor. Before he left, he called ten of his servants and gave them each three month's wages, telling them, 'Trade with these until I come back.'

"But his new subjects hated him and sent representatives after him to say, 'We don't want this man to be our king.'

"After being crowned, he returned home and ordered that the servants to whom he had given the money be called to him to find out what they'd earned by trading.

"The first came up and said, 'Master, I've increased the money tenfold.'

"His master responded, 'Well done, good servant. Because you've been trustworthy in a very small matter, you'll have authority over ten cities.'

"The second came and said, 'Master, I've increased the money fivefold.'

"His master answered, 'You'll have authority over five cities.'

"Then another servant came and said, 'Master, look, here's your money. I stored it in a piece of cloth. I was afraid of you because you're a stern man, taking profits from what you didn't invest in and reaping where you didn't sow.'

"His master replied, 'I'll judge you by your own words, you wicked servant! Do you really know that I'm a stern man—taking out of what I didn't put into and reaping what I didn't sow? Why then didn't you put my money on deposit, so when I returned, I could have collected it with interest?' Then he ordered his attendants, 'Take the money from him and give it to the one who made the tenfold profit.'

"They protested, 'Master, he already has three year's wages!'

"The king replied, 'I'm telling you, everyone who has will be given more, but as for the one who doesn't have much, even what he has will be taken away. But as for these enemies of mine, those who don't want me to reign over them, bring them here and execute them in front of me.'"

თ

Some time later, the disciples found a favorable campsite along the Jericho-Bethany Road. The crowd dispersed in different directions, some to find lodging or food and others to camp with their own supplies. They would be back the next day—that was certain.

Jesus went to a remote area within a nearby forest to pray. He would need his Father's strength for the journey ahead.

As he was making his way back to camp, Peter was running to meet him. "Lord, we just got an urgent message from Martha and Mary! Lazarus is sick with a serious illness! Their message said, 'Lord, help! He whom you love is sick.'"

The disciples were surprised when Jesus didn't seem that concerned, especially considering how close he and Lazarus were. Then he replied, "This sickness won't end in death but is for the glory of God so that God's Son may be glorified by it."

Now Jesus loved Martha and her sister and Lazarus. But despite having heard that Lazarus was sick, he stayed where he was two more days. Then he said to his disciples, "Let's go back to Judea."

But they objected, "Rabbi, a little while ago the Jews there tried to stone you to death—and you're going back there?"

Jesus answered, "Aren't there twelve hours of daylight in the day? Those who walk in the daytime don't stumble. They see by this world's light. But anyone who walks at night stumbles because the light is not in them." After he said these things, he said, "Our friend Lazarus has fallen asleep, but I'm going to wake him up."

The disciples replied, "Lord, if he's sleeping, he'll get better."

Now Jesus had been speaking of Lazarus' death, but his disciples thought he meant literal sleep. So then he told them plainly, "Lazarus has died. For your sake, I'm glad I wasn't there so that you may believe. But let's go to him."

Then Thomas (also called the Twin) said to his fellow disciples, "Let's go too—and die with him."

They set out for Bethany with the crowd following them.

When they arrived there, Jesus found that Lazarus had already been in the tomb for four days. Many Jews had come to comfort Martha and Mary concerning their brother's death. When Martha heard that Jesus was coming, she met him, but Mary remained sitting at home. Martha told him between sobs, "Lord, if you'd been here, my brother wouldn't have died. But even now I know that whatever you ask of God, God will give you."

Jesus replied, "Your brother will rise again."

Martha answered, "I know he'll rise again in the resurrection on the last day."

Jesus said to her, "I am the resurrection and the life. Anyone who believes in me will live eternally, even though they die physically. And whoever lives and believes in me will never die. Do you believe this?"

Martha wiped the tears from her eyes. "Yes, Lord. I believe you're the Messiah, the Son of God, who comes into the world."

After saying this, she went and called her sister, Mary, and secretly told her, "The Teacher's here asking for you." When she heard this, Mary got up quickly and went to him.

Now Jesus hadn't yet entered the village but was still in the place where Martha had met him. When the Jews who were consoling her in the house saw Mary get up quickly and leave, they followed her, thinking she was going to the tomb to mourn there. When Mary saw Jesus, she fell at his feet and said the same thing her sister did: "Lord, if you'd been here, my brother wouldn't have died."

When Jesus saw her weeping, and the Jews who had come with her also weeping, he was troubled and deeply moved in spirit. He asked, "Where have you laid him?"

"Lord, come and see," they replied.

Jesus wept.

The Jews were saying, "Look how much he loved him."

But some of them said, "Couldn't this man, who opened the eyes of the blind man, have kept this man from dying?"

Jesus, deeply moved within himself again, came to the tomb, a cave with a stone across it. He said, "Take away the stone."

But Martha objected: "Lord, by now it stinks. It's been four days!"

Then Jesus said, "Didn't I tell you that if you believe, you'll see the glory of God?" So they removed the stone. Then Jesus lifted his eyes and said, "Father, I thank you that you've heard me. I know that you always hear me, but I said this because of the crowd standing here, that they may believe you sent me."

When he had said this, Jesus shouted, "Lazarus, come out!"

The sisters, the disciples, and all the mourners became silent and peered into the open tomb. Not even a minute passed, but it seemed like an eternity while they waited. Still nothing. Then suddenly— movement! To everyone's shock, Lazarus, who had been dead for four days, came out, bound hand and foot with strips of linen. A cloth was wrapped around his face. Awestruck, the spectators gasped.

Jesus told them, "Unbind him and let him go."

"My Lord!" Lazarus exclaimed, shielding his eyes from the bright sun. Lazarus wiped a tear from his eye and embraced Jesus. "Until we meet again," Jesus said then let him go.

Many of the Jews who had come to console Mary, having seen what Jesus had done, believed in him. But some of them went to the Pharisees to tell them what happened. As a result, the chief priests and the Pharisees convened a Sanhedrin council meeting. "What are we doing," they asked, "since this man is performing many miracles? If we let him continue, everyone will believe in him, then the Romans will come and take away our place and our nation."

Then one of them, Caiaphas, that year's high priest, spoke up: "Don't you know anything! Don't you realize it's better for us that one man dies for the people than that the whole nation perishes at the hands of Caesar?" He didn't say this on his own, but being the high priest, he prophesied Jesus would die for the nation, and not only for the nation but also to gather into one the children of God who had been scattered abroad.

From that day on they plotted to kill him, so Jesus stopped walking openly among the Jews. Instead, he withdrew to a region near the wilderness, to a village called Ephraim, where he stayed with his disciples until it was time to enter Jerusalem.

⁊

Since it was near the time for the Jewish Passover, many people from the countryside headed to Jerusalem to purify themselves. They were looking for Jesus, and as they stood in the temple courts, they asked one another, "What do you think—will he come to the festival?" For the chief priests and the Pharisees had given orders that anyone who knew where Jesus was should report it, so he could be arrested. Unknown to them, Jesus was on his way.

Meanwhile, Jesus ministered in the villages around Jerusalem. He often taught in the synagogues. One traveler saw him and asked, "Lord, will only a few be saved?"

He replied, "Strive to enter through the narrow door. I'm telling you, many people will try to enter and won't be able to. Once the head of the house gets up and closes the door, you'll be left standing outside, knocking at the door and pleading, 'Lord, open up the door to us.' But he'll answer, 'No,' and tell you, 'I don't know where you come from.' Then you'll begin to say, 'We ate and drank with you, and you taught in our streets.'

"But he'll reply, 'I'm telling you, I don't know you or where you come from. Get away from me, all you evildoers!' There will be weeping and great pain when you see Abraham, Isaac, Jacob, and all the prophets in the kingdom of God while you're being thrown out. People will come from all over the world and eat in the kingdom of God. Mark this: Some who are last will be first, and some who are first will be last."

Just then some Pharisees approached Jesus and warned him, "Get away from here because Herod wants to kill you."

But he replied, "Go tell that fox I'll continue casting out demons and performing healings today and tomorrow, and on the third day I'll have accomplished my goal. I must keep traveling today, tomorrow, and the next day, for it's unthinkable that a prophet should perish outside Jerusalem!

"O Jerusalem, Jerusalem, you who kill the prophets and stone those sent to you. How often I've longed to gather your children together as a hen gathers her chicks under her wings, but you weren't willing. I'm telling you, you'll never see me again until the time when you say, 'Blessed is he who comes in the name of the Lord.'"

☙

One Sabbath day, Jesus was outside a village synagogue waiting to go in when he noticed people helping a woman enter the building. She was completely bent over and couldn't straighten up at all. He perceived it was an evil spirit causing the condition and was filled with sorrow for all she'd suffered. As she passed him slowly, she looked up at him with pleading in her eyes.

When Jesus sat down to teach, he looked over at the woman then noticed the synagogue leader watching him intently, as if trying to catch him in something. He called the woman forward and said to her, "You are set free from your ailment." Then he laid his hands on her, and immediately she stood straight and praised God.

The synagogue leader, indignant that Jesus had healed on the Sabbath, responded by telling the crowd, "There are six days for work, so come to be healed on them, not on the Sabbath!"

Jesus answered back, "You hypocrites! Wouldn't any one of you untie your ox or donkey from the stall and lead it to water on the

Sabbath? Then shouldn't this woman, a daughter of Abraham kept in bondage by Satan for eighteen years, be set free on the Sabbath day?"

When he said this, all his opponents were humiliated, but the whole crowd was rejoicing over all the glorious things he was doing.

On another Sabbath, Jesus went for a meal at the house of a leading Pharisee, and the guests were watching him carefully. There was a man with edema seated right in front of him. Jesus, answering their stares, asked the experts in the law and Pharisees, "Is it lawful to heal on the Sabbath or not?" But they didn't answer. So he took hold of the man, healed him, and sent him away. Then he asked them, "If one of you has a son or an ox fall into a well on the Sabbath day, wouldn't you immediately pull him out?" And they couldn't figure out what to say.

Then Jesus noticed how some guests chose to sit in the places of honor at the table, so he pointed out their mistake: "When someone invites you to a wedding feast, don't take the place of highest honor, for someone more distinguished than you may have been invited. If so, the one who invited both of you will come and tell you, 'Give this person your place.' Then, embarrassed, you'll begin to move to the place of lowest honor. But when you're invited, go and sit at the lowest place, so when your host comes, they'll tell you, 'Friend, come up higher,' and you'll be honored in the presence of all those eating with you. Everyone who exalts themselves will be humbled, and whoever humbles themselves will be exalted."

Then Jesus said to his host, "Whenever you give a luncheon or dinner, don't invite your friends or your siblings or relatives or your rich neighbors; otherwise they may invite you in return and that becomes your repayment. But whenever you give a banquet, invite the poor, the crippled, the lame, and the blind, and you'll be blessed. Because they have nothing to repay you, you'll be repaid at the resurrection of the just."

When one of those eating with him heard this, he said to him, "Blessed is the person who will dine in the kingdom of God."

Jesus responded with another parable:

"A man was preparing to give a banquet and invited many guests. At the time of the dinner, he sent his servant to tell those who had been invited, 'Come, everything is ready now.' But they all began to make excuses.

The first said, 'Please excuse me because I've just bought a field, and I must go and see it.'

Another said, 'Please excuse me because I've just bought five pairs of oxen, and I'm going to try them out.'

And another said, 'I can't come because I just got married.'

The servant returned and reported this to his master. Then the owner of the house became angry and ordered his servant, 'Go quickly into the streets and alleys of the town and bring in the poor, the crippled, the blind, and the lame.'

Later the servant reported: 'Sir, what you ordered has been done, and there's still room.'

So the master told him, 'Go out to the main routes and the side roads and compel them to come in so my house will be full. I'm telling you, not one of those who were invited will get a taste of my dinner.'"

After dinner, large crowds surrounded Jesus. Turning to them he said, "It's the same for all believers, just as I have told the disciples: If you come to me and do not hate your father and mother, your spouse and children, brothers and sisters, yes, even your own life, you cannot be my disciple."*

Jesus continued, "And if you do not carry your own cross and follow me, you cannot be my disciple. Take up your cross."**

"Which of you, if you want to construct a tower, won't first sit down and estimate the cost, whether you have enough money to

---

* Because Scripture teaches we are to honor our parents and love our siblings, spouses, children, neighbors, and so on, here Jesus' use of the term *hate* is understood in the greater sense of hating whatever demands, counsel, opposition, and so forth, of others stand between our being obedient to Christ and having their love and cooperation.

** Your cross is whatever task God gives you no matter how uncomfortable or humiliating.

complete it? Otherwise you may lay its foundation and not be able to finish it. Everyone who sees it will ridicule you, saying, 'This person began to build and was not able to finish.'

"Or what king, when he sets out to battle another king, won't first sit down and consider whether he's able with ten thousand men to oppose the one coming against him with twenty thousand? If he's not able, he'll send a delegation while the other is still a long way off and ask for terms of peace." In this way, he warned people to make peace with God.

"So then, every one of you who doesn't give up all they possess is not able to be my disciple. Whoever has ears to hear should listen."

Now all the tax collectors and other sinners were coming close to hear him. But both the Pharisees and scribes were muttering, "This man welcomes sinners and eats with them."

Jesus answered with a parable: "What one among you, if he had a hundred sheep and lost one of them, wouldn't leave the ninety-nine in the open country and go after the lost one until he found it? And when he found it, wouldn't he joyfully put it on his shoulders, go home, and call together his friends and neighbors and tell them, 'Celebrate with me. I've found my lost sheep'? I'm telling you, in the same way, there will be more joy in heaven over one sinner who repents than over ninety-nine righteous people who don't need to repent.

"Or think of it this way: What woman who has ten silver coins and loses one, a day's wages, wouldn't light a lamp, sweep the house, and search carefully until she finds it? And when she finds it, won't she call together her friends and neighbors and tell them, 'Celebrate with me. I've found the silver coin I lost'? I'm telling you, in the same way, there is joy in the presence of the angels of God over one sinner who repents."

Jesus continued with another example:

"A man had two sons. The younger of them said to his father, 'Father, give me the share of the estate that's mine.' So the father divided the property between them. After a few days, the younger son gathered all he had and went off to a distant country. There he squandered his wealth in wasteful living.

After he'd spent everything, there was a severe famine throughout that country, and he began to be in need. So he went to work for a citizen of the country, who sent him into his fields to feed pigs. He became so hungry that he longed to fill his stomach with the carob pods the pigs were eating, but no one gave him anything.

When he came to his senses, he thought, 'How many of my father's hired men have an abundance of food! But I'm here dying of hunger! I'm going to return to my father and tell him, "Father, I've sinned against heaven and against you. I'm no longer worthy to be called your son. Treat me like one of your hired men."' And he got up and went to his father.

But while he was still a long way off, his father saw him and was filled with compassion for him. He ran to him, threw his arms around his neck, and kissed him. His son said to him, 'Father, I've sinned against heaven and in your sight. I'm no longer worthy to be called your son.'

But the father told his servants, 'Quick! Bring out the best robe and put it on him. Put a ring on his finger and sandals on his feet. Bring the fattened calf and kill it. Let's have a feast and celebrate, for this son of mine was dead and is alive again, was lost and is found.' So they began to celebrate.

Meanwhile, the older son was working in the field. When he came up to the house, he heard music and dancing. So he called one of the servants and asked him, 'What's going on?'

He replied, 'Your brother has returned, and your father has killed the fattened calf because he has gotten him back safe and sound.'

But the older brother became angry and wouldn't go in. So his father went out and pleaded with him. And he answered his father, 'Look, for years I've served you and never disobeyed your orders, yet you've never given me even a young goat for a feast with my friends. But when this son of yours, who has eaten through your wealth with prostitutes, comes home, you kill the fattened calf for him!'

And the father told him, 'Son, you're always with me, and all that I have is yours, but we had to celebrate and rejoice because this brother of yours was dead and is alive again, was lost and has been found.'"

Jesus then told his disciples this parable:

"A rich man had a manager who was accused of wasting his possessions. So he called him in and asked him, 'What's this I hear about you? Give a financial accounting of your stewardship because you can no longer be my manager.' The manager thought, 'What will I do? My master is terminating me! I'm not strong enough to dig, and I'm ashamed to beg.' Then he thought, 'I know what I'll do so that when I'm removed from management here, people will welcome me into their homes.' So he summoned each of his master's debtors. He asked the first, 'How much do you owe my master?' 'Six hundred gallons of olive oil,' he replied. The manager said, 'Take your bill, sit down quickly, and make it 300.' Then he asked another, 'And how much do you owe?' And he replied, 'Six hundred bushels of wheat.' The manager told him, 'Take your bill and make it 480.'"

"Now we're talking!" Judas said. "That manager was a shrewd businessman."

Jesus answered, "You're right. The people of this world are more shrewd in dealing with their own kind than the people of the light. The master commended the dishonest manager because he'd acted wisely. I'm telling you, use the wealth of this world to make friends for yourselves so that when it's all gone you'll be welcomed into eternal homes. Whoever's trustworthy in the smallest matter is also trustworthy in large matters, and whoever's dishonest with a little thing is also dishonest with large things."

Judas shrunk back after this statement, then James spoke up. "Master, why are you praising this dishonest man? Isn't it wrong to do what he did?"

Jesus explained, "Yes, of course it's wrong, but you're missing the point. The manager was doing what people of the world do—lay up treasures for themselves to protect their future, a future that will end when they die. I'm saying that those who follow me should use their treasure for eternal purposes, not temporal comfort. They should think about their future in eternity and lay up eternal treasures for themselves, not strive for treasures in this world but in the next."

"I think I get it," James answered. "After all, we can't take it with us!"

By now a group of Pharisees had joined them, so Jesus went on teaching: "Now let me ask you: If you haven't been trustworthy in handling worldly wealth, who will trust you with true riches? And if you haven't been trustworthy with another person's property, who will give you your own? No servant can serve two masters, for either they'll hate the one and love the other, or they'll be devoted to the one and despise the other. You can't serve both God and wealth."

The Pharisees, who loved wealth, heard all this and ridiculed him, saying, "You're wrong about this. God blesses us with wealth just like he did the patriarchs because we act righteously."

Jesus responded, "You're the ones who justify yourselves before people, but God knows your hearts. What's highly prized among people is a foul thing in God's sight. The Law and the Prophets were proclaimed until John came. Since then, the good news of the kingdom of God is being proclaimed, and everyone is trying to force their way into it. It's easier for heaven and earth to go out of existence than for the smallest mark to drop out of the law. For example, it's still true that anyone who divorces his wife and marries another commits adultery, and he who marries a divorced woman commits adultery."

Some of the Pharisees walked away in disgust.

Jesus turned to his disciples and said, "Listen to this story to further illustrate the importance of laying up eternal treasures instead of worldly ones:

"There was a rich man who dressed in purple and fine linen and feasted sumptuously every day. A beggar named Lazarus laid at his gate, covered with sores, longing to eat whatever fell from the rich man's table. But the only care he got was from dogs, who came and licked his sores.

"Now the beggar died and was carried by the angels to Abraham's side. The rich man also died and was buried. In torment in hell, he looked up, and far away he saw Abraham with Lazarus in his arms. So he called out to him, 'Father Abraham, have mercy on me. Send Lazarus to dip the tip of his finger in water and cool my tongue because I'm in agony in this fire.'

"But Abraham replied, 'Son, remember that in your lifetime you received good things while Lazarus received bad things. Now he's being comforted here, and you're in agony. And besides all this, there's a great chasm fixed between us and you so that those who want to go from here over to you can't, and no one can cross over from there to here.'

"The rich man answered, 'Then I beg you, father Abraham, send Lazarus to my father's house. I have five brothers, and I want him to warn them so that they don't also come to this place of torment.'

"Abraham replied, 'They have the writings of Moses and the Prophets. They can listen to them.'

"'No, father Abraham,' he pleaded, 'if someone from the dead goes to them, they'll repent.'

"And Abraham told him, 'If they don't listen to Moses and the Prophets, they won't be convinced even if someone rises from the dead.'"

The apostles were clearly disturbed by the story and were talking among themselves.

Jesus turned to them and said, "Stumbling blocks are inevitable, but woe to whoever brings them. It would be better for those people to have a millstone hung around their neck and be thrown into the sea than that they should cause one of little means to sin." So watch yourselves, and if your fellow believers sin, rebuke them. If they repent, forgive them. If they sin against you seven times in a day and come back to you seven times saying, 'I repent,' forgive them."

The apostles said to the Lord, "Give us more faith!"

Jesus pointed to a tree and said, "If you had faith as small as a mustard seed, you'd say to this mulberry tree, 'Be uprooted and planted in the sea,' and it would obey you. Which of you, if you had a servant plowing or tending sheep, would tell him when he comes in from the field, 'Come now and eat'? Wouldn't you instead tell him, 'Make my supper. Get yourself ready and serve me while I eat and drink, then you may eat and drink'? Would you thank the servant for doing what was ordered? So it should be with you too. When you have only done everything you were ordered to do, you should say, 'We are unworthy servants. We have only done what we ought to have done.'"

Chapter 13

A Few Good Days

The next day, six days before Passover, Jesus returned to Bethany, the hometown of Lazarus, whom Jesus had raised from the dead. Simon the leper was giving a dinner in Jesus' honor. Martha was serving, and Lazarus was among those invited. While Jesus was eating, Lazarus' other sister, Mary, came to him with an alabaster jar containing almost a pint of expensive perfume made from oil of spikenard. In tribute to Jesus, she snapped the neck of the jar. Then she poured the perfume on his head and feet and wiped his feet with her hair. And the house filled with the perfume's fragrance.

Judas objected. "Why wasn't this perfume sold for a year's wages and the money given to the poor?"

Jesus knew he wasn't saying this because he cared about the poor but because he was a thief. He had been appointed keeper of the money box, and he was stealing from it.

When the other disciples saw what Mary had done, they were indignant too. They asked one another, "Why did she waste this perfume? It could have been sold for a high price, and the money could have been given to the poor."

When they scolded her harshly, Jesus interrupted, "Leave her alone! Why are you bothering her? She's done a beautiful thing to me. You will always have the poor with you, and you can do good for them whenever you want. But you won't always have me. She's done what she could—anointed my body in advance to prepare it for burial. I'm telling you the truth, wherever the good news is preached in the whole world, what she's done will also be told in memory of her."

Meanwhile a large crowd of Jews learned Jesus was in town. They came not only because of him but also to see Lazarus, whom he'd raised from the dead. So the chief priests planned to kill Lazarus, too, because on account of him many Jews were leaving them and believing in Jesus.

ℂℂ

The next day after they'd left Bethany and approached Bethphage near the Mount of Olives, Jesus told two of his disciples, "Go to the next village. As you enter it, you'll find a donkey's colt tied there, which no one has ever ridden. Untie it and bring it here. If anyone asks you, 'Why are you untying it?' tell them, 'Because the Lord needs it, and he'll send it back soon.'"

They went to the village and found a colt outside in the street, tied up at a doorway, just as he'd told them. As they were untying the colt, some bystanders asked them, "Why are you untying the colt?"

They replied, "The Lord needs it." And they let them go.

They brought it to Jesus, threw their cloaks on it, and put Jesus on it. A large crowd had come for the Passover Festival and heard that Jesus was entering Jerusalem. Romans presented palm branches to champions, and only royalty walked on cloth. So to show that Jesus was their champion and king, they spread their cloaks on the road ahead of him. Others cut branches from palm trees in the fields, went out to meet him, and spread them on the road. When he was approaching Jerusalem, the whole crowd of disciples began to joyfully praise God in loud voices for all the miracles they'd seen. Everyone in front and behind him cried out:

"Hosanna to the Son of David!"

"Blessed is he who comes in the name of the Lord!"[39]

"Peace in heaven and glory in the highest heaven!"

"Blessed is the coming kingdom of our father David!"

"Blessed is the king of Israel!"

"Hosanna in the highest heaven!"

Some of the Pharisees in the crowd called to Jesus, "Teacher, rebuke your disciples!"

He called back, "I'm telling you, if they keep quiet, the stones will cry out!"

This took place to fulfill what Zechariah prophesied more than five hundred years ago: "Do not be afraid, Daughter of Zion.* Look, your king is coming, gentle and mounted on a donkey's colt."[40]

At first his disciples didn't understand these unusual events. But when Jesus was glorified, they realized these things had been written about him and why they had happened.

Now the crowd, who had been with him when he called Lazarus out of the tomb and raised him from the dead, continued to testify about it. So the Pharisees said to one another, "We're accomplishing nothing. Look how the world has gone after him!" For the whole city was stirred, asking "Who is this?" The crowds were responding, "This is the prophet Jesus, from Nazareth in Galilee."

When Jesus entered Jerusalem, he went directly to the temple courtyard. But because it was already late, he only gave it a quick glance then went back to Bethany with the twelve apostles to stay the night with their friends Mary, Martha, and Lazarus. Jesus savored this time with his friends more than ever, knowing his time was short.

⌘

The next morning, they got back on the road to Jerusalem before sunrise. Because they hadn't had time to eat, Jesus was hungry. Seeing a fig tree in full leaf in the distance, he went to see if he'd find any fruit on it. When he reached it, he found nothing but leaves because it wasn't the season for figs. In response he said to it, "May no one ever eat fruit from you again!" And his disciples heard him say it.

When Jesus saw Jerusalem from a distance, he was overwhelmed by intense emotion and couldn't stop himself from crying. All choked up, he said, "If you, even you, had known today what actually brings you peace—but now it's hidden from your eyes. The days will come

---

* "Daughter of Zion": an idiomatic expression referring to either the people of Jerusalem or of all Israel.

upon you when your enemies throw up an embankment against you, surround you, and hem you in on every side. They'll dash you to the ground, you, and your children within your walls. They won't even leave one stone upon another because you didn't recognize the time when God visited you."

When they arrived in Jerusalem, Jesus entered the temple courts and saw the same vendors he'd driven out before, buying and selling there again. Outraged, he overturned the tables of the money changers and the seats of those selling doves. And he stopped people from carrying merchandise through the temple courts to sell at exorbitant prices. Then he said, "Isn't it written: 'My house will be called a house of prayer for all nations'? But you've made it a den of thieves!"[41]

He continued teaching daily in the temple courts. The chief priests, scribes, and other leaders were trying to destroy him, but they couldn't find any way to do it because everyone was listening to him eagerly. Blind and lame people came to him in the temple, and he healed them. When the chief priests and the scribes saw the wonderful things he did and heard the children shouting, "Hosanna, Son of David," they were indignant.

So they asked Jesus, "Do you hear what they're saying?"

"Yes," Jesus replied. "Haven't you read David's prophecy: 'Out of the mouths of children and nursing infants you have ordained praise'?"[42] And when evening came, he and his disciples left them and went back to Bethany for the night.

☙

On their return to Jerusalem the next morning, they passed the fig tree on which Jesus hadn't found any fruit. The disciples were amazed to see it had withered from the roots up. Peter remembered and said, "Rabbi, look! The fig tree you cursed has completely withered! How did it dry up so quickly?"

Jesus replied, "I'm telling you the truth: If you have faith and do not doubt, not only will you do what was done to the fig tree, but if you say to this mountain, 'Be lifted up and thrown into the sea,' it will happen.* Whatever you ask for in prayer believe that you've received it, and it will be yours. And whenever you stand praying, if you have anything against anyone, forgive that person, so your Father in heaven may forgive your sins. But if you don't forgive, neither will your Father in heaven forgive your sins."

☙

When Jesus arrived at the temple, as he did every day, he went to one of the courts to teach. There was already a crowd there as they came early every morning to hear him. So he decided it would be better to camp close by, on the Mount of Olives each night, rather than make the two-mile trip between Bethany and Jerusalem twice a day.

As he began to teach and proclaim the good news about the kingdom of God, the chief priests, scribes, and some elders, came up to him and asked, "Tell us by what authority you're doing these things and who gave you this authority."

He replied, "I'll also ask you a question. Did the baptism of John originate from heaven or was it from people?"

Jesus heard them discussing it among themselves: "If we say, 'From heaven,' he'll ask, 'Then why didn't you believe him?' But if we say, 'Of human origin,' all the people will stone us because they're convinced that John was a prophet." So they answered, "We don't know."

So Jesus said to them, "Then I won't tell you by what authority I'm doing these things. Instead, I will tell you a story:

"A man had two sons. He went to the first and said, 'Son, go work in the vineyard today.'

"He answered, 'I won't,' but later changed his mind and went.

---

* Like today, "mountain" was a metaphor for a huge problem. The top Jewish leaders (those with spiritual insight or records of great accomplishment) were referred to as "rooters of mountains" (able to root out great problems, as a rotary rooter works through a clogged drain). So Jesus was saying that if a person has great faith, God will help them work through even the most mountainous problem.

"Then the man went to his other son and said the same thing.

He answered, 'I will, sir,' but he didn't go."

Then Jesus asked, "Which of the two did the will of his father?"

They answered, "The first."

Jesus responded, "I'm telling you the truth: The tax collectors and prostitutes will get into the kingdom of God before you. John came to show you the way of righteousness, and you didn't believe him, but the tax collectors and the prostitutes did. And you, even after seeing this, didn't repent and believe him.

"Let me give you another example:

There was a landowner who planted a vineyard. He put a wall around it, cut out a shallow pit in which to press the grapes to make wine, and built a watchtower. Then he leased it to tenant farmers and went abroad for a long time. When harvest time approached, he sent a servant to the tenants, so they would give him his share of the grapes and wine. But the tenants beat him and sent him away empty-handed. So he sent another servant, and they beat him, treated him shamefully, and sent him away empty-handed. He sent a third, and they wounded him and threw him out. Then the owner of the vineyard said, 'What should I do? I'll send my son, whom I love. Perhaps they'll respect him.' But when the tenants saw him, they said to each other, 'This is the heir. Let's kill him, and the inheritance will be ours.' So they threw him out of the vineyard and killed him!"

Jesus turned to the crowd. "Now, when the owner of the vineyard comes, what do you think he'll do to those tenants?"

The religious leaders replied, "He'll bring those wretches to a miserable end, and he'll lease the vineyard to other vine growers who will give him his share of the fruit at the proper time."

And the people heard this and reacted: "May such a thing never happen!"

Jesus looked straight at them and said, "Then what's the meaning of this Scripture: 'The stone the builders rejected has become the cornerstone. The Lord did this, and it's marvelous in our eyes'?[43]

Everyone looked at each other and couldn't hazard a guess.

Jesus continued: "I'm telling you, everyone who falls on that stone will be broken to pieces, but whoever it falls on will be crushed. The kingdom of God will be taken away from you and given to a people who will produce its fruit."

When the chief priests, scribes and elders, and other Pharisees heard Jesus' parables, they realized he was talking about them. They looked for a way to arrest him, but they were afraid of the crowd because the people regarded him as a prophet. Then they left him and went away, but they continued observing him.

ᏉᏗ

Later that day Jesus spoke again to the chief priests and some members of the Sanhedrin: "The kingdom of heaven is like this:

> A king prepared a wedding feast for his son. He sent his servants to those who had been invited to tell them it was time to come, but they wouldn't come. Then he sent some more servants and said, 'Tell those who have been invited that I've prepared my dinner—my oxen and prime cattle have been butchered. Everything is ready. Come to the wedding dinner.'
>
> Some who were invited paid no attention and went off: one to their farm, another to their business. The rest seized his servants, mistreated them, and killed them. The king was so enraged he sent his army and killed those murderers and burned their city.
>
> Then he told his servants, 'The wedding feast is ready, but those I invited weren't worthy. So go into the streets and invite everyone you find.' So the servants went out and gathered everyone they found, both good and bad, and the wedding was filled with guests. But when the king came in

to see the guests, he saw one man who wasn't wearing wedding clothes and asked him, 'Friend, how did you get in here without wedding clothes? The man had nothing to say.

Then the king ordered the attendants, 'Tie him hand and foot, and throw him outside into the outer darkness where there will be weeping and gnashing of teeth.' For many are invited, but few are chosen."

Taking this story as an insult rather than a warning about their behavior, the Pharisees were outraged. They stormed out and plotted to trap Jesus in his words. The scribes and chief priests had some of their own disciples and some Herodians spy on Jesus. They pretended to be righteous, hoping to catch Jesus in something he said so they could hand him over to the governor.

The spies queried him, "Teacher, we know you teach correctly and are truthful—that you're not influenced by men or partial to any person or group. You teach the true way of God. Tell us then—is it right to pay the poll tax to Caesar or not? Should we pay, or shouldn't we?"

But Jesus, perceiving their craftiness and knowing their evil intentions, answered, "You hypocrites! Why are you trying to trap me? Show me the coin used to pay the tax. Bring me a denarius to look at."

They brought him the coin, and he asked them, "Whose portrait is this and whose inscription?"

"Caesar's," they replied.

Then he told them, "Give to Caesar that which is Caesar's and to God that which is God's." When they heard this, they were so amazed at his answer, they were speechless and went away shaking their heads. They were simply unable to trap him in an incriminating statement.

ᑎ

That same day the Sadducees, who don't believe in the resurrection of the dead, came to Jesus with this question: "Teacher, Moses told us if a married man dies childless, his brother as next of kin must marry the widow and have children for his brother.[44] Now there were seven

178

brothers. The first one married and died. Having no children, he left his wife to his brother. The second one married her but also died leaving no child. It was the same with the third through the seventh. Finally, the woman died too. Since all seven had married her, whose wife will she be at the resurrection?"

Jesus replied, "Isn't this why you're led astray—because you know neither the Scriptures nor the power of God? Those considered worthy of sharing in the resurrection from the dead, when they rise, will neither marry nor be given in marriage. For they can no longer die because they're like angels and are God's children, being children of the resurrection. Haven't you read in the writings of Moses in the account about the burning bush what was spoken to you by God? Even Moses showed that the dead are raised when he recorded that the Lord said to him, 'I am the God of Abraham, the God of Isaac, and the God of Jacob,' so he's not the God of the dead but of the living.[45] To him all are living. You're misguided, thinking the dead don't rise! Abraham, Isaac, and Jacob are alive in heaven."

Some of the scribes, who did believe in the resurrection, responded, "Well said, Teacher!"

When the crowds heard all this, they were amazed at his teaching too.

Hearing that Jesus had silenced the Sadducees, the Pharisees came together. One of the scribes, who was an expert in the law, heard them debating and noticed that Jesus had answered them well. So he tested him: "Teacher, which is the greatest, the most important commandment in the law?"

Jesus replied, "The most important one is this: 'Hear, O Israel, the Lord our God, the Lord is one. You shall love the Lord your God with all your heart and with all your soul and with all your mind and with all your strength.'[46] This is the first and greatest commandment. And the second is like it: 'Love your neighbor as yourself.'[47] There are no other commandments greater than these. All the Law and the Prophets hang on these two commandments."

The man replied, "Well said, Teacher! You've spoken the truth that God is one, and there's no one else but him. Loving him with all your heart, understanding, and strength and your neighbor as yourself are more important than all the burnt offerings and sacrifices."

When Jesus saw the man had answered wisely, he told him, "You are not far from the kingdom of God." Jesus then turned to some Pharisees who had gathered there and asked them, "What do you think about the Messiah? Whose son is he?"

They replied, "The son of David."

So Jesus asked, "Why do the scribes say the Messiah is the descendant of David? How is it then that David himself, led by the Holy Spirit, calls the Messiah 'Lord' in the psalms? It says, 'The Lord said to the Messiah, "Sit at my right hand until I make your enemies a footstool for your feet."'[48] If David calls him 'Lord,' in what way can he be his son?"*

No one could answer him, and from that day on, none of them dared ask him a question. And the large crowd of spectators enjoyed listening to him.

Then Jesus told the crowds and his disciples: "The scribes and the Pharisees sit in Moses' seat, teaching and interpreting his laws. But don't do what they do, for they speak and don't do. They tie up heavy loads and lay them on men's shoulders, but they themselves are unwilling to lift a finger to move them. Everything they do is a show for the public. Watch out for those scribes who

widen their phylacteries,**

love to walk around in the long, flowing robes of scholars,

lengthen the tassels on their garments,***

love the places of honor at banquets,

love the first seats in the synagogues,

devour widows' property,

love being greeted with honor in the marketplaces,

---

* Jesus, a descendant of David, was pointing out that though he had an earthly genealogy, he was God himself and should be honored as such.

** "Phylactery": a small leather box containing verses of Scripture that was worn on the head or arm.

*** "Tassels": probably referring to what many Jews consider the holiest part of a cloak, the tassels that were hung at the bottom to remind people of God's commands (see Numbers 15:37–41).

pray long prayers just for a show, and
love to have people call them 'Rabbi.'

Such people will be judged as more guilty than others and will receive greater condemnation. You scribes should not be called 'Rabbi, for it means "master." You have only one master, God, and both clergy and laypeople are all equal brothers. And don't call anyone on earth 'father.' You have one Father, who is in heaven. And you shouldn't be called 'teacher.' You have one teacher, the Messiah. The greatest among you will be your servant. Whoever exalts himself will be humbled, and whoever humbles himself will be exalted."

ↄ⳩

The next morning, Thursday, just a day before his crucifixion, Jesus continued to teach at the temple, pouring out warnings about false religion.

"Woe to you, scribes and Pharisees, you hypocrites!
You've taken away the key to knowledge. You lock
people out of the kingdom of heaven. You yourselves
don't go in, and when others are going in, you stop
them.
"Woe to you, scribes and Pharisees, you hypocrites!
You devour widows' houses and pray long prayers just
for a public show. Therefore you will receive greater
punishment.
"Woe to you, scribes and Pharisees, you hypocrites!
You travel across land and sea to win a single convert,
and when he becomes one, you make him twice as much
a son of hell as yourselves.
"Woe to you, you blind guides!
You say, 'When someone swears by the temple, it's
meaningless, but if anyone swears by the gold of the
temple, they're obligated.' You blind fools! Which is
greater: the gold or the temple that makes the gold
sacred? You say, 'If someone swears by the bronze altar

in the temple courtyard, it's meaningless, but if anyone swears by the offering on it, they're obligated.' You blind men! Which is greater: the offering or the altar that makes the offering sacred?

"Understand this: Anyone who swears by the altar swears by it and by everything sacrificed on it. And anyone who swears by the temple swears by both it and by God, the one who dwells in it. And anyone who swears by heaven swears both by God's throne and by him who sits on it.

"Woe to you, scribes and Pharisees, you hypocrites! You give a tenth of your mint and spice and every garden herb to the priests, but you've neglected the weightier matters of the law: justice, mercy, faithfulness, and the love of God. These latter things you should have done without neglecting the former. You blind guides who strain out a gnat yet swallow a camel!

"Woe to you, scribes and Pharisees, you hypocrites! You clean the outside of both the cup and the dish, but inside you're full of greed and self-indulgence. You blind Pharisees! First clean the inside of the cup and the dish so that the outside may also become clean.

"Woe to you, scribes and Pharisees, you hypocrites! You're like unmarked graves that men walk over and so make themselves unclean without knowing it."[49] You're like whitewashed tombs that look beautiful on the outside, but inside are full of dead men's bones and all kinds of uncleanness. You, like them, appear righteous on the outside, but on the inside you're full of hypocrisy and lawlessness.

"Woe to you, scribes and Pharisees, you hypocrites! You build tombs for the prophets and decorate the graves of the righteous, whom your ancestors killed. You claim, 'If we'd been living in the days of our forefathers,

we wouldn't have participated with them in shedding
the blood of the prophets.' This behavior serves as your
own testimony against yourselves that you truly are the
descendants of those who murdered the prophets. Finish
what your forefathers started!

"You snakes! You brood of vipers! How will you escape being
sentenced to hell?

"Because of this, I'm going to send you prophets and
wise men and scribes. Some of them you'll kill and
crucify; others you'll flog in your synagogues and put
to flight from town to town. And so the guilt of all the
righteous blood shed on earth, from the blood of righteous Abel to the blood of Zechariah (the son of Bere-
kiah, whom you murdered between the temple and the
altar) will come upon you. I'm telling you the truth: This
generation will be held responsible."

Jesus stepped down from the bench he'd been standing on, leaving
the Pharisees and scribes aghast. He went to the Court of Women
and sat down across from one of the offering boxes in the temple and
watched how people put their money into it. He looked up and saw
wealthy people putting large amounts into it. Then a poor widow
came and put in two of the smallest Roman coins, worth only a frac-
tion of a cent. Jesus called his disciples over and said, "I'm telling you
the truth: This poor widow has put more into the offering box than all
the others. They all gave out of their excess, but she out of her want.
She put in everything she owned, all she had to live on."

❧

Jesus left the temple and was walking away when his disciples came
up to him to point out the magnificence of the temple building, how
it was adorned with beautiful stones and expensive gifts given as offerings to God: "Look, at all these things, Teacher, the massive stones
and the magnificent buildings!"

Jesus responded, "See all these great buildings? Not one of these stones will be left on another. They'll all be torn down. I'm telling you the truth: Not one stone here will be left standing."*

The group returned to their camp on the Mount of Olives. Peter, James, John, Andrew, and the other disciples came to Jesus and asked him, "Teacher, when will this happen? What will be the sign that all these things are going to be fulfilled—that they're about to take place? What will be the sign of your coming and the end of the age?"

Jesus answered, "Watch out that no one misleads you. Many people will come in my name, claiming, 'I'm the Messiah. The time is near.' They'll deceive many. Make sure you don't follow them. You'll also hear of wars and rumors of wars and turmoil. But don't be alarmed. These things must happen first, but the end won't come immediately."

Mary and the other women brought them something to eat then sat down to listen. The disciples broke off pieces of bread and dipped it into a bowl of olive oil and spices being passed around. Their attention was fixed on Jesus, and they didn't want to miss a word.

Jesus continued his warning: "Nation will rise against nation, and kingdom against kingdom. There will be major earthquakes and famines in various places, pestilences and terrifying sights—and great signs from heaven." He lifted his arms and motioned to the sky. "All these are merely the beginning of the end's birth pains."

Mary asked, "Will this happen soon—in our lifetimes?"

Jesus made no response regarding the timing, then he said, "I've told you before that many of you will suffer for being my followers. Be on your guard because they'll arrest you and persecute you. They'll hand you over to the local councils, you'll be flogged in the synagogues, and they'll kill you. They'll deliver you to prisons to be tortured. For my sake, you'll stand before governors and kings as my witnesses to them."

---

* When Titus conquered Jerusalem in AD 70, he built fires against the walls of the temple to crumble the stones. The entire wall was destroyed. Only a portion of the retaining wall on the western side remains. Today that portion, known as the "Wailing Wall," is the holiest place for a Jew to pray.

James spoke up. "I remember this—I'm not supposed to worry about what to say."

Jesus said, "I'm pleased you took to heart what I told you before. Whenever you're arrested and brought to trial, don't worry about what to say. Just say whatever is given to you then, for it's not you speaking but the Holy Spirit. So make up your minds not to prepare ahead of time how you'll defend yourselves, for I'll give you such words and wisdom that none of your adversaries will be able to resist or refute them."

"I definitely could use that help every day," Peter said, trying to lighten the somber mood, but there was no doing that considering the seriousness of Jesus' statements.

Jesus stood up and started walking around them. He didn't like having to deliver all this dire news, but they had to be prepared. "You will be hated by everyone, all nations, because of me and because of my name, but not a hair of your head will perish. Many will fall away from God and will betray one another and even hate each other. Most people's love will grow cold because of the increase of wickedness."

John interjected, "But surely many people will be saved too."

Jesus answered, "By enduring, you'll secure your lives. Whoever endures to the end will be saved. And the good news of the kingdom will be preached in the whole world as a testimony to all nations. Then the end will come. Jerusalem will be trampled on by the Gentiles until the times of the Gentiles are fulfilled. When you see Jerusalem being surrounded by armies, know its desolation is near. Its residents will fall by the sword and be taken as prisoners to all the nations."

Jesus let out a long sigh. "There will be suffering. When you see 'the abomination that causes desolation' standing where it should not be, in the holy place, as prophesied by Daniel, those in Judea better flee to the mountains, those in the city get out, and those in the country not enter the city.[50] This is the time of God's vengeance to fulfill everything written in the Scriptures.

"Woe to those who are pregnant and nursing babies in those days. Pray your flight won't be in winter or on the Sabbath. For in those days, there will be great tribulation, such as has never yet nor ever again will occur. If the Lord had not cut short those days, no life would have been saved. But for the sake of the elect, whom he's chosen, those days will be cut short.

"There will be false prophets. When they appear, they'll lead many astray. If anyone says to you, 'Look, here's the Messiah!' or 'Look, he's over there!' don't believe it. False 'anointed ones' and false 'prophets' will rise and perform great signs and wonders to deceive, if possible, even God's chosen ones.

"So watch out! I've told you everything ahead of time. If anyone tells you, 'Look, he's out in the wilderness,' don't go, or 'Look, he's in the inner rooms,' don't believe it.

"Nations will be distressed and perplexed at the roaring of the sea and its waves. The universe will be disrupted. Immediately after the tribulation of those days, following that suffering, the sun will be darkened, and the moon will not give its light. The stars will fall from the sky,[51] and the spiritual powers in the heavens will be shaken. People will faint from fear and their expectation of what's coming on the world, for truly, the heavenly bodies will be shaken."

The group was reeling from all Jesus had said. "This sounds terrifying!" Matthew concluded. "So after all this, is that when you'll return?"

Jesus responded, "Just as lightning comes out of the east and is visible even in the west, that's how it will be when the Son of Man returns. His sign will appear in the sky, and all the people of the earth who have survived will mourn, for they'll see the 'Son of Man coming on the clouds of the sky' with power and great glory. He'll send his angels with a great trumpet call, and they'll gather his elect from the four winds, from the farthest ends of the earth to the farthest ends of the heavens. When these things begin to happen, stand up and lift your heads because your redemption is drawing near.

"Now learn from the lesson of the parable about the fig tree and all the trees:* As soon as each year's new shoots fill with sap and put forth their leaves, you know summer is near. In the same way, when

---

* "Fig tree" may be a metaphor for Israel.

you see all these things, know he's near, right at the door. Truthfully, this generation won't pass away until all these things happen.* Heaven and earth will pass away, but my words will never pass away."

Jesus turned toward Mary and said, "Now to answer your question about the timing. No one knows the day or hour except the Father alone, not even the angels in heaven or the Son. So watch out! Stay alert and pray, for you don't know when that time will come. Your situation is like a man going on a trip: When he leaves his house, he orders the doorkeeper to stay alert and puts his servants in charge, giving each their responsibilities. Since you don't know when the owner of the house will return—whether in the evening, at midnight, in the morning when the rooster crows, or at daybreak—you also must stay alert in case he comes suddenly and finds you sleeping. What I say to you, I say to everyone: 'Keep alert!'

"I'm telling you, watch yourselves, or your hearts will be weighed down with unrestrained sensual pleasure, drunkenness, and the anxieties of life. That day will come suddenly, like a trap. For it will come upon all who live on the face of the whole earth. So keep watching, praying that you may have strength to escape all that must happen and be able to stand before the Son of Man. Remain alert because you don't know on what day your Lord is coming."

Since they'd been sitting so long, and there was a lot for them to take in, Jesus stopped talking for a while to let them absorb everything.

Ↄↄ

After a while, Jesus sat down by the fire and told them a parable: "On the day your Lord comes, those who want to enter the kingdom of heaven will be like this:

> Ten virgins took their lamps and went out to meet the
> bridegroom. Five were foolish, and five were wise. The
> foolish ones took their lamps but didn't take any oil to refill
> them. The wise ones, however, took oil in jars along with

---

* "Generation" may refer to the Jewish race or to the generation that sees the signs Jesus just talked about (or something else).

their lamps. When the bridegroom lingered, the bridesmaids became drowsy and fell asleep.

At midnight someone shouted: 'Look, the bridegroom! Come out to meet him!'

All the virgins woke up and trimmed their lamps. The foolish ones said to the wise, 'Give us some of your oil. Our lamps are going out!'

But the wise answered, 'No! There won't be enough for both us and you too. Go to the sellers and buy some for yourselves.'

While they were going away to buy oil, the bridegroom came, and those who were ready went in with him to the wedding feast. Then the door was shut.

Later the other virgins came, pleading 'Lord! Lord! Let us in!'

But he replied, 'Truly, I don't know you.'

"As I said, stay alert, for you don't know the day or the hour when the Son of Man is coming."

"I'm going to be scared to go to sleep after this!" James said.

"We all will," Nathanael added.

John corrected them. "You're missing the point. It doesn't mean we can't go to sleep again—just that we need to be ready, spiritually speaking, for our Lord's return."

"Whatever that means," Judas said.

Jesus answered, "It means you want your heart to be right with God. When the Son of Man comes in his glory, and all the angels with him, he'll sit on his glorious throne. All the nations will be gathered before him, and he'll separate people one from another as a shepherd separates the sheep from the goats. He'll put the sheep on his right and the goats on his left. Then the King will say to those on his right,

'Come, you who are blessed by my Father, inherit the kingdom prepared for you from the creation of the world. For

I was hungry, and you gave me food to eat.
I was thirsty, and you gave me water to drink.
I was a stranger, and you invited me in.
I was naked, and you clothed me.
I was sick, and you took care of me.
I was in prison, and you came to visit me.'

"Then the righteous will say back to him, 'Lord, when did we see you hungry and feed you? Or see you thirsty and give you something to drink? When did we see you as a stranger and invite you in, or see you needing clothes and clothe you? And when did we see you sick or in prison and visit you?'

"The King will reply, 'I'm telling the truth: Whatever you did for one of the least of my brothers and sisters, you did for me.'

Then the King will say to those on his left,

'Depart from me, you who are doomed, into the eternal fire prepared for the devil and his angels. For
I was hungry, and you gave me nothing to eat.
I was thirsty, and you gave me nothing to drink.
I was a stranger, and you didn't invite me in.
I was naked, and you didn't clothe me.
I was sick and in prison, and you didn't visit me.'

"They, too, will answer, 'Lord, when did we see you hungry or thirsty or a stranger or needing clothes or sick or in prison and didn't attend to your needs?'

"He'll reply, 'I'm telling you the truth: Whatever you didn't do for the least of these, you didn't do for me.' And these will go away into eternal punishment, but the righteous to eternal life."

When Jesus had finished saying these things, he told his disciples, "As you know, the Passover is tomorrow, and the Son of Man will be handed over to be crucified." Then the disciples went back into the city.

Chapter 14

Betrayal, Arrest, and Trial

Meanwhile, the chief priests and elders of the people were meeting with the high priest, Caiaphas, at his palace to discuss the best time to arrest Jesus secretly and kill him.

"Not during the Passover Festival, or the people may riot." Caiaphas advised the chief priests and elders. "If you want to have Jesus arrested, you need to do it quietly. The people see him as a prophet."

"A false one," they answered. "But still, we need to wait for the right opportunity."

A guard entered the room and said to Caiaphas, "There's someone here to see you. I think you'll want to hear what he has to say." Caiaphas looked up to see Judas Iscariot standing there.

"What do you want?" Caiaphas demanded. "We're in the middle of an important meeting."

"What will you give me to betray Jesus to you?" Judas asked.

Caiaphas was taken aback. "Aren't you one of his disciples? Why would you want to betray your own master?"

"I have my reasons," Judas answered. Little did they know Satan had entered him and put the idea of betraying Jesus into his heart. "Now how much will you pay me to deliver him to you?"

They were all delighted at this turn of events. It was just the opportunity they were looking for. So they promised to pay him thirty pieces of silver, about four months' wages.

"Fair enough," Judas said, and they weighed out the money for him. "I'll let you know when I find a good time to hand him over when he's away from the crowd." Judas left and returned to the apostles near the temple.

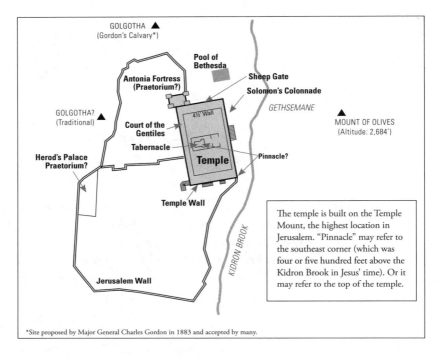

GOLGOTHA ▲
(Gordon's Calvary*)

Pool of
Bethesda

Antonia Fortress
(Praetorium?)

Sheep Gate

Solomon's Colonnade

GETHSEMANE

GOLGOTHA? ▲
(Traditional)

4½' Wall

Court of the
Gentiles

Tabernacle

▲
MOUNT OF OLIVES
(Altitude: 2,684')

Herod's Palace
Praetorium?

Temple

Pinnacle?

Temple Wall

KIDRON BROOK

Jerusalem Wall

The temple is built on the Temple Mount, the highest location in Jerusalem. "Pinnacle" may refer to the southeast corner (which was four or five hundred feet above the Kidron Brook in Jesus' time). Or it may refer to the top of the temple.

*Site proposed by Major General Charles Gordon in 1883 and accepted by many.

Where Did Jesus Walk? Where Was He Taken?

The "Jesus' Last Two Days" map shows almost every location in Jerusalem mentioned in the four Gospels. Some places are omitted because their location is purely speculative (e.g., Annas' house, Caiaphas' house). That is, they have neither archaeological evidence nor strong tradition supporting their location. So we do not attempt to show the route that Jesus walked/was taken from place to place. The reality is that we have a general idea but are uncertain.

Sometimes our uncertainty is because of ambiguity of the text. For instance, when he was "taken to Caiaphas" is the text referring to his home or his headquarters (or were they the same place)? And while we are reasonably confident that Pilate lived at Herod the Great's former palace, we do not know if it was "the Praetorium" (i.e., his military headquarters, which may have been at the Antonia Fortress). Even where the text is clear, the location is oftentimes uncertain. There are strong traditions about the location of Golgotha and the Garden of Gethsemane.

Day	Time	Location – *Significant Event*
Thursday, 4/26/31	Afternoon 7:00 p.m. 11:00 p.m.	Jerusalem Temple – *Taught* House in Jerusalem – *Taught, instituted the Lord's Supper* On the way to Gethsemane – *Final time teaching the apostles* *– Prayed his high priestly prayer*
Friday, 4/27/31	Midnight	Garden of Gethsemane – *Prayed his Father's will be done* *– Betrayed and arrested*
	1:00 a.m.	House (?) of Annas – *Interrogated by Annas*
	2:00 a.m.	House (?) of Caiaphas – *Informal Sanhedrin hearing* *– Peter denied knowing Jesus.* *– Sanhedrin decided to plot Jesus' death.*
	3:00 a.m.	Praetorium – *Interrogated by Pontius Pilate*
	Daybreak	Herod Antipas' Palace – *Interrogated by Herod* *– Mocked by Herod's guards*
	7:00 a.m.	Praetorium – *Interrogated again by Pilate, found innocent* *– Flogged and mocked by soldiers* *– Handed over for crucifixion* *– Soldiers mocked him.*
	8:00 a.m.	Jerusalem street – *Walked to Golgotha*
	10:00 a.m.	Golgotha – *Crucified*
	3:00 p.m.	*– Died*
	4:00 p.m.	A nearby garden – *Buried*

However, despite much work, there is no definitive evidence that the sites currently shown tourists are correct.

While it would be nice to know these things, it is not necessary to know them to understand what Jesus went through after he was arrested. His longest walk was probably the one after he was arrested, from Gethsemane to Annas' house. Whatever the distance, he was healthy and could do it easily. And we can say with confidence that he was probably moved three hundred to six hundred yards each time he was taken from one building to another, perhaps a four- to five-minute walk each time. Because he was beaten several times, the walks may have been slower and slower. Or maybe the soldiers quick-marched him.

By the time Jesus had been condemned, flogged once, and beaten other times, he had been awake for about thirty hours (from sunrise Thursday until noon Friday). Surely the walk from the Praetorium to Golgotha (1,000 to 2,000 feet) was quite slow and seemed miles long to him.

Just as Judas arrived at the temple, some God-fearing Gentiles among those who had gone up to worship at the festival approached Philip and said, "Sir, we'd like to meet Jesus."

Philip went and told Andrew, and Andrew and Philip went and told Jesus. They found him back at the temple, talking as usual with a crowd surrounding him.

"The time has come for the Son of Man to be glorified. I'm telling you the truth: Unless a grain of wheat falls to the ground and dies, it remains alone, a single seed. But if it dies, it produces much fruit, a head with many seeds. Those who love their life here will lose it, and those who hate their life in this world will keep it for eternal life. Whoever wants to serve me must follow me, and where I am, there my servant will be also. If anyone serves me, the Father will honor them. Now my soul is troubled, and what should I say? 'Father, save me from this hour'? No, for this very reason I've come to this hour." Then he called out, "Father, glorify your name!"

Then a booming voice came from heaven: "I have glorified it and will glorify it again."

The crowd stood there awestruck. Some said the voice sounded like thunder. Others said an angel had spoken to him.

Jesus said, "This voice wasn't for my benefit but for yours. Now's the time of judgment on this world when Satan, the prince of this world, will be cast out. When I'm lifted from the earth on the cross, I will draw all people to myself." He said this to point to the kind of death he was going to die.

The crowd answered, "We've heard from the law that the Messiah will remain forever, so how can you say, 'The Son of Man must be lifted up'? Who is this 'Son of Man'?"

As usual, Jesus didn't answer directly. "The light is among you for a little while longer. Walk while you have the light, so darkness won't overtake you. Whoever walks in the darkness doesn't know where they're going. While you have the light, believe in the light, so you may become children of light."

❧

After he'd finished speaking, he left and hid himself from them for a short while. Even though he had performed many miraculous signs in front of the Jews, most still didn't believe in him. This fulfilled Isaiah's prophecy: "Lord, who has believed our message, and to whom has your power been revealed?"[52] They couldn't believe because, as Isaiah also said, "He has blinded their eyes and hardened their hearts, so they cannot see with their eyes or understand with their hearts and turn that I might heal them."[53] Isaiah said these things because he saw God's glory and spoke about him.

Nevertheless, many, even among the Jewish leaders, did believe in Jesus. But because of the Pharisees, they didn't speak of their faith openly, so they wouldn't be put out of the synagogue. They loved receiving glory from people more than from God.

ↀ

Jesus went back out among the crowds and cried out, "Whoever believes in me doesn't believe only in me but in God the Father who sent me. Whoever looks at me sees the one who sent me. I've come to the world as a light so that everyone who believes in me will no longer remain in darkness.

"If anyone hears my words but doesn't keep them, I don't pass judgment on them. I didn't come to judge the world but to save the world. Anyone who rejects me and doesn't receive my words has one who judges them. The words I have spoken will judge them on the last day. I didn't speak from within myself, but the Father who sent me has himself given me a commandment—what to say and what to speak. I know that his commandment is eternal life. Therefore whatever I say, I say just as the Father has told me to say it."

Jesus knew the time had come to leave this world and go to the Father. Having loved his own who were in the world, he loved them to the end.

ↀ

Earlier that day, the day on which the Passover lamb is sacrificed, the disciples had asked Jesus, "In whose home do you want us to go and prepare for you to eat the Passover meal?"

Jesus said to Peter and John, "You go and prepare the meal for us, so we can eat it together."

They asked, "Where do you want us to make preparations for it?"

He replied, "Go into the city. When you enter it, a man carrying a jar of water will meet you. Follow him, and tell the owner of whatever house he enters, 'The Teacher says, "My appointed time is near, and I will observe the Passover with my disciples at your house."' He'll show you a large room upstairs, furnished and ready. Make the preparations for us there."

The two disciples went into the city and found things just as Jesus had told them, so they prepared the Passover meal there. After sundown, about 7:00 p.m., Jesus arrived with the twelve apostles, and they reclined at the table for their Passover meal.

Jesus knew the Father had given him power over everything, and he'd come from God and was returning to God, so he got up from the meal, took off his cloak, and wrapped a towel around his waist. Then he poured water into a basin and began to wash the feet of his disciples. Then he dried them with the towel he had wrapped around himself.

As he started to wash Peter's feet, he protested, "Lord, are you going to wash my feet?"

Jesus replied, "Right now you don't understand what I'm doing, but later you will."

Peter responded, "No! You shall never wash my feet."

Jesus answered, "Unless I wash you, you have no place with me."

Peter said. "Then not just my feet, Lord, but wash my hands and my head also!"

Jesus responded, "A person who's had a bath doesn't need to do anything except wash their feet. Then their whole body is clean." He looked around at them. "You are clean—but not every one of you." He already knew who would betray him.

After washing their feet and putting his cloak back on, Jesus took his place back at the table along with the apostles. He asked them, "Do you understand what I've done for you? You call me 'Teacher' and 'Lord,' and rightly so, for this is who I am. If then I, your Lord and Teacher, have washed your feet, you also ought to wash one another's feet. I've set an example so that you'll do what I've done for you. I'm telling you the truth: A servant isn't greater than their master, nor is the messenger greater than the one who sent them. If you know these things, you'll be blessed if you do them."

He looked around the table at each one of them, and his eyes lingered on Judas a little longer than the rest. "I'm not speaking of all of you," Jesus continued. "I know whom I've chosen. But the Scripture will be fulfilled that says, 'He who eats my bread has lifted up his heel against me.'[54] I'm telling you this now, before it happens, so when it does, you will believe that I am he. I'm telling you the truth: Whoever receives anyone I send receives me, and whoever receives me receives the one who sent me."

Later, while they were still reclining at the table and eating, Jesus said, "I'm telling you the truth: One of you will betray me, one of you who is eating with me."

Deeply grieved, one by one they said to him, "Surely not I, Lord?"

He replied, "One of you twelve, the one who dips his hand into the bowl with me, will betray me; for the Son of Man goes to die just as it is written about him in Scripture. But woe to the man who betrays the Son of Man! It would be better for him if he had not been born."

Peter and John got up to serve the lamb and the herbs, and Jesus motioned for them to sit back down. Then he served each person their portion. "I've wanted so much to eat this meal with you before I suffer," he said, "and I won't eat another Passover meal until it's fulfilled in the kingdom of God."

While they were eating, Jesus took some of the unleavened bread, said a blessing, broke it, and gave it to his disciples, saying, "Take, eat; this is my body, which is given for you. Do this in remembrance of me." In the same way, he filled a cup with wine, gave thanks to God, and gave it to them, saying, "Take this and share it among yourselves. All of you drink from it, for this is my blood of the new covenant, which is poured out for you and for many for the forgiveness of sins. I'm telling you the truth: I'll no longer drink of this fruit of the vine from now on until the kingdom of God comes, until the day when I drink it anew with you in my Father's kingdom. Do this, as often as you drink it, in remembrance of me."[55] And they all drank from the cup.

Then they started disputing once again about which one of them should be considered the greatest. Jesus told them, "The kings of the Gentiles lord it over them, and those with authority over them are called 'benefactors.' But it's not to be this way with you. As I've told you before, the one who's greatest among you must become like the youngest, and the one who leads like the one who serves. For who's greater, the one who's eating at the table or the one who serves? Isn't it the one who's eating? But think about this: I'm here with you as the one who serves.

"You are the ones who have stood by me in my trials. And just as my Father has granted me a kingdom, I grant that you may eat and drink at my table in my kingdom and sit on thrones judging the twelve tribes of Israel."

After saying this, Jesus became troubled in spirit and said, "I'm telling you the truth: One of you twelve is going to betray me! His hand is with mine on the table."

The disciples looked at one another, asking which one of them would possibly betray him. John was eating with his head on Jesus' breast. Peter motioned to him to ask Jesus whom he was speaking about, so John leaned back on Jesus' breast and said, "Lord, who is it?"

Jesus answered, "It's the one I'll give this piece of bread to after I've dipped it." Then he dipped the piece of bread in the bowl and gave it to Judas. After Judas took the bread, Satan entered him again.

Then Judas said, "Surely not me, Rabbi?"

Jesus answered, "You've said it yourself!"

Then Jesus told him, "What you're about to do, do quickly."

None of the others at the table knew why Jesus said this to him. Because Judas handled their money, some thought Jesus was telling him to buy whatever was needed for the Passover Festival or to give something to the poor. Judas left immediately after taking the bread.

After Judas had left, Jesus said, "Now the Son of Man is glorified, and God is glorified in him. If God is glorified in him, God will glorify the Son in himself and glorify him at once. My dear disciples, I'm going to be with you only a little longer. You'll look for me, and as I also told the Jews at the temple, I'm telling you now: where I'm going, you can't come.

"I'm giving you a new commandment: Love one another. Just as I have loved you, you should love one another. Everyone will know you're my disciples by this: if you love one another."

Peter asked him, "Lord, where are you going?"

Jesus replied, "Where I'm going you can't follow now, but you'll follow later."

So Peter asked, "Lord, why can't I follow you now? I would lay down my life for you."

Jesus answered, "Will you really lay down your life for me? I'm telling you the truth: Before the rooster crows twice, you'll deny knowing me three times."

Then Jesus told them all, "Tonight you will all desert me on account of who I am. The Scripture says, 'I will strike down the shepherd, and the sheep of the flock will be scattered.'"[56] But after I have been raised, I will go ahead of you to Galilee."

Peter declared, "Though everyone else may desert you, I never will."

Jesus responded, "Peter, Peter, listen! Satan has asked to sift all of you like wheat. But I have prayed for you, Peter, that your faith may not fail. And when you've turned back, strengthen your fellow believers."

But he objected, "Lord, I'm ready to go with you, both to prison and to death."

Jesus replied, "I'm telling you, Peter, the rooster won't crow twice today until you've denied knowing me three times."

But Peter persisted: "Even if I have to die with you, I'll never deny knowing you." And all the other disciples said the same thing.

Jesus knew what he'd told them would be difficult to accept and even more difficult to endure. To comfort them, he said, "Don't let your hearts be troubled. Believe in God the Father. Believe also in me. There are many rooms in my Father's house. If there were not, would I have told you I'm going there to prepare a place for you? And if I go and prepare a place for you, I'll come back and take you to be with me, so you, too, can be where I am. You know the way to where I'm going."

Thomas said, "Lord, we don't know where you're going, so how could we know the way?"

Jesus answered, "I am the way and the truth and the life. No one comes to the Father except through me. If you'd known me, you'd have known my Father too. From now on, you do know him and have seen him."

Philip said, "Lord, show us the Father, and that's enough for us."

Jesus replied, "I've been with you for so long, and yet you still don't know me, Philip? Anyone who's seen me has seen the Father. How can you say, 'Show us the Father'? Don't you believe I'm in the Father and the Father is in me? The words I speak to you I don't speak from within myself, but the Father lives in me and does his work through me. Believe me when I say I'm in the Father, and the Father's in me. But if you don't, believe because of the evidence of the miraculous works themselves.

"I'm telling you the truth: Anyone who believes in me will do the works I've done and do greater works than these because I'm going to the Father. And whatever you ask in my name, I'll do it so that the Father may be glorified through the works of the Son. Remember this: If you ask me for anything in my name, I'll do it.*

"If you love me, you'll obey my commandments. And I'll ask the Father, and he'll give you another helper to be with you forever— the Spirit of truth—whom the world is not able to receive because

---

* He was referring to the scope and size and number of works Jesus' disciples would perform, as they lived for years spreading the gospel well beyond what Jesus did before he ascended to heaven.

it neither sees him nor knows him. But you do know him, for he remains with you and will be in you. I won't leave you as orphans; I'm coming back to you. In a little while, the world won't see me anymore, but you'll see me. Because I live, you'll also live. On that day, you will realize I am in my Father, you are in me—and I am in you.* The one who has my commandments and keeps them is the one who loves me, and the one who loves me will be loved by my Father. And I will love them and reveal myself to them."

Then the other disciple named Judas (not Judas Iscariot) said, "Lord, what's happened that you're going to reveal yourself to us and not to the world?"

Jesus replied, "Anyone who loves me will obey my words. My Father will love them, and we will come to them and make our home with them. Anyone who doesn't love me won't obey my words. The words you hear are not mine but those of the Father who sent me.

"I've told you these things while I'm still with you. But the Helper, the Holy Spirit, whom the Father will send in my name, will teach you all things and remind you of all I've said to you. Peace I leave you. I give you my peace. I'm not giving it to you as the world gives. So don't let your hearts be troubled, and don't be afraid.

"You heard me say, 'I'm going away and coming back to you.' If you loved me, you would have rejoiced that I'm going to the Father, for the Father is greater than I am. I have told you now, before it happens, so that when it does happen you will believe. I won't talk with you much longer because the ruler of this world is coming—though he has no power over me. I'm doing exactly as the Father has commanded me, so the world may learn that I love the Father."

After supper, Jesus asked them, "When I sent you out preaching and healing without a money bag, without a traveler's bag, or extra sandals, you didn't lack anything, did you?"

"No, nothing," they replied.

He continued, "Now, whoever has a money bag should take it and a traveler's bag too. And if you don't have a sword, sell your cloak

* "On that day" is a reference to Pentecost, the day believers received the Holy Spirit (see Acts 2).

and buy one. For I'm telling you the Scripture 'and he was numbered with the transgressors' must be fulfilled in me.[57] And it's about to be fulfilled."

The disciples said, "Look, Lord, here are two swords."

He told them, "That's enough."

Then, after they sang a hymn, Jesus said, "Now, get up! Let's leave here."

ℰ℔

Around 11:00 p.m., Jesus went out as usual to the Mount of Olives, and his disciples followed him. On the way there, Jesus had them gather closely around him as they walked, so he could share what would be his final teaching to them:

"I am the true vine, and my Father is the vineyard keeper. He removes every branch in me that does not produce fruit, and he prunes every branch that produces fruit, so it will produce more fruit. You're already cleansed because of the word I've spoken to you. Remain in me, as I also will remain in you. Just as a branch cannot bear fruit by itself—it has to remain attached to the vine—you cannot bear fruit unless you remain attached to me. I am the vine, and you are the branches. Whoever remains in me, and I in them, that person will bear much fruit. Apart from me you cannot produce anything. If someone doesn't remain in me, that person will be thrown away and dry up like an unattached branch—workers gather them up, throw them into the fire, and they're burned. If you remain in me and my words remain in you, ask whatever you wish, and it will be done for you. My Father is glorified by this, that you bear much fruit and so prove you're my disciples.

"I have loved you just as the Father has loved me. Now remain in my love. If you keep my commandments, you'll remain in my love, just as I have kept my Father's commandments and remain in his love. I've told you these things so that my joy may be in you and your joy may be complete. This is my commandment: Love one another as I've loved you. Greater love has no one than this: that they lay down their life for their friends. You are my friends if you do what I command

202

you. I no longer call you servants because the servant doesn't know what their master's doing. Rather, I've called you friends because I've made known to you everything I learned from my Father. You didn't choose me, but I chose you and appointed you so that you would go and bear fruit, and your fruit should remain so that the Father will give you whatever you ask for in my name. These things I command you, that you love one another.

"If the world hates you, know that it hated me before it hated you. If you belonged to the world, the world would love you as its own. But because you don't belong to the world—for I have chosen you out of the world—the world hates you. Remember the word I spoke to you: 'A servant isn't greater than their master.' If they persecuted me, they'll also persecute you. If they obey my teaching, they'll also obey yours. They're going to do all these things to you because of your association with my name, for they don't know God, the one who sent me.

"Anyone who hates me hates my Father also. If I hadn't come and spoken to them, they wouldn't have been guilty of sin, but now they don't have any excuse for their sin. If I hadn't done miraculous works in their midst that no one else did, they wouldn't have been guilty of sin. As it is, they've seen all these things and still hate both me and my Father. But the word written in their law, 'They hated me without a cause,' must be fulfilled.[58]

"When the Helper comes, the Holy Spirit of truth who goes out from the Father, whom I'll send to you from the Father, he will testify about me. And you will also testify because you've been with me from the start."

One of the apostles asked, "Lord, why are you telling us these things?"

Jesus replied, "So you won't fall away. They're going to expel you from the synagogue. In fact, the time is coming when those who kill you will think they are offering a service to God! They'll do these things because they haven't known the Father or me. I've told you these things, so you will remember at the time they happen that I warned you about them.

"I didn't tell you about these things at the beginning because I was staying with you. But now I'm going to him who sent me. Yet not one of you is asking me, 'Where are you going?' Because I've said these things to you, sorrow has filled your heart. But I'm telling you the truth: It's better for you that I leave. If I don't leave, the Holy Spirit, the Helper, won't come to you. But when I go, I'll send him to you. When he comes, he'll convict the world:

about sin—because they don't believe in me;

about righteousness—because I'm going to the Father (and you'll no longer see me); and

about judgment—because Satan, the prince of this world, now stands condemned.

I have much more to say to you, but you can't bear it right now. But when he, the Spirit of truth, comes, he will guide you into all the truth. He won't speak from within himself. Rather, he will only tell you what he hears from the Father. And he'll tell you what's coming. He will glorify me by receiving from me and disclosing it to you. All the Father has is mine. Because of this, I said the Spirit will take and declare to you what's mine."

Jesus continued, "In a little while you won't see me anymore because I go to the Father, and then after a little while, you will see me again."

Some of his disciples said to one another, "What's this he's telling us, 'In a little while, you won't see me anymore, and then after a little while, you will see me again' and 'because I'm going to the Father'?" They were asking, "What's this, 'a little while'? We don't understand what he's saying."

Jesus knew they wanted to ask him about these things, so he said, "Are you asking each other what I meant by saying, 'In a little while, you won't see me anymore, and then after a little while, you will see me again'? I'm telling you the truth: You'll weep and lament, but the world will rejoice. You'll grieve, but your grief will turn into joy. When a woman gives birth, she has pain because her time has come. But when her baby is born, she forgets the anguish because of her joy that a person is born into the world. In the same way, you have grief now; but your heart will rejoice when I see you again, and no one will take away your joy. In that day, you won't ask me for anything. I'm telling you the truth: My Father will give you whatever you ask for in my name. Up till now you haven't asked for anything in my name. Ask and you will receive so that your joy may be complete!

"I've spoken these things to you figuratively. A time is coming when I'll no longer speak figuratively, but I will tell you about the Father plainly. In that day you'll make requests directly to the Father in my name. I'm not telling you that I'll ask the Father on your behalf, for the Father himself loves you, because you have loved me and have believed that I came from God. I came from the Father and entered the world. Again I'm leaving the world and going to the Father."

Then his disciples said, "Finally, now you're speaking plainly, without using a figure of speech. We know that you know all things, and you don't need to have anyone question you to prove it. By this we believe you came from God."

Jesus responded, "Do you believe now? Look, the time is coming—in fact it's already come—when you will be scattered, each one of you to your own home. You'll leave me all alone. Yet I'm not alone because the Father is with me. I've told you these things so that in me you may have peace. In this world you have trouble. But take heart! I have overcome the world."

***

When they were almost to the Garden of Gethsemane, Jesus stopped and turned to them all and said, "I'm about to leave you, and I want to pray for you before I go."

They all circled around him, kneeled, and bowed their heads. Jesus lifted his eyes to heaven and prayed his farewell prayer:

"Father, the hour has come. You granted me authority over all people, that I should give eternal life to all those you have brought to me. Now this is eternal life: that they know you, the only true God, and me, Jesus Christ, whom you have sent.

"Now glorify me, your Son, that I may glorify you. I glorified you on earth by finishing the work you gave me to do. And now,

Father, glorify me together with yourself—with the glory I had with you before the world existed.

"I have revealed your name to the people whom you gave me. They were yours, and you gave them to me, and they have kept your word. Now they know that everything you've given me truly is from you—for I gave them the words you gave me, and they accepted them. They truly understand that I came from you, and they believed that you sent me. I pray for them. I am not praying for the world but for those you have given me, for they are yours. All that I have is yours, and all that you have is mine. I have been glorified among them. I am no longer in the world, but they're still going to be in the world after I come to you.

"Holy Father, keep them safe in the power of your name—the name you've given me—so that they may be united just as we are one. While I was with them in the world, I watched over them and kept them safe in your name. Not one of them was lost except the son of destruction (that the Scripture would be fulfilled).

"Now I am coming to you. I'm saying these things while I'm still in the world so that my joy will be made complete in them. I've given them your message, and the world has hated them because just as I don't belong to the world, they don't belong to the world. I am not asking you to take them out of the world but for you to protect them from the evil one. Sanctify them in the truth, knowing that your word is truth.* As you sent me into the world, I have also sent them into the world. For their sakes I have sanctified myself, that they, too, may be truly sanctified.

"I'm not praying only for these but also for those who will believe in me in the future through their message—that they all may be one, just as you, Father, are in me, and I am in you—that they may also be in us so that the world may believe that you have sent me.

"I have given them the glory that you gave me, that they may be one as we are one—I in them and you in me—that they may be

---

* "Sanctify": to set apart a thing or person to be used to fulfill God's purposes.

completely unified so that the world may know that you sent me and have loved them in the same way that you have loved me.

"Father, I want those you've given to me to be with me where I am, so they can see my glory, the glory that you have given me, because you loved me before laying the foundation of the world.

"O righteous Father, though the world doesn't know you, I know you, and these disciples know that you sent me. I have made your name known to them and will continue to make it known so that the love with which you've loved me may be in them, and I in them."

When he finished praying, they continued to the Garden of Gethsemane.

❧

Meanwhile, Judas was at the home of Caiaphas, the high priest. Caiaphas, still in his night clothes, said, "Do you know what time it is? What was so important that you had to wake me?"

"There won't be a better time than this to arrest Jesus," Judas said. "And I know right where he'll be."

Caiaphas started pacing then asked, "What do you need?"

"Soldiers to make the arrest."

Caiaphas opened the door and called in his assistant, Malchus, who had gotten up when he did. Caiaphas said to him, "We have an opportunity to arrest Jesus tonight."

Malchus was shocked. "But what about what you said about not doing this during Passover? This completely goes against our customs!"

Caiaphas was not deterred. "Look, we may not get the chance again, and I want this man taken care of. More and more people are believing in him, and I'm not going to risk the Romans thinking we are rebelling and taking back our nation."

"As you wish," Malchus relented. "I'll gather the chief priests, Pharisees, and elders. Then what do you want us to do?"

"Take Judas with you to the palace and ask for some soldiers. If they give you any trouble, tell them to tell Pilate that 'Joseph Caiaphas needs them.' That should get you whatever you want."

⌘

Back in Gethsemane, it was already midnight. Jesus said to his disciples, "Sit here while I go over there and pray." Then he took Peter, James, and John with him to a secluded part of the garden and began to be deeply distressed and experience agonizing sorrow. He told them, "My soul is deeply grieved to the point of death. Stay here and keep watch with me."

He went a little farther, fell on his face, and prayed, "Abba, Father, could you take away this ordeal I'm about to face? With you all things are possible. Take this cup from me. Yet not what I will but what you will be done."

Then he returned to his three disciples and found them sleeping! He exclaimed, "Peter! Are you asleep? Couldn't you keep watch with me for even an hour? Stay alert and pray, so you don't fall into temptation. The spirit is willing, but the body is weak."

He went about a stone's throw away a second time, knelt, and prayed, "My Father, if you're willing, take this cup of suffering from me. But if this cup can't pass away unless I drink it, may your will be done."

When he returned, he found them sleeping again. They couldn't keep their eyes open, and they didn't know what to say to him.

So he left them again and prayed the same prayer a third time. Then an angel from heaven appeared and strengthened him. Filled with dread and agony, he prayed even more earnestly, and his sweat became like great drops of blood falling to the ground. When he was finished, he got up and went back to the disciples. He found them sleeping again, exhausted from grief, and said, "Are you still sleeping and resting? Why are you sleeping? Get up and pray so that you won't fall into temptation! Look, the hour is near and has come! The Son of Man is being betrayed into the hands of sinners. Get up! Let's go! The one who's betraying me is approaching."

While Jesus was still speaking, he looked up to see Judas Iscariot leading a large crowd and a detachment of soldiers toward him with lanterns, torches, swords, and clubs. Judas had known how to find him because Jesus often met at Gethsemane with the disciples.

Judas had instructed the soldiers and some officials from the chief priests and Pharisees, "Arrest the one I kiss and lead him away under guard."

Immediately, Judas approached Jesus to kiss him and said, "Greetings, Rabbi."

Jesus said, "Judas, are you betraying the Son of Man with a kiss?"

Then Judas kissed him.

Jesus replied, "Friend, go ahead and do what you came for."

Knowing everything that was going to happen to him, Jesus stepped forward and asked the officials, "Who are you looking for?"

"Jesus of Nazareth," they replied.

"I am he," he said, while Judas was standing right there with them.

When Jesus said this, they drew back, and suddenly losing all their strength, they fell to the ground.

Jesus asked again, "Who are you looking for?"

Trying to get back up, they replied, "Jesus of Nazareth."

Jesus answered, "I told you that I am he. If you're looking for me, let the others go their way." This happened to fulfill the words he had just spoken to God the Father: "Not one of them was lost."

Then they stepped up and took hold of Jesus and arrested him.

When those around him saw what was about to happen, they said, "Lord, should we strike with swords?" Then Peter drew his sword and struck the high priest's servant, Malchus, cutting off his right ear.

But Jesus answered, "No more of this! Shouldn't I drink the cup of suffering the Father's given me? Put your sword back in its place. Those who take up the sword will die by the sword. Don't you know I can call on my Father, and he'll immediately send me more than sixty thousand angels? But then how would the Scriptures, which say it must happen this way, be fulfilled?" And he touched Malchus' ear and healed him.

Then he said to the chief priests, the officers of the temple guard, and the elders who had come for him, "Have you come out with swords and clubs like you would to arrest an outlaw? I was teaching daily in the temple courts, and you didn't lay a hand on me. But this is your hour and that of the power of darkness. All this has taken place to fulfill the writings of the prophets."

The soldiers, their commander, and the Jewish officials seized him, and the soldiers bound him. Then all his disciples deserted him and fled. A certain young man who was wearing only a linen garment was following Jesus. They grabbed him, but he fled naked, leaving his garment behind.

Jesus looked at his disciples running and sighed deeply. If it were not for his Father, he would be completely alone. Even though he knew this would happen, it was hard to take. These men had been his closest friends. Tears fell from his eyes, and he couldn't wipe them away because his hands were tied.

⁊

The soldiers led Jesus to Annas, the former high priest and father-in-law of Caiaphas, the current high priest. Annas questioned Jesus about his disciples and his teaching. Jesus responded, "I've spoken openly to the world. I've always taught in synagogues or the temple courts, where all the Jews gather. I've said nothing in secret. So why question me? Ask those who heard me speak. They know what I said."

When he said this, one of the officials near him slapped his face and said, "Is that the way you answer a former high priest?"

Jesus answered, "If I said something wrong, tell me what it is. But if I spoke truthfully, why did you hit me?"

At about 2:00 a.m., Annas sent him to the home of Caiaphas, the current high priest, who had advised the Jewish leaders that it would be better if just one man died for the people. All the chief priests, scribes, and members of the Sanhedrin had assembled there for an informal meeting. (Formal meetings, ones at which binding judgments could be made, had to be held during daytime.)

Peter and John were following Jesus at a distance. Because Caiaphas was acquainted with John, he was able to go with Jesus into the courtyard, but Peter had to stay outside at the door. John came out, spoke to the doorkeeper, and brought Peter in.

Now the chief priests and the whole Sanhedrin kept looking for false testimony against Jesus, so they could put him to death. But though many false witnesses came forward, their testimonies were inconsistent. The council found nothing usable to condemn him until some stood up and testified falsely. Though Jesus had told the Jewish leaders that if they destroyed the temple he would raise it up in three days, the false witnesses claimed, "We heard him say, 'I will destroy this man-made temple of God, and in three days. I'll build another one, one not made by man.' But their testimony wasn't consistent even about this."

So Caiaphas stood up, came forward, and asked Jesus, "Have you no answer to what these men are charging you with?"

But Jesus kept silent.

Then Caiaphas questioned him again: "I demand you testify under oath by the living God. Are you the Messiah, the Son of the Blessed One—the Son of God?"

Jesus replied, "You've said it yourself. I am, and I say to you all: In the future you will see the Son of Man sitting at the right hand of the all-powerful God and coming on the clouds of heaven."*

Caiaphas was so horrified at this seeming blasphemy that, though the high priest was normally forbidden from doing it, he tore his clothes, in horror exclaiming, "He's blasphemed! Why do we need any other witnesses? Look, you heard him blaspheme. What's your verdict?"

They answered, "He deserves death!" And they all decided to condemn him to death—and some even spit in his face. Then they blindfolded him and struck him with their fists. Some slapped him and taunted, "Prophesy to us, Anointed One. Who hit you?"

Then the guards mocked him and beat him. They kept on demanding, "Prophesy!" And they shouted a lot of other insults at him.

Meanwhile, outside in the courtyard, Peter was warming himself around the charcoal fire the servants and officers of Caiaphas had made because of the cold. The servant girl who was the doorkeeper looked closely at Peter in the firelight and said, "This man was with him."

---

* So here again, by claiming God's name (i.e., "I am"), he was claiming to be God—a blasphemy punishable by death.

Then she spoke directly to Peter, "You, too, were with Jesus of Galilee, the Nazarene. You're one of this man's disciples, too, aren't you?"

He denied it, saying, "No, I am not. I don't know what you're talking about." Then he went out onto the front porch, and a rooster crowed.

When the servant girl spotted him there, she again told those standing around, "This is one of them."

Another woman agreed, "This man was with Jesus of Nazareth."

Someone else noticed him and said, "You, too, are one of them."

Peter denied it again with an oath: "I swear I don't know the man!"

About an hour later, the bystanders went up to Peter and insisted, "Surely this man was with him. He's a Galilean too." They looked at Peter and said, "Your accent gives you away."

Then one of the high priest's servants, a relative of Malchus, the one whose ear Peter had cut off, asked, "Didn't I see you with him in the Garden of Gethsemane?"

Peter began to utter curses and affirm them with oaths: "I don't know the man! I don't even know what you're talking about." And immediately a rooster crowed a second time.

Jesus turned and looked straight at Peter, and Peter remembered his Lord's words, how he'd told him, "Before the rooster crows twice, you'll deny knowing me three times." Then Peter broke down and wept bitterly. He fled the area, sobbing as he ran. He fell to his knees and cried out to God for forgiveness. He felt unworthy of being Jesus' disciple anymore.

❧

Around daybreak, though their meeting did not meet the regulatory requirement to make such a decision, the whole Sanhedrin council made the decision to execute him and plotted to put Jesus to death.

They assembled yet again and led Jesus into their council meeting. "If you're the Messiah," they said, "tell us."

Jesus replied, "If I tell you, you won't believe me. And if I ask you a question, you won't answer. But from now on the Son of Man will be seated at the right hand of the power of God."

They all shouted, "Are you the Son of God then?"

He replied, "You say that I am."

Then they said, "What other testimony do we need? We've heard it ourselves from his own lips."

Then they took him, still tied up, from Caiaphas to the Praetorium, where they handed him over to Pontius Pilate, the Roman governor. To remain ceremonially clean so they could eat the Passover meal, they stayed outside the palace.

Pilate came out to them and asked, "What charge are you bringing against this man?"

The crowd who brought him replied, "We wouldn't have handed him over to you if he weren't a criminal." Then they began to accuse him of many things: "We've found this man is subverting our nation. He opposes tax payments to Caesar and claims to be the Messiah, a king."

So the governor asked, "Are you the king of the Jews?"

Jesus replied, "You've said so." Then when the chief priests and elders accused him, he still didn't respond.

So Pilate asked, "Look how many charges they're bringing against you. Aren't you going to answer?"

Jesus didn't reply to even a single charge, and the governor was astounded. This fulfilled what Isaiah prophesied more than seven hundred years earlier:

"He was oppressed and afflicted,
Yet he did not object or even open his mouth.
He was led like a lamb to the slaughter,
Yet like a sheep that is silent before his shearers, he did not
open his mouth."[59]

The crowd insisted Pilate do something, claiming, "He stirs up the people, and he's been teaching all over Judea. He started in Galilee and has now arrived here."

But Pilate told the chief priests and the rest of the crowd, "I find no reason to charge this man. Take him yourselves and judge him under your own law."

They objected: "But under Roman law, as native Israelites, we have no right to execute anyone. Only Romans can execute."

When Pilate heard this, he asked if the man was a Galilean. When he learned Jesus was from Herod Antipas' jurisdiction, Pilate sent him to Herod.

Now Herod, who lived on the coast in Caesarea, was in Jerusalem for the Passover Festival, so they took Jesus to him. When he saw Jesus, he was delighted because he had wanted to meet him for a long time, hoping to see him perform some miracle like those he'd heard about. He asked him lots of questions, but Jesus gave him no answer. The chief priests and the scribes stood there vehemently accusing him of many crimes. Then Herod and his soldiers ridiculed and mocked him and sent him back to Pilate. Now that same day, Herod and Pilate, who had previously been enemies, became friends.

Pilate went back into the Praetorium around 7:00 a.m., had Jesus brought to him, and asked him again, "Are you the king of the Jews?"

Jesus asked him, "Is that your idea, or did others tell you about me?"

Pilate replied, "Am I a Jew? Your own people and chief priests handed you over to me. What have you done?"

Jesus told him, "My kingdom is not of this world. If it were, my followers would have fought so that I wouldn't have been handed over to the Jewish leaders."

Pilate exclaimed, "You really are a king then!"

Jesus responded, "You say it correctly, that I'm a king. I was born and came into the world for this reason, to testify to the truth. Everyone who's on the side of truth listens to me."

Pilate replied, "What is truth?"

Pilate called together the chief priests and other leaders and told them, "You brought me this man as one who has turned the people from allegiance to Caesar. Look, I've examined him in your presence and haven't found any guilt in him as you've charged. Neither has Herod because he sent him back to us. He's done nothing to deserve the death penalty. So I'll have him flogged and let him go."

క్ర

Now it was the governor's custom to release to the crowd any prisoner they wanted around the time of the Passover Festival. And the crowd was asking Pilate to do that. So he told the Jewish leaders, "I find no guilt in him, and you do have a custom that I release someone to you every year at Passover. Do you want me to release 'the king of the Jews'?"

The leaders replied, "No, not him. Give us Barabbas" (a notorious thief and freedom fighter who was in prison with the rebels who had killed people in an anti-Roman uprising).

But Pilate, knowing the religious leaders had handed Jesus over to him out of envy, asked the crowd, "Which one do you want me to release: Barabbas or Jesus, the king of the Jews, who's called the Messiah?"

The chief priests and the elders had stirred up the crowd and persuaded them to ask for Barabbas' freedom and Jesus' execution. So when Pilate asked them, "Which of the two do you want me to release for you?" all together the crowd cried out, "Away with him! Release Barabbas to us!"

Then Pilate asked, "What shall I do then with this man you call the king of the Jews—Jesus, who's called the Messiah?"

They all shouted, "Crucify him!"

But Pilate, wanting to release Jesus, appealed to them again, "Why? What crime has he committed?"

But they kept shouting even louder, "Crucify him! Crucify him!"

Pilate called out to them a third time: "Why? What crime has this man committed? I've found no guilt in him to justify the death penalty. So I'm going to have him flogged and then release him."

But they were insistent, demanding with loud shouts that he be crucified. And their shouts prevailed.

When Pilate saw he was getting nowhere, and a riot was starting to break out, he took water and washed his hands in front of the crowd and said, "I'm innocent of this man's blood. The responsibility is yours!"

All the people called out, "Let his blood be on us and on our children!" They were willing to take full responsibility. Desiring to satisfy the crowd, he released Barabbas to the crowd and Jesus to the guard to be flogged.

The soldiers dragged Jesus away and stripped his clothes off him to further humiliate him. They scourged him with a leather whip with lead weights on the end, hitting him over and over. The metal ripped into his skin, tearing it to pieces. The pain shot through him, searing him to the core. He gritted his teeth, calling out silently to his Father for the endurance to bear the pain—to bear the humiliation of his nakedness in front of the mocking soldiers. After they'd finished whipping him, they dragged him upright, put his clothes back on, and brought him back to Pilate.

Pilate himself grimaced when he saw his bloodied body and again went out to the Jewish leaders and said, "Look, I'm bringing him out to you so that you'll truly understand I find no guilt in him." Shoving Jesus in front of them, he said, "Behold, the man!"

When the chief priests and their officers saw him, they shouted, "Crucify him! Crucify him!"

But Pilate told them, "You take him and crucify him. As for me, I find no guilt in him."

The Jewish leaders persisted, "We have a law, and according to it he must die because he claimed to be the Son of God." For the law of Moses required that anyone who blasphemed be stoned to death.[60] When Pilate heard this, he was even more afraid. As a Roman official, he had the responsibility of keeping peace and eliminating any threat to Caesar's rule.

He asked Jesus, "Where do you come from?"

But Jesus didn't answer him.

Pilate asked, "Are you refusing to speak to me? Don't you know I have the power to free you or to crucify you?"

Jesus answered, "You'd have no power over me unless it was given to you from above. So the one who handed me over to you is guilty of greater sin than you are."

As a result of this, Pilate tried to release him, but the Jewish leaders kept shouting, "If you release this man, you're no friend of Caesar. Anyone who claims to be a king opposes Caesar."

When he heard those words, Pilate took Jesus out to the place where judgments were pronounced. There he sat on the judgment seat and proclaimed to the Jewish leaders, "Behold your king!"

But they shouted back, "Away with him! Away with him. Crucify him!"

Pilate asked, "What! You want me to crucify your king?"

The chief priests answered, "We have no king but Caesar."

So Pilate handed him over to the Roman soldiers to do the people's will and crucify him. Pilate did all this, despite the message his wife sent him while he was sitting on the judge's seat: "Don't have anything to do with that righteous man. Today, I suffered a great deal in a dream because of him."

Then Pilate's soldiers took Jesus back into the Praetorium and gathered the detachment around him. The soldiers stripped him and put a purple robe on him. Then after twisting together a crown of thorns, they jammed it on his head. The thorns pierced his scalp, and blood started trickling down his face into his eyes. They put a reed staff in his right hand, knelt before him, and mocked him—saluting and saying, "Hail, king of the Jews!" They spit on him and took the staff and beat him on the head with it, while continuing to kneel and bow before him. The blood and spit mixed with his own tears, burning his eyes, fulfilling the words of the prophet Isaiah:

> I gave my back to those who beat me and my cheeks to
> those who plucked out my beard.
> I didn't hide my face from insults and spitting,
> for the Lord God helps me.
> Therefore
> I will not be disgraced.
> I have set my face like a stone, like flint,
> for I will not be put to shame.[61]

All this happened to fulfill Jesus' prophecy about the kind of death he was going to die. For he had said he would be "handed over to the Gentiles to be mocked, spit upon, flogged, and crucified."

After they mocked him, they took the purple robe off him and put his own clothes back on. Then they led him away to crucify him.

Pilate had a notice of the charge against him posted above his head on the cross. It read: JESUS OF NAZARETH, THE KING OF THE JEWS.

The chief priests of the Jews protested, saying to Pilate, "Don't write 'The King of the Jews' but write that he said, 'I am King of the Jews.'"

Pilate answered, "What I've written, I've written."

Judas, who betrayed Jesus, stood at a distance, watching what was happening. When he saw that Jesus had been condemned to death, he was filled with remorse. He returned the thirty pieces of silver to the chief priests and the elders and said, "I've sinned by betraying innocent blood."

They replied, "Who cares? That's your concern."

So Judas threw the money into the temple sanctuary and left. Inconsolable and unable to bear the shame of his sin, he went to a potter's field and hanged himself.

Later, the chief priests heard what happened—that his body, after rotting, had fallen headfirst, burst open, and all his intestines had spilled out. They took the thirty pieces of silver and said to each other, "Since this is blood money, it's not lawful to put this into the treasury." So they conferred together and used it to buy the potter's field as a burial place for strangers. That's why to this day it's been called the Field of Blood. This fulfilled what the prophet Jeremiah spoke: "And they took the thirty pieces of silver, the price of the one whose price had been set by the sons of Israel, and they gave them for the potter's field, as the Lord directed me."[62]

Chapter 15

Crucifixion and Burial

A round 8:00 a.m. they took Jesus out to a place then referred to as Golgotha. But first the soldiers dragged Jesus to the Antonia Fortress where they stripped off his clothes, only adding further to his public humiliation. They laid the heavy wooden crossbeam upon which he'd be crucified onto his shoulders. Then they offered him wine mixed with gall and myrrh. But after tasting it, he didn't drink it. He knew the pain would be unbearable. This mixture may have dulled the pain a bit, but he would rely on his Father to sustain him.

He was forced to carry the cross down the streets of Jerusalem like a common criminal. By then it was full daylight, and everyone could see his shame. Weakened from the scourging and lack of sleep and buckling under the hundred-pound weight of the cross, Jesus fell to his knees several times. When he could no longer get up, they took the cross off him and made a passerby coming in from the country—Simon, a man from Cyrene, the father of Alexander and Rufus—carry it behind Jesus. Two other criminals were also being led away to be executed.

The same crowd who had worshiped Jesus with praises and palm branches when he arrived in Jerusalem now threw insults at him as they followed behind him. The few friendly faces he saw registered shock and despair at his condition, including the women mourning and crying for him. He turned and said to them, "Daughters of Jerusalem, don't weep for me. Weep for yourselves and your children. The time will come when you'll say, 'Blessed are the barren women, the wombs that never bore and the breasts that never nursed!' Then they'll say to the mountains, 'Fall on us,' and to the hills, 'Cover us!' If they do these kinds of things when the tree is alive, what will happen when it's dead?"

At Golgotha they took the cross from Simon of Cyrene's shoulders and laid it on the ground. Then they tied Jesus' arms to it. He couldn't bear to look as he saw a soldier coming with a hammer in hand and large iron spikes. He tried not to cry out as they pounded them into each of his hands and into his feet. It was an excruciating pain, but it became even worse when they lifted the cross and set it upright. He could barely catch his breath, and the nails further pierced his hands when he tried to lift himself to take a breath. He cried out to his Father silently for strength to endure the hours ahead. He was in agony from the physical pain, and the emotional torture was just as unbearable. How could the Jewish people—the very people he came to save—turn on him like this?

Two criminals were crucified with him, one on his right and one on his left, fulfilling the Scripture that says, "He was numbered with lawbreakers."[63]

After the soldiers crucified him, they took his outer garments and divided them into four shares, one for each of them. This left the seamless one-piece tunic, which was woven from top to bottom. They said to one another, "Let's not tear it but cast lots to decide who will get it." Little did they know, they did this to fulfill the Scripture: "They divided my outer garments among them and cast lots for my clothing."[64] Then they sat down and kept watch over him.

Jesus looked their way and said, "Father, forgive them, for they don't know what they are doing."

Then he looked at the crowd and saw four women watching and weeping:

his mother Mary,

Salome (her sister, the mother of James and John, the sons of Zebedee),

another Mary (sister of Cleopas, mother of his cousins James and Joseph), and Mary Magdalene.

These women had supported him during his entire ministry. They would not lose their reward.

When Jesus saw his mother and the disciple whom he loved standing nearby, he said to her, "Dear woman, here's your son," and to the disciple, "Here's your mother." From then on, John took her into his home.

The place where Jesus was crucified was near the city. Anyone who passed by could read Pilate's notice of the charges against Jesus because it was written in Hebrew (the language of the Jews), Latin (the language of Rome), and Greek (the international language). They stood watching and showed contempt for him. Some shook their heads and said, "You who would destroy the temple and build it in three days! Save yourself! If you're the Son of God, come down from the cross."

The chief priests, scribes, and elders stood by themselves and mocked him in the same way, saying to each other: "He saved others, but he can't even save himself!

"He's the king of Israel? Let this self-appointed Messiah of God, the so-called Chosen One, this pretend king of Israel, come down from the cross now so that we may see and believe in him.

"He trusts in God? Let God rescue him now if he delights in him, for he claimed, 'I am the Son of God.'"

The soldiers also mocked him by coming up to him and offering a common worker's drink, wine that had gone sour. And they said, "If you're the king of the Jews, save yourself!"

At first, the two criminals who were crucified with him hung there and mocked and insulted him in the same way. One of the criminals said, "Some Christ! Save yourself and us!"

But then the other rebuked him: "Don't you fear God since you're under the same death sentence? We're suffering justly. We're getting what we deserve for what we did, but this man has done nothing wrong." Then he said, "Jesus, remember me when you come into your kingdom."

Jesus told him, "I'm telling you the truth—today you will be with me in paradise."

Then the sun's light failed, and darkness fell over all the land from about noon until three o'clock. Suddenly, Jesus felt a dark void overtake him as his Father's comforting presence was withdrawn from him. The weight of the world's sins was laid upon him. The pain of the cross was excruciating, but this spiritual darkness was pure agony. He was truly alone, and for the first time, he understood how lost people felt without God. He panicked, struggling to catch his breath, but only causing the nails to drive deeper into his skin. Never having experienced this separation from his Father before, he cried out the words King David had written in Psalm 22 over a thousand years earlier: "Eli, Eli, lema sabachthani?" meaning, "My God, my God, why have you forsaken me?"

Some who were standing there thought he had cried out, "Eliyahu, Eliyahu," the Hebrew name of the prophet Elijah. They said, "Listen, he's calling Elijah." Immediately one of them ran and got a sponge, filled it with wine vinegar, put it on a stick, and offered it to Jesus to drink.

But the rest said, "Leave him alone. Let's see if Elijah will come to take him down and save him."

Later, knowing everything had been accomplished and to fulfill the Scripture, Jesus said, "I'm thirsty."[65]

A jar full of wine vinegar was still there, so the soldiers soaked a sponge in it, put it on a hyssop stalk, and held it to his lips, fulfilling the Scripture. When he'd received it, he said, "It is finished."

❧

At 3:00 p.m. Jesus cried out in a loud voice, "Father, into your hands I commit my spirit." Then he bowed his head, breathed his last, and he gave up his spirit.

Right at that moment, a half mile away in the temple, the sixty-foot-high, four-inch-thick curtain separating the Holy Place from the Holy of Holies was torn in two from top to bottom. The earth shook, and rocks split apart. Tombs broke open, and the bodies of many saints who had died were raised to life. After Jesus' resurrection they came out of the tombs and went into the holy city of Jerusalem and appeared to many people. When those with him who were keeping guard saw how he died and the earthquake and all that happened, they were terrified.

The centurion standing right in front of Jesus praised God and said, "Surely this man was innocent. Truly he was the Son of God!"

When all the crowd that had gathered to witness the spectacle saw what took place, they returned home beating their breasts in grief and shame.

At the end, all those who knew him, including the four women who had been standing close and the women who had followed him from Galilee and ministered to him, stood watching these things from a distance. And many other women who had come up with him to Jerusalem were there too.

Meanwhile, the Jewish leaders were arriving at Pilate's headquarters, unaware that Jesus had already died. After asking to see the governor, they were ushered inside.

"Can we make one more of request of you?" they asked Pilate.

"Haven't you done enough?" Pilate responded, fuming. He'd already gone against his conscience and condemned an innocent man to death.

One of them stepped forward to speak for the group. "Your excellency, tonight at sundown, we celebrate the first night of the Jewish Passover, an exceptionally holy day for us."

"I'm aware," Pilate said impatiently. "So?"

The man continued, "At sundown it will be the Sabbath, the day when we are unable to work. For this reason, today is the day we do any work required to prepare for a day of no work tomorrow. And Jewish law requires that when a person has been put to death by "hanging on a tree," they are to be buried that same day.[66] So we need those three men to die today, so we can bury them today. Can you have soldiers break their legs to speed up their deaths. That way the bodies can be taken down from the crosses and buried before sundown." They knew that crucified people with broken legs suffocated quickly because they were unable to push up so they could breathe.

Pilate saw no reason not to grant the request. Why should Jesus suffer longer than necessary? "It will be done," he said and dismissed them.

So soldiers came and broke the legs of the two men who had been crucified with Jesus. But when they came to Jesus and saw he was already dead, they didn't break his legs. Instead, one of the soldiers pierced Jesus' side with a spear, and immediately blood and water flowed out.

These things happened to fulfill the Scripture: "Not one of his bones will be broken," and, "They will look on the one they have pierced."[67] John saw all this happen and wrote an account of it so that all may believe.

ℝ

There was a rich man, Joseph from Arimathea, who was both a prominent member of the Sanhedrin and a secret disciple of Jesus. He was waiting for the kingdom of God as Jesus described it, but he feared the Jewish leaders. Being a good and upright man, he hadn't consented to the council's plan and to what they'd done. So on this Friday evening on the day of preparation, despite his fear, he went boldly to Pilate and asked if he could take away the body of Jesus.

But Pilate wasn't sure if Jesus was already dead, so he summoned a centurion and asked him if Jesus had already died. Upon confirming his death, he ordered that the body be given to Joseph, and he gave him permission to bury Jesus.

So Joseph went to Golgotha and took down Jesus' body from the cross. Nicodemus, who had first come to Jesus secretly at night, also went, taking about seventy-five pounds of spices (aloes mixed with myrrh). They took the body and bound it in accordance with Jewish burial customs, putting the spices around the body in clean, fine-linen wrappings. Then they took it to a garden near where he was crucified, where Joseph had his own new tomb—one that he'd ordered cut out of rock, and in which no one had ever been laid. Because the tomb was nearby, and the Sabbath was about to begin, they laid Jesus there. Then they rolled a big stone across its entrance and left.

The women who'd accompanied Jesus from Galilee, including Mary Magdalene and Mary, the mother of Joseph, stayed behind, sitting there opposite the tomb. They'd followed Joseph and Nicodemus and had seen the tomb and how his body was placed in it. Then they returned home to prepare fragrant spices and perfumed anointing oils for Jesus' body before they rested on the Sabbath in obedience to the commandment.

Later that same day, the chief priests and the Pharisees gathered before Pilate once again and said, "Sir, we remembered that while he was still alive the deceiver said, 'After three days I will rise.' So give an order that the tomb be made secure until the third day. Otherwise, his disciples may come and steal his body and tell the people he's risen from the dead. This last deception will be worse than the first."

Pilate answered, "You have a guard. Go make the tomb as secure as you know how." So they went and secured the tomb by posting a guard and putting a seal on the stone.

Chapter 16

Resurrection Day and After

Early on Sunday morning, when it was still dark, Jesus' mother Mary and Mary Magdalene headed to the tomb with fragrant spices to anoint Jesus' body. When they arrived at the gravesite, Mary Magdalene asked, "Who will roll the stone from the entrance of the tomb?"

But suddenly there was a violent earthquake. An angel of the Lord descended from heaven, rolled back the stone, and sat on it. His appearance was like lightning, and his clothes were white as snow. The guards shook with fear and became like dead men.

When the women saw that the stone, which was quite large, had been rolled away from the entrance, they entered the tomb. But they couldn't find the body. Suddenly two men in dazzling white garments stood beside them. The women were terrified and bowed down with their faces to the ground. The men asked, "Why do you look for the living among the dead? He's not here. He has risen! It happened just as he told you back in Galilee: 'The Son of Man must be delivered into the hands of sinful men, be crucified, and rise again on the third day.'" And the women remembered Jesus' words.

One of the angels had gone to sit on the right side and, sensing their fear, said, "Don't be alarmed. You're looking for Jesus the Nazarene, who was crucified. He's not here. He's been raised, just as he said. Come and see the place where he was lying." He took them to the spot and said, "Look, here's where they laid him. Go quickly and tell his disciples, and especially Peter, that Jesus has been raised from the dead and is going ahead of you into Galilee. You'll see him there."

Elated, the women quickly fled from the tomb and ran to tell Jesus' eleven apostles. They said nothing to anyone on the way because they were still afraid.

About that time, Peter was pacing around the courtyard of the house the apostles were staying at in Jerusalem. After what happened to Jesus, they wanted to remain there so they could visit his tomb. Peter wasn't sure where they'd go after that, what they'd do, or even if he'd be included as a believer after the way he'd denied even knowing Jesus. Would he ever be forgiven? He remembered how Jesus had called him a rock. Right now, he felt like a pebble. Maybe he could go back to fishing?

Andrew called out to him, "Join us inside. After all the lessons Jesus gave you about forgiving people, you must know he'll forgive you too. Didn't we all run when he was arrested? None of us is without guilt."

Just as Peter was heading into the main room, Mary Magdalene burst inside and ran up to him and John.

Frantic, she said, "They've taken the Lord out of the tomb, and we don't know where they've laid him!"

"What? This is unbelievable!" they said. Her words seemed like nonsense. But Peter and John got up anyway and ran to the tomb, followed by Mary Magdalene. At first the men ran together, but John outran Peter and reached the tomb first. He stooped down, looked in, and saw the strips of linen lying there but didn't go in. Then Peter arrived. He stooped down and went into the tomb and saw the linen wrappings lying by themselves. The facecloth that had been on Jesus' head was not lying with the wrappings; it was rolled up by itself. And he left, wondering what had happened. Then John went inside too. He saw and believed. But regardless of this, neither one realized yet that the Scriptures said Jesus had to rise from the dead. Then they went home.

Mary remained standing outside the tomb, crying. As she wept, she stooped down and looked into the tomb. She saw the two angels in white sitting where Jesus' body had been laid, one at the head and the other at the foot. They asked her, "Why are you crying?"

She replied, "They've taken my Lord away, and I don't know where they've put him."

Then she turned around and saw a man standing behind her, but she didn't recognize him. He asked her, "Why are you crying? Who are you looking for?"

Thinking he was the gardener, she said, "Sir, if you've carried him away, tell me where you've put him, and I'll take him."

"Mary!" Jesus said, revealing himself. She was the first one he appeared to after his resurrection.

She turned toward him and cried, "Rabboni!" (which is Jewish for "teacher"). Then she hugged him and couldn't let go.

Jesus said, "Stop clinging to me! I haven't yet gone up to the Father. Go to my brothers and tell them I'm going up to my Father and your Father, to my God and your God." And he left.

ᕤ

Meanwhile, the other women who had run from the tomb were on the way back to see the apostles. Suddenly Jesus appeared before them and greeted them.

They went up to him, took hold of his feet, and worshiped him in fear and wonder.

Then he said, "Don't be afraid. Go and take word to my followers to go to Galilee, and I'll meet you there."

Later, Mary Magdalene and Joanna, along with Mary the mother of James, and the other women with them told these things to the apostles and all the others who were mourning and weeping with Peter.

Mary Magdalene announced, "I've seen the Lord!" And she told them the things he'd said to her.

When they heard Jesus was alive and she'd seen him, they still didn't believe it.

While the women were going to the disciples, some of the guards went into the city and reported to the chief priests all that had happened. After they'd met with the elders and formed a plan, the elders gave the soldiers a large sum of money and told them, "Say that his disciples came during the night and stole his body while you were asleep.

If the governor hears this, we'll convince him not to blame you and keep you out of trouble." So the soldiers took the money and did as they were instructed. And this story was commonly told among the Jews everywhere at that time and is even believed by many people today.

∽

Now that same day, two of the disciples were going to a village called Emmaus, about seven miles from Jerusalem. They were talking to each other about everything that had happened. While they were discussing these things, Jesus himself came up and walked along with them. But they were prevented from recognizing him.

Post-Resurrection Appearances

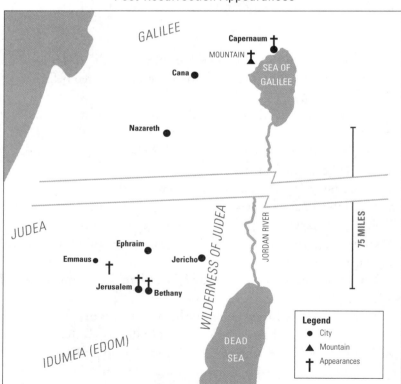

He asked them, "What are you talking about as you walk?"

They stopped, dejected with downcast faces. One of them, named Cleopas, replied, "Are you the only visitor to Jerusalem who doesn't know the things that recently happened there?"

"What things?" he asked.

They replied, "The things about Jesus of Nazareth, who was a prophet, mighty in deed and word before God and all the people— how the chief priests and our rulers handed him over to be condemned to death, and they crucified him. But we'd hoped he was the one who was about to redeem Israel. And now it's the third day since these things happened. Then some of the women of our group told

Post-Resurrection Appearances[a]

Date, Est. Time	Location – *Significant Event*	Days after Resurrection
Sun., 4/29/31 Daybreak	Jerusalem, tomb – *Appeared to Mary Magdalene, appeared to Jesus' mother Mary and several women*	0
Afternoon	Road from Jerusalem to Emmaus – *Appeared to Cleopas and one other disciple*	0
Afternoon?	Jerusalem – *Appeared to Peter*[b]	0
Evening	Jerusalem – *Appeared to eleven disciples when they were eating, reassured Peter*	0
Mon., 5/7/31	Jerusalem – *In the house, appeared to the eleven and Thomas*	8
???	Jerusalem – *Appeared to James (his half brother)*[c]	?
???	Location unknown – *Appeared to more than five hundred people at one time*[d]	?
???	By the Sea of Galilee – *Appeared to seven disciples – Brought about a miraculous catch of fish*	?
???	Mountain Jesus designated – *Appeared to the eleven disciples – Issued the Great Commission*	?
Thur., 6/7/31 Fri., 6/8/31	Jerusalem – *Promised baptism with the Holy Spirit* Bethany – *Ascended to heaven*	40

a Acts 1:3 says that during the forty days before he ascended Jesus appeared to the disciples and gave "many proofs" that he was alive. We only list the few appearances recorded in the Bible. Appearances not recorded in the four Gospels are footnoted.

b See 1 Corinthians 15:5.

c See 1 Corinthians 15:6.

d See 1 Corinthians 15:7.

us an incredible story. They were at the tomb early this morning and couldn't find his body! They came and told us they'd seen a vision of angels who said he was alive! Then some who were with us went to the tomb and found it exactly as the women said, but they didn't see him."

He said to them, "How foolish you are, how slow of heart to believe all the prophets have spoken! Wasn't it necessary for the Messiah to suffer these things and then enter his glory?" Then, beginning with Moses, and from all the prophets' writings, he explained to them the passages about himself in all the Scriptures.

As they approached the village where they were going, Jesus acted as if he were going farther. But they urged him, "Stay with us. It's almost evening."

So he went in to stay with them. When he was eating with them, he took the bread, blessed it, broke it, and gave it to them. Then their eyes were opened, and they recognized him. But he immediately vanished from their sight. They asked each other, "Weren't our hearts burning within us while he talked with us on the road and opened the Scriptures to us?"

At that same hour, they got up and returned to Jerusalem to find the apostles and others with them. Then they told them what had happened on their trip, how they recognized Jesus when he broke the bread.

❧

That evening the apostles gathered to discuss the reports of how Jesus had appeared to people after his death. Peter said, "I have no idea why he appeared to me and not the rest of you. I turned around and there he was. He just looked at me with those see-into-your-soul eyes of his," Peter explained.

"And what did you see in those eyes?" Matthew prodded. "Anger? Disappointment? Sorrow?"

"Love," Peter answered. "I saw love."

"I don't get it," Philip lamented. "He appears to the women, the disciples going to Emmaus, and Peter but not to us. Why?"

Right then, Jesus himself suddenly appeared—startling, even terrifying them. At first, they thought they were seeing a ghost because, fearing the Jewish leaders, they'd locked the doors.

Jesus said, "Peace be with you!" Then he asked them, "Why are you troubled, and why are your hearts filled with such doubts?"

Then he showed them his hands, feet, and his pierced side, and said, "Look at my hands and my feet. It's really me. Touch me and see. A ghost doesn't have flesh and bones like I do."

After seeing the Lord, the disciples were amazed and filled with joy. They couldn't believe it!

So he asked them, "Do you have anything here to eat?" They gave him a piece of broiled fish, and he ate it in front of them.

Then he told them, "This is what I told you would happen while I was still with you—that everything written about me in the law of Moses, the Prophets, and the Psalms must be fulfilled." Then he opened their minds, so they could understand the Scriptures, telling them, "This is what's written: The Messiah was to suffer and rise from the dead on the third day, and that forgiveness of sins for all who repent is to be proclaimed in his name to all nations, beginning in Jerusalem. You are witnesses to these things. Now, just as the Father sent me, I'm sending you." Then he breathed on them and said, "Receive the Holy Spirit. If you forgive the sins of anyone, they're forgiven. If you don't forgive them, they are not forgiven."

Later when Thomas (nicknamed "The Twin") returned from a trip, John said to him, "We've seen the Lord!" Thomas had been away when Jesus appeared to them.

Thomas was doubtful. "Unless I see the nail marks in his hands and put my finger where the nails were and put my hand into the wound on his side, I won't believe it."

☙

Eight days later the disciples were together in the house, and this time Thomas was with them. Though the doors were locked again, Jesus appeared and said, "Peace be with you!" Then he motioned to the nail marks in his hands and said to Thomas, "Look at my hands.

Put your finger here. Reach out and put your hand into my side. Don't be unbelieving but believe!"

Thomas exclaimed, "My Lord and my God!"

Then Jesus told him, "You've believed because you've seen me. Blessed are those who haven't seen and yet have believed."

Jesus presented himself alive to them and his half-brother James by many convincing proofs, appearing to them during forty days, speaking about the kingdom of God. One time, according to the apostle Paul, he appeared to more than five hundred believers.[68]

☙

Several days after Jesus' first appearances, Peter, Thomas, Nathanael, James and John (the sons of Zebedee), and two other disciples were together near the Sea of Galilee.

Peter told them, "I'm going fishing," and headed toward the fishing boats at the shore. He was glad for some time alone after all that had happened. As he reached the boat, he looked out over the calm sea. He felt more a sense of peace in this familiar place doing this familiar task than he had since Jesus was arrested. How could he have betrayed him that way! He still couldn't get over the shame. He was thrilled Jesus had risen from the dead, but when he saw him, he couldn't get past his sense of unworthiness to be called his disciple. Maybe it was for the best he returned to fishing. He started to push the boat away from shore when he heard the others behind him.

"We'll go with you," they said and got into the boat with him. But that night they caught nothing.

At daybreak, Peter saw a man standing on the shore about a hundred yards away. None of them recognized him from that distance. The man called out, "Men, do you have any fish?"

"No," they yelled back.

He shouted, "Throw your net on the right side of the boat, and you'll find some." So they cast the net there and were unable to haul it in because there were so many fish.

Then John, the disciple whom Jesus loved so much, said to Peter, "It's the Lord!"

When Peter realized it was Jesus, he wrapped his fisherman's cloak around his nakedness and jumped into the water. Peter couldn't help but remember the first time he met Jesus in the same set of circumstances. He had come full circle.

When they landed, they saw some bread and a charcoal fire with fish on it.

Jesus invited them, "Bring some of the fish you've just caught."

Peter went aboard and dragged the net to the shore. It was full of more than 150 fish! Even though there were so many, the net hadn't torn.

Jesus called them, "Come on, let's have breakfast."

Though they wanted to, none of the disciples dared ask, "Is it really you?" They knew it was.

Jesus came to them, took the bread, and gave it to them, and he did the same with the fish. The disciples were talking nonstop about how Jesus was raised from the dead and the miraculous catch of fish, but Peter remained silent. He didn't dare say anything because of embarrassment. How could he have been so weak to fall into temptation when Jesus even warned him ahead of time?

After they'd eaten, he got up to go off by himself, but Jesus started walking down the beach next to him. He asked, "Simon, son of John, do you love me more than these?" He motioned toward the other apostles.

At first, Peter wasn't sure how to answer. He thought he had loved Jesus more than his own life, but when he was tested, he had failed. He looked down, thinking. Then, once it was settled in his mind, he responded, "Yes, Lord, you know that I love you."

Then Jesus told him, "Feed my lambs." And then Jesus asked him again, "Simon, son of John, do you love me?"

He answered, "Yes, Lord, you know that I love you."

And Jesus told him, "Take care of my sheep."

Then he asked a third time, "Simon, son of John, do you love me?"

Peter was hurt because Jesus asked him this a third time, but then he realized he was allowing him to say he loved him one time for every time he'd denied him. He sighed deeply, finally feeling forgiven and released from his shame. He smiled and said, "Lord, you know all things. You know that I love you!" And this time he was saying it with all his heart.

Jesus told him, "Feed my sheep. I'm telling you the truth: When you were younger, you dressed yourself and went wherever you wanted, but when you're old, you'll stretch out your hands and someone else will dress you and take you where you don't want to go." Jesus said this to indicate the kind of death by which Peter would glorify God.*

Last of all, Jesus told Peter, "Follow me."

Peter was relieved to know Jesus hadn't rejected him as his disciple. He could still serve his Lord! Even knowing how he'd die, somehow he also knew this time he'd be up to the task. Then he turned around and saw that John, the disciple Jesus loved so much, was following them. Peter asked, "Lord, what's going to happen to him?"

Jesus answered, "If I want him to live until I return, what's that to you? You need to follow me."

Consequently, a rumor spread among the believers that John would never die. But Jesus didn't say he'd never die. He only said, "If I want him to live until I return, what's that to you?"

❧

Then the eleven disciples went to Galilee, to the mountain Jesus had designated. They worshiped him when they saw him, but some still had doubts. Then Jesus came to them and said, "All authority in heaven and on earth has been given to me. Go therefore and make disciples of all nations, baptizing them in the name of the Father and of the Son and of the Holy Spirit, teaching them to observe everything I've commanded you."

❧

On their last day with him, they were together in Jerusalem. Jesus instructed them, "Don't leave this city, but wait for the Father's

---

* While there are several theories as to how Peter died, the most believed is probably that of Roman Catholic tradition: Peter was crucified in Rome and buried there in about AD 64 as part of Nero's persecution of Christians.

promise, which I told you about. John baptized you with water, but you'll soon be baptized with the Holy Spirit—clothed with power from on high."

They asked him, "Lord, at this time are you restoring the kingdom of Israel?"

He replied, "It's not for you to know the times or seasons the Father has set by his own authority. But you will receive power when the Holy Spirit comes upon you, and you will be my witnesses in Jerusalem, Judea, Samaria, and to the ends of the earth."

Then Jesus led them to Bethany, lifted his hands, and blessed them. While he was blessing them, he left them and was taken up into heaven. They worshiped him as he rose upward until he disappeared from sight. As they were staring into the sky as he was going, suddenly two men dressed in white robes stood beside them. "Men of Galilee," they said, "why are you standing here looking in the sky? This Jesus, who has been taken up from you into heaven, will come back in the same way you watched him go into heaven." They returned to Jerusalem with great joy, staying continually at the temple, praising God.

So the words of Isaiah written more than seven hundred years ago had been fulfilled:

> He was pierced because of our transgressions;
> he was crushed for our iniquities;
> the punishment that brought our peace was on him, and
> by his wounds we are healed.

> All of us have wandered like sheep.
> Each one has turned to their own way, and
> the LORD has laid on him the iniquity of us all.

> He was oppressed and afflicted,
> but he didn't open his mouth.
>   Like a lamb led to the slaughter,
>   like a sheep before its shearers is silent,
> he didn't open his mouth.

He was taken away by oppression and judgment.
Who among his generation cared
    that he was cut off from the land of the living,
    that he was stricken because of my people's transgression?
He was assigned a grave among the wicked,
    but he laid with the rich after his death,
    because
        he had done no violence, and
        no deceit was in his mouth.
But though the Lord determined to crush him, causing him
    to suffer,
    he made his life an offering for guilt.
Because of this,
        he will see his descendants,
        he will prolong his days, and
        the will of the Lord will be accomplished through
            him.
Because of the anguish of his soul,
    he will see light and be satisfied.
By his knowledge the Righteous One, my Servant, will
    justify many,
and he will bear their iniquities.
Therefore
    I will give him a portion among the great,
    and he will divide the spoil with the strong,
    because he
        abandoned his life to death,
        was numbered with the transgressors,
        carried the sins of many, and interceded for the
            transgressors.[69]

Epilogue

This ends the account of Jesus' life as told by men who walked with him for more than a thousand days and as commented upon by several others whose writings are considered authoritative by the Christian church. These four men, and many others who walked with Jesus, suffered the consequences of standing for him as Lord in a time when those who ruled the nations embraced other gods. Many of them died difficult deaths.

The apostle John attested to the truth of his writing this way: "I am the disciple who declares these things are true and who wrote them down. We know that the things he said are true." They have been "recorded so that you may believe that Jesus is the Messiah, the Son of God, and that by believing, you may have life in his name."

Jesus' life and its meaning for human beings can be summed up in the words of the last apostle, a man called Paul. He was a leading Pharisee who persecuted Christians after Jesus' death but who then met the resurrected Jesus, repented, and chose to follow him. He wrote:

> Jesus, although existing in the very nature of God, did not consider equality with God something to be held on to. Rather, he emptied himself, taking the very nature of a servant, being made in human likeness, and being found in appearance as a man; he humbled himself. Therefore God exalted him to the highest place and gave him the name that is above every name so that at the name of Jesus every knee should bow, in heaven and on earth and under the earth, and every tongue confess that Jesus Christ is Lord—to the

glory of God the Father.[70] He died for all so that those who live might no longer live for themselves but for him who died and rose again for their sake.[71]

Jesus' life (what he said and what he did), his death and resurrection, and his purpose for coming to earth can be summed up this way:

Jesus, both God's son and God himself, created all things. Due to man's sin and the break in fellowship it brought between God and humanity, he emptied himself of all that made him equal to God the Father, and he came to earth in human form—in the flesh, to reconcile human beings to his Father.

Jesus led a perfect life on earth, spreading the good news that people can find forgiveness for their sin if they believe in him. He proved that he was God by the miracles he performed, and by coming back from the dead and appearing to over five hundred people (many of whom gave up their lives to spread the truth about his life).

Because he lived a sinless life, he was able to offer himself to his Father as a pure, spotless sacrifice on behalf of every person on earth. When he was on the cross, he took upon himself every person's sin, sin which caused God the Father to withdraw his presence from him (for God cannot have fellowship with sin). Jesus, in agony, experiencing separation from his Father for the first time, cried out, "My God, my God, why have you forsaken me?" God the Father accepted his sacrifice as atonement for the sins of all people and raised Jesus up to sit at his right hand, the side of honor, to reign forever and ever. And he appointed him to judge the living and the dead.

The Christian church sums it up in the Apostles' Creed:*

I believe in God,
>   the Father Almighty,
>   Creator of Heaven and earth;
>   and in Jesus Christ, His only Son Our Lord,
> Who was conceived by the Holy Spirit,
>   born of the virgin Mary,
>   suffered under Pontius Pilate,
>   was crucified, died, and was buried.
> He descended into Hell.
>   The third day He rose again from the dead;
> He ascended into Heaven,
>   and sits at the right hand of God, the Father almighty.
>   From there He shall come to judge the living and the
>   dead.
> I believe in the Holy Spirit,
>   the holy catholic church**
>   the communion of saints,
>   the forgiveness of sins,
>   the resurrection of the body
>   and life everlasting.
> Amen.

---

* "Creed": a statement of belief in which one has trust; from the Latin *credo*, which translates as "I believe and trust."

** "Catholic": the transliteration of the Latin word *catholicus*, which means "universal." The earliest known record of the term "catholic church" is in Ignatius of Antioch's *Letter to the Smyrneans*, written about AD 107. It refers to the universal church, all believers throughout the world, as opposed to a local church congregation.

Invitation to Respond

Jesus said, "This is the will of my Father, that everyone who looks on the Son and believes in him should have eternal life, and I will raise them up on the last day." Believing means to believe not only that he exists but also that what he says is true. Believing leads to accepting him as Lord and Savior and doing what he says. The alternative is to not believe, to experience the alternative to eternal life, to die in your sins and experience death in the worst way.

God says in the book of Romans, "There is no one who is righteous, not even one person." We all need a Savior to pay the price for our sins, so we are "not guilty" before God. That Savior is Jesus. And his offer is forgiveness to all who repent and believe.

To "repent" means

1. to change your attitude toward God and sin, to move from putting yourself first to putting God first by respecting him as your master, and

2. to turn from sin: to change your conduct, thoughts, and actions from self-centeredness and rebellion against God to God-centered cooperation with his work and obedience to his will.

To believe means to put complete trust in what God and his Son, Jesus, have said and done (as revealed by Scripture) and in what they do today.

What's amazing is that salvation is offered as a gift. The Bible says our salvation is by grace (i.e., undeserved favor) "through faith, and this is not from yourselves; it is the gift of God, not the result of any good works."

Jesus paid the price for our sins and offers us salvation as a gift if we will turn to him and believe. Will you accept Jesus' offer of forgiveness for your sins? Will you believe he died to save you and give you the promise of eternal life with God? Make your decision now and express your belief and commitment to God by saying a prayer like this:

God,

I believe that Jesus Christ is the Son of God who died to pay the price for my sins. I believe he was buried and three days later was raised from the dead. I repent, call upon God for forgiveness, and accept Jesus Christ today as my Lord and Savior, recognizing that you accept his sacrifice on my behalf for the forgiveness of all my sins.

If you have prayed this prayer, take an extra moment and recite the Apostles' Creed above as a believer.

We hope you will follow through in your new faith by attending a Bible-believing church, reading the Bible, praying, and serving him for the rest of your life. And don't forget to tell others about your faith.

Appendix

When Did Jesus Live?

Because of the difficulty and lack of agreement about the dating of events that occurred almost two thousand years ago, before historians were concerned about recording exact dates, all dates in *The Anointed One* are estimates. The only way of dating Jesus' birth is to relate it to other events. Matthew 2:1 tells us Jesus was born during the "reign of Herod." There is disagreement over the date Herod died. Some scholars believe he died as late as 1 BC; some believe his death was in 4 BC.

Matthew 2:16 tells us Herod, in an attempt to kill Jesus, set out to slay all the male children "two years old and younger." So the latest Jesus could be born is two years before Herod's death, which gives us a birth year range of 6–3 BC. Many people argue for dates based upon celestial and Jewish calendar events at about that time. But none of this is beyond doubt, and the disagreements are numerous. Still, the exact year is unimportant.

We do not know Jesus' birthday or even his birth month. All we know is on the day of his birth some shepherds were outside watching over their flock at night. Some scholars believe this was unlikely in December, saying that sheep were ordinarily kept in a shelter at this time of year. They suggest a spring date is more likely.

Then there are the questions of how old he was when he began his ministry and the length of his ministry. And when did he die? *The Anointed One* includes the biblical text about Jesus' life in approximate chronological order. It is impossible to know the exact chronological order of the events in three of the four Gospels because the writers were not concerned with that. Luke may have presented the events he describes in chronological order, but that is uncertain. The text fits into

a four-year period from Jesus' baptism in May of his first year of ministry until his death almost four years later. It is reasonable to assume
he was born in AD 3. The dating of our maps assumes Jesus started his
ministry in April of AD 27 and that he died in April of AD 31.

Frankly, these things are unimportant. For thousands of years
people did not even know in what year they lived. Such knowledge
was not universal in the Western world until the fourteenth century.*
Most believers could not find Israel on a map until recent centuries.
Many believers in undeveloped countries cannot find Israel on a map
today. Yet they understand the Scriptures and can faithfully follow
Christ. The Christian walk with God is not dependent upon knowledge of geography or time.

Note on Content, Translation and Presentation

The Anointed One integrates the text of the Gospels and includes other
Scriptures about Jesus in his life, based upon the text of The Readable Bible translation. It is a "complete biography" in the sense that it
includes everything written about his life by those who witnessed it.
However, his biographers only wrote about events that took place on
about 90 of the roughly 1,400 days he ministered (from about June,
AD 27 to his death in April, AD 31).

Most scholars believe Mark wrote his Gospel first. Then Matthew
began with Mark's account and added explanatory words. Then Luke
began with both accounts and added more explanation, and John
built on these three. Each chose to not include all the previous writer's
material and added new material of their own. Our goal is to present
a complete account of the life of Jesus with as few distractions as possible, so we have not given any indication of which writers supplied
which words.

---

* The Anno Domini system of numbering years (i.e., BC and AD) was invented by a monk,
Dionysius Exiguus, who calculated he was living in AD 525. It is universally agreed that his
calculation was incorrect. The system began to be embraced by Western nations two hundred
years later, after Venerable Bede wrote his *Ecclesiastical History of the English People* in AD 731.
Charlemagne endorsed the system later in the eighth century, but it was not universal in western Europe until the fifteenth century. Before adopting the BC/AD system, people kept track
of years by the regnal system, tying events to the year of the reigning king or governor (e.g.,
"in the fifteenth year of Tiberias Caesar"). People simply were not concerned about time.

On occasion we have added explanatory, fictional material to help the reader understand the context of what is being said or happening. The source of Scriptures drawn from outside the four Gospels is listed in the endnotes.

The Gospel writers presented different accounts of the same stories for two reasons. First, Jesus told the same story many times and in many ways. Popular speakers commonly tell a story to one group in a way that will relate to them, and they tell it another way to a different group. And that's what Jesus and the Gospel writers did. Second, when two people hear the same story at the same time, they remember different facts. In *The Anointed One*, we have combined the differing accounts of each story into one account with all the information. While this seems to make it easier to grasp all the facts, it may present a story in a way Jesus never told it.

So this is not Scripture. If you are seeking to study the Scriptures, use this book as a tool next to a Bible.

The ancient weights and measures in the biblical text are in most cases presented in current equivalents. It is not uncommon for such estimates to differ by significant amounts, as ancient measures varied by time and place, and archaeological information is incomplete. We have used values commonly accepted today. Coinage can be expressed somewhat accurately in weight, but it is more difficult to translate its value into terms that relate to today. The exact amount does not appear to be critical to the meaning of any text.

Note on Maps

The maps are provided to give you a general idea of Jesus' travels. The chronological order of events is uncertain, and we do not know what routes Jesus took, just the destinations. Several times the text tells us Jesus "went through all the towns and villages." But we do not know exactly what area that refers to, and "all" is in the general sense (as in "We toured all of New England to see the fall foliage.")

Every location cited in the text is located on the map presented for that year of Jesus' ministry. All the Jerusalem and temple locations mentioned in the text are noted in the Jerusalem area map.

Jewish Calendar

In addition to the Levitical festivals below, there are twelve new moon festivals (on the first day of each month), and every Sabbath is a day of complete rest.

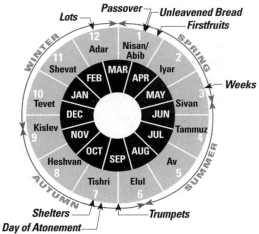

Jewish Day

The Jewish "hour" was 1/12th of the time from sunrise to sunset. Thus it varied from day to day, being shorter in the winter and longer in the summer. The time from sunset to sunrise was divided into four watches.

The Festivals of the Lord[a]

A sacred convocation is held on the first day of each festival. The offerings are in addition to the regular daily offerings, Sabbath offerings, and new moon offerings (see Numbers 28:3–15).

	Spring Festivals				Fall Festivals		
English Name	Passover[c]	Unleavened Bread[c]	Firstfruits	Weeks[c] (Pentecost, Harvest)	Trumpets	Day of Atonement	Shelters[c] (a.k.a. Tabernacles, Booths, Ingathering)
Hebrew Name	Pesach	Hag Hamatzot	Bikkurim	Shavuot	Rosh Hashanah	Yom Kippur	Sukkot
Purpose	Remember God passed over the Israelites when, to free them, he killed the firstborn of Egypt.	Remember leaving Egypt.	Recognize God's goodness in providing a crop.	Celebrate the grain harvest and God's giving of the Ten Commandments.	Celebrate the beginning of the new year.	Mourn sin, afflict the soul, and seek atonement.	Remember the exodus and forty years of wandering.
Dates[b] Hebrew	Abib 14	Abib 15–21	Abib 16	50th day after Passover	Tishri 1	Tishri 10	Tishri 15
Gregorian		Late March to late April		Mid-May to mid-June	Mid-September to mid-October		
Number of Days	One day	Six or seven days	One day	One day	One day	One day	Seven days
Offerings and Practices	Burnt and sin offerings. Seder meal. Eat no leavened bread. Rest, no work.	Daily offerings by fire. Eat no leavened bread. Rest, no work on 1st and 7th days.	Wave offering of sheaf of firstfruits. Burnt, grain, and wine offerings. Rest, no work.	Burnt and sin offerings. Rest, no work.	Burnt and sin offerings. Trumpet blasts.[d] Rest, no work.	Burnt, grain, and drink offerings. A complete fast. Rest, no work.	Burnt and sin offerings. Live in shelters. Rejoicing.
Scripture References	Exodus 12:1–14; Leviticus 23:5; Numbers 9:9–14; 28:16; Deuteronomy 16:1–8	Exodus 12:15–20; 13:3–10; 23:14–15; Leviticus 23:6–8; Numbers 28:17–25; Deuteronomy 16:1–8	Leviticus 23:9–14	Exodus 23:16; 34:22, 26; Leviticus 23:15–21; Numbers 28:26–31; Deuteronomy 16:9–12	Leviticus 23:23–25	Leviticus 23:26–32	Leviticus 23:33–43; Deuteronomy 16:13–17

a In addition to the Sabbath. See Leviticus 23:3.

b Because the dates are set according to the Jewish calendar, which is controlled by the phases of the moon, the dates vary from year to year in the Gregorian (today's) calendar.

c Pilgrimage festivals, meaning that all Jewish men were to come to Jerusalem to celebrate the festival. Some people consider Passover and Unleavened Bread to be one long event because they are next to each other.

d Unless it is on the Sabbath, in which case there are no trumpet blasts.

The Herod Family

Rulers mentioned in the four Gospels and Acts are in bold type.

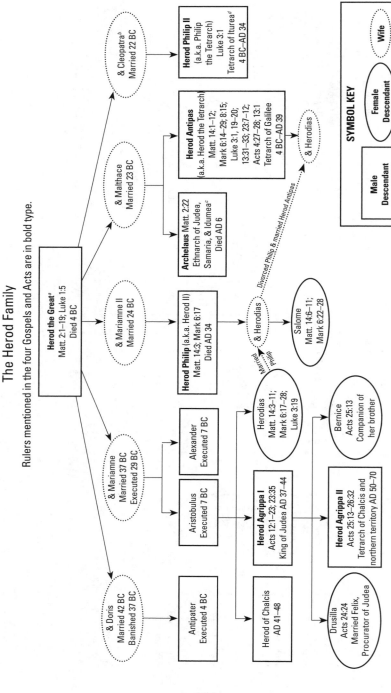

Herod the Great[a]
Matt. 2:1–19; Luke 1:5
Died 4 BC

& Cleopatra[b]
Married 22 BC

Herod Philip II
(a.k.a. Philip
the Tetrarch)
Luke 3:1
Tetrarch of Iturea[d]
4 BC–AD 34

& Malthace
Married 23 BC

Herod Antipas
(a.k.a. Herod the Tetrarch)
Matt. 14:1–12;
Mark 6:14–29; 8:15;
Luke 3:1, 19–20;
13:31–33; 23:7–12;
Acts 4:27–28; 13:1
Tetrarch of Galilee
4 BC–AD 39

Archelaus Matt. 2:22
Ethnarch of Judea,
Samaria, & Idumea[c]
Died AD 6

& Herodias

& Mariamne II
Married 24 BC

Herod Philip (a.k.a. Herod II)
Matt. 14:3; Mark 6:17
Died AD 34

& Herodias

Salome
Matt. 14:6–11;
Mark 6:22–28

Married
Philip

Divorced Philip, & married Herod Antipas

& Mariamne
Married 37 BC
Executed 29 BC

Alexander
Executed 7 BC

Aristobulus
Executed 7 BC

Herodias
Matt. 14:3–11;
Mark 6:17–28;
Luke 3:19

Herod Agrippa I
Acts 12:1–23; 23:35
King of Judea AD 37–44

Bernice
Acts 25:13
Companion of
her brother

Herod Agrippa II
Acts 25:13–26:32
Tetrarch of Chalcis and
northern territory AD 50–70

& Doris
Married 42 BC
Banished 37 BC

Antipater
Executed 4 BC

Herod of Chalcis
AD 41–48

Drusilla
Acts 24:24
Married Felix,
Procurator of Judea

SYMBOL KEY

Wife

Female
Descendant

Male
Descendant

a Herod had five other wives, none of whom appear in the biblical story.
b Of Jerusalem; not to be confused with Cleopatra of Egypt.
c The province south of Judea.
d Iturea: the province northeast of the Sea of Galilee.

Division of the Kingdom of Herod the Great

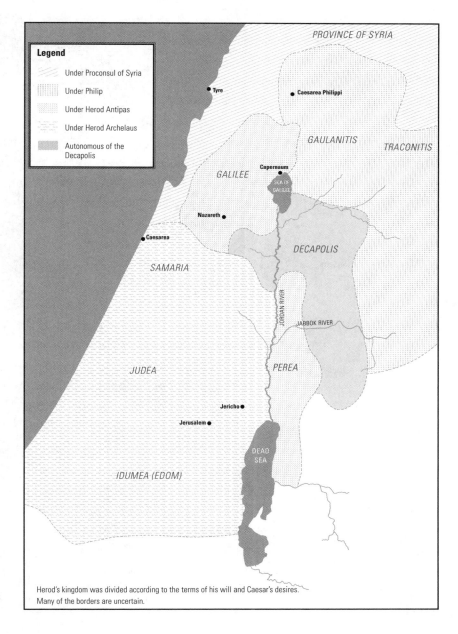

Herod's kingdom was divided according to the terms of his will and Caesar's desires.
Many of the borders are uncertain.

Travels: First Year of Ministry

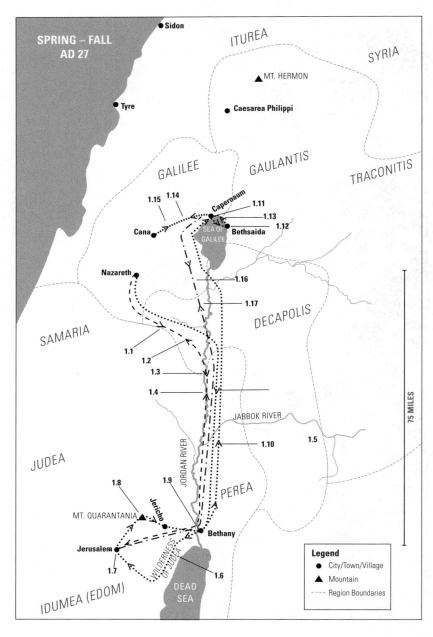

Travels: First Year of Ministry
April – October, AD 27

Journey	Season	Location – *Significant Event* [a]
– – – – 1.1	April	Nazareth – *Lived most of his youth* Jerusalem – *Festival of Passover* [b]
1.2		Nazareth
1.3	May	Jerusalem – *Festival of Weeks* [b]
1.4		Nazareth
·········· 1.5		Jordan River near Bethany [c] – *Baptized by John the Baptist* *– Holy Spirit of God descended upon him.*
1.6	Months of these events are uncertain	Wilderness of Judea – *Fasted forty days* *– Tempted by the devil to turn stones into bread*
1.7		Jerusalem – *Tempted on the pinnacle of the temple*
1.8		Mt. Quarantania [d] – *Tempted looking over kingdoms*
1.9		Jordan River near Bethany *– John the Baptist identified him as the Lamb of God.*
1.10		On trip to Capernaum – *Recruited Andrew and John*
1.11		Capernaum – *Recruited Simon Peter*
1.12		Bethsaida – Recruited *Philip and Nathanael*
·············· 1.13		Capernaum (assumed stay)
1.14		Cana – *Turned water into wine*
1.15		Capernaum – *Visited with his family and disciples*
· — · — · – 1.16	October	Jerusalem – *Festival of Shelters* [b]
1.17		Capernaum

a This table lists all the recorded movements of Jesus but not all the events at each location.
b There is no record of Jesus making this trip, but because all Jewish men were required to be in Jerusalem for the festival, we assume he made it.
c The exact location of this village is unknown, but it must have been not far from where the Jordan River enters the Dead Sea.
d Mt. Quarantania is the traditional place cited as the "high mountain" where the devil took Jesus to look over "the kingdoms."

Travels: Second Year of Ministry

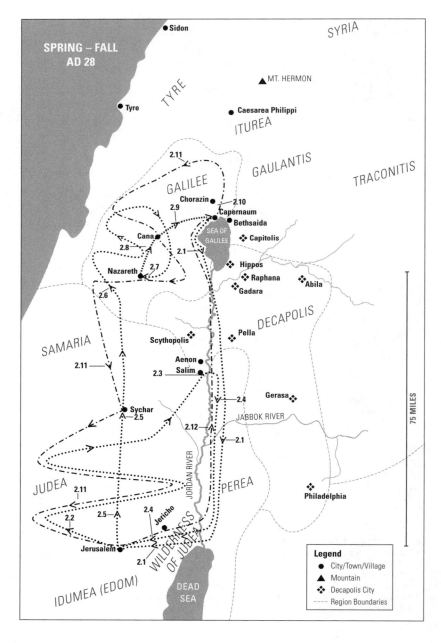

Travels: Second Year of Ministry

April, AD 28 – October, AD 28

Journey	Season	Location – *Significant Event*[a]

•••••• 2.1	April	Capernaum
		Jerusalem – *Chased merchants from the temple*
		    – *Festivals of Passover and Unleavened Bread*
		    – *Camped on the Mt. of Olives and taught the disciples*
		    – *Told Nicodemus he must be born again*

2.2	May/June	Judean countryside – *Taught*
2.3		Salim near Aenon – *Baptized many*
2.4		Jerusalem – *Festival of Weeks*[b]
2.5		Sychar – *Led Samaritan woman to faith, and other Samaritans became believers*
2.6		Galilee – *Taught in synagogues*
2.7		Nazareth – *Welcomed at first, chased out for saying he is the Messiah*
••••••• 2.8		Cana – *Began his healing ministry*
2.9		Capernaum – *Made Capernaum his home* – *Taught, healed, and began his deliverance ministry (casting out demons)*
–•–•• 2.10		Villages near Capernaum
2.11		Throughout Galilee and Judea – *Preached, healed, and drove out demons*
2.12	September	Capernaum/Sea of Galilee – *Recruited Matthew*
2.13	October	Jerusalem – *Festival of Shelters* – *Claimed to be God's Son and healed on the Sabbath*
Not mapped		Sea of Galilee/Capernaum – *Chose the twelve apostles* – *Taught and healed*

(Months of these events are uncertain)

---

a This map shows all the recorded movements of Jesus but not all the events at each location.

b There is no record of Jesus making this trip, but because all Jewish men were required to be in Jerusalem for the festival, we assume he made it.

Travels: Third Year of Ministry

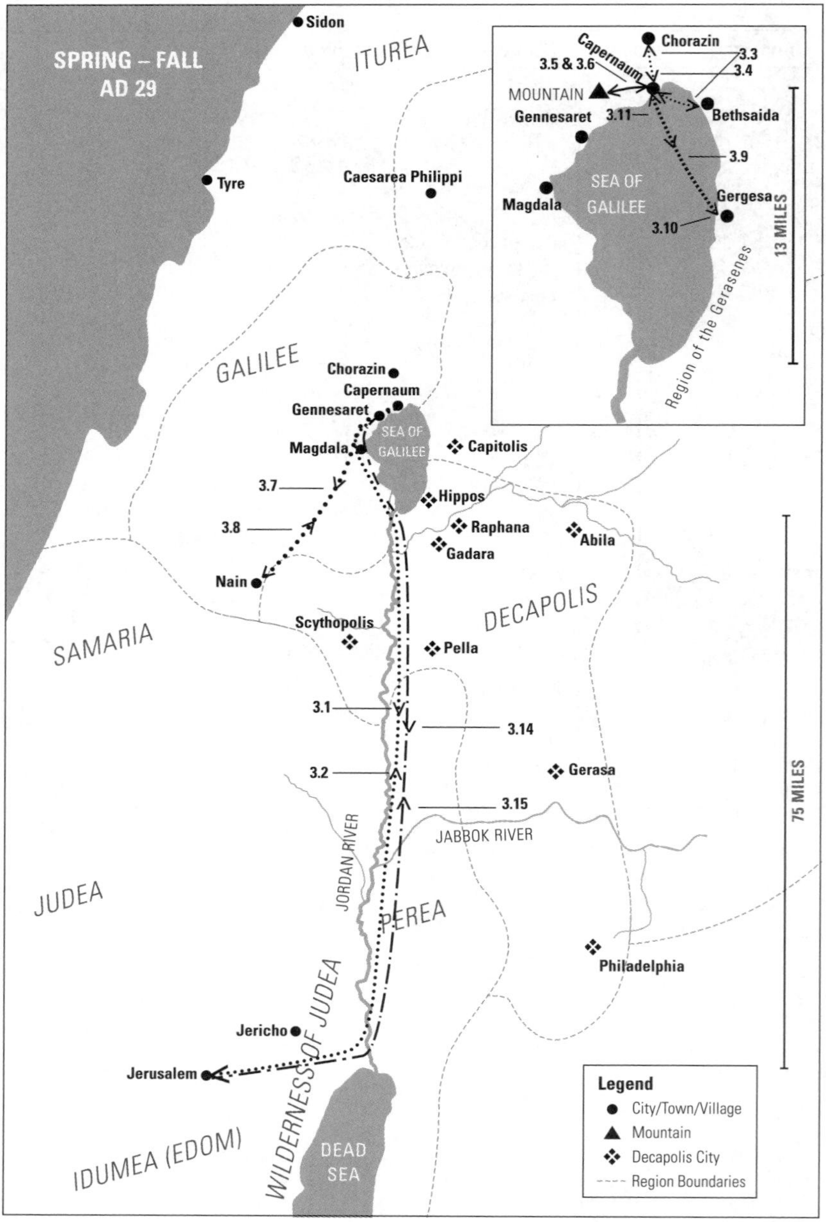

Travels: Third Year of Ministry

April – October, AD 29

Journey	Season	Location – *Significant Event*[a]
······· 3.1	April	Capernaum Jerusalem – *Festival of Passover*[b] – *Festival of Weeks*[b]
3.2	May	Capernaum and around Sea of Galilee
·········· 3.3		Chorazin and Bethsaida[c] – *Performed miracles, but they did not repent*
3.4		Capernaum
—— 3.5		Nearby mountain – *Sermon on the Mount*[d]
3.6		Capernaum
····· 3.7		Nain – *Raised a widow's son from the dead*
3.8		Way to Capernaum – *Taught, healed, met with John the Baptist's disciples*
▪▪▪▪▪▪▪▪ 3.9		On the sea of Galilee – *Calms a storm*
3.10		Southeast side of the Sea of Galilee, region of the Gerasenes – *Delivered Gaderene demoniac*
3.11		Capernaum – *Raised Jairus' daughter from death* – *Stopped a woman's chronic bleeding*
not mapped 3.12		By the Sea of Galilee – *Began using parables*
not mapped 3.13	September	Capernaum and surrounding communities – *Preached and healed*
·—·—· 3.14	October	Jerusalem – *Festival of Shelters*[b]
3.15		Capernaum

Months of these events are uncertain

a This map shows all the recorded movements of Jesus but not all the events at each location.

b There is no record of Jesus making this trip, but because all Jewish men were required to be in Jerusalem for the festival, we assume he made it.

c There are no records of either of these visits. But Jesus later mentions that though he did miracles there, they did not repent. He visited Bethsaida again in his fourth year of ministry.

d The map shows the traditional location, but its accuracy is uncertain.

Travels: Fourth Year of Ministry

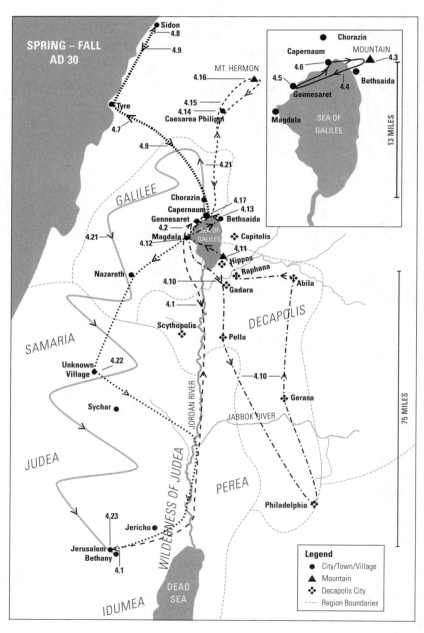

Travels: Fourth Year of Ministry

March – Nov., AD 30

Journey	Season	Location – ***Significant Event***[a]
		Capernaum
- - - - 4.1	March	Jerusalem – *Festival of Passover*[b]
		– *Festival of Weeks*[b]
4.2		Around the Sea of Galilee – *Taught*
——— 4.3	April	Mountain outside Bethsaida – *Fed 5,000+ with five loaves and two fish*
4.4	↓ Months of these events are uncertain	Sea of Galilee – *Walked on water to the boat*
4.5		Gennesaret – *Healed many*
4.6		Capernaum – *Said "I am the bread of life"*
⋯⋯ 4.7		Tyre – *Cast out a demon*
4.8		Sidon
4.9		Around the Sea of Galilee
· – · – · 4.10		Decapolis[c] – *Healed a deaf man*
4.11		Mountain by Sea of Galilee – *Fed 4,000+ with seven loaves and a few small fish*
4.12		Near Magdala[d] – *Shortened his visit because people demanded a miraculous sign.*
4.13		Bethsaida – *Healed*
- - - - - - 4.14		Caesarea Philippi and nearly villages – *Preached and taught*
		– *Peter and disciples realize Jesus truly is the Messiah.*
4.15		Camp outside of town – *Predicted his death and resurrection*
4.16		Mt. Hermon[e] – *Transfigured, taught*
4.17		Capernaum – *Taught*
not mapped 4.18		Galilee – *Taught his disciples privately*
not mapped 4.19		Capernaum – *Taught*
not mapped 4.20		Judea – *Taught*
═══ 4.21	September	Throughout Galilee – *Taught and healed*
4.22	October	Samaria – *Rejected because he was going to Jerusalem*
4.23		Jerusalem – *Festival of Shelters*
		– *Spares an adulterous woman*
		– *Taught and healed*
	November	– *Festival of Dedication, taught in the temple courts*
not mapped 4.24		Bethany
not mapped 4.25		Capernaum

a This map shows all the recorded movements of Jesus but not all the events at each location.

b There is no record of Jesus making this trip, but because all Jewish men were required to be in Jerusalem for the festival, we assume he made it.

c Which cities of the Decapolis Jesus visited are unknown.

d Literally, "Magadan." Magadan and Magdala may be two names for the same place, or Magadan may be a village close to Magdala. Mark's Gospel refers to this location as Dalmanutha.

e The record says "a high mountain." Some scholars locate the Transfiguration on Mt. Tabor (east-southeast of Nazareth). But Mt. Hermon better fits the term "high mountain" as it is 9,232' high (versus Mt. Tabor, 1,886' high).

In and Around Jerusalem
March – April, AD 31

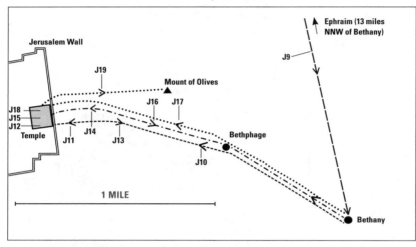

Journey	Date	Location – *Significant Event*
not mapped J1	March	Bethany – *Taught Martha what is important*
not mapped J2		Perea – *Sent out 72 disciples ahead of him*
not mapped J3		Many towns and villages – *Taught*
not mapped J4		Jericho – *Zacchaeus saved.*
not mapped J5		Road to Bethany – *Healed blind Bartimaeus*
not mapped J6	April	Bethany – *Raised Lazarus*
not mapped J7	Sun., 4/22	Village of Ephraim – *Retreated because of plot to kill him*
not mapped J8		Villages around Jerusalem
J9	— — —	Bethany – *Anointed by Mary*
	Mon., 4/23	On way to Jerusalem via Bethphage
J10	---------	*– Disciples got a donkey colt for Jesus to ride upon*
J11		*– Entered Jerusalem triumphantly*
J12		Jerusalem temple – *Made a short visit*
J13		Bethany – *Stayed overnight*
	Tue., 4/24	
J14	·–·–·–··	Outside Jerusalem – *Cursed a fig tree, predicted destruction*
J15		Jerusalem temple – *Drove the merchants out, taught daily*
J16		Bethany – *Stayed overnight*
	Wed., 4/25	
J17	············	On way to Jerusalem – *Taught on faith and forgiveness*
J18		Jerusalem – *Preached and taught the good news about the kingdom of God*
J19		Mount of Olives – *Stayed overnight, taught the disciples*

References

1. Psalm 89:27–29, 35–37
2. Isaiah 7:14
3. Micah 5:2
4. Hebrews 1:6
5. Micah 5:2
6. Isaiah 53:2
7. Deuteronomy 8:3
8. Psalm 91:11–12
9. Deuteronomy 6:16
10. Deuteronomy 6:13. Many other Scriptures say to only worship God and/or to serve only him.
11. Malachi 4:5
12. Isaiah 40:3
13. Leviticus 18:16; 20:21
14. 1 Kings 17:10
15. 2 Kings 5
16. Isaiah 9:1–2
17. Isaiah 53:4
18. Hosea 6:6
19. Hosea 6:6
20. Jonah 1:17
21. Jeremiah 6:16
22. Isaiah 6:9
23. Psalm 78:2
24. Micah 7:6
25. Leviticus 18:16; 20:21
26. Exodus 16:15; Numbers 11:7–9
27. Exodus 20:12; 21:17
28. Isaiah 29:13
29. Deuteronomy 19:15
30. Micah 5:2
31. Isaiah 58:11
32. Deuteronomy 18:15, 18
33. Psalm 82:6
34. Deuteronomy 6:5
35. Leviticus 19:18
36. Leviticus 14:1–32
37. Genesis 18:20–19:29
38. Genesis 19:26
39. Psalm 118:26
40. Zechariah 9:9
41. Jeremiah 7:11
42. Psalm 8:2
43. Psalm 118:22–23
44. Deuteronomy 25:5
45. Exodus 3:6
46. Deuteronomy 6:4–5; 10:12; 30:6
47. Leviticus 19:18
48. Psalm 110:1
49. Numbers 19:16
50. Daniel 9:27; 11:31; 12:11
51. Isaiah 13:10; 34:4
52. Isaiah 53:1
53. Isaiah 6:10
54. Psalm 41:9
55. 1 Corinthians 11:25
56. Zechariah 13:7
57. Isaiah 53:12
58. Psalms 35:19; 69:4
59. Isaiah 53:7
60. Leviticus 24:16
61. Isaiah 50:6–7
62. Zechariah 11:12–13
63. Isaiah 53:12
64. Psalm 22:18
65. Psalm 69:21
66. Deuteronomy 21:22–23
67. Psalm 34:20; Zechariah 12:10
68. 1 Corinthians 15:5–7
69. Isaiah 53:4–12
70. Philippians 2:6–11
71. 2 Corinthians 5:15